D0945470

Temporal Dimensions of Development Administration

Comparative Administration Group Series

Ralph Braibanti, *General Editor*

Editorial Board

Don L. Bowen

Frederic N. Cleaveland

James Guyot

James Heaphey

Warren F. Ilchman

John D. Montgomery

Francine Rabinovitz

Fred W. Riggs

Peter Savage

William J. Siffin

Clarence Thurber

Dwight Waldo

Temporal Dimensions of Development Administration

Dwight Waldo   Peter Savage   John G. Gunnell

Alfred Diamant   Warren F. Ilchman   Hahn-Been Lee

Frank P. Sherwood   Kenneth T. Jowitt   Edwin A. Bock

Edited by Dwight Waldo

Published in cooperation with the Comparative Administration
Group of the American Society for Public Administration
Duke University Press, Durham, North Carolina   1970

St. Mary's College Library
Winona, Minnesota

© 1970, Duke University Press
LCC Card Number 73–97215
ISBN 0–8223–0220–9

Printed in the United States of America
by the Kingsport Press, Inc., Kingsport, Tennessee

350.08
T28

Preface

104567

The essays in this volume are the product of a summer seminar sponsored by the Comparative Administration Group of the American Society for Public Administration. The seminar met at the University of California, Berkeley, in the summer of 1965. It was planned and conducted as a companion to a seminar meeting simultaneously at the University of Pittsburgh, dealing with the spatial dimension in development administration. The product of the Pittsburgh seminar, edited by James J. Heaphey, *Spatial Dimensions of Comparative Administration,* appears as a companion volume to this.

In the introductory chapter, there is some discussion of the Berkeley seminar as it pertains to an understanding of the essays. A few words of further explanation, however, need to be added.

Indeed, "time and chance happeneth to all [men]," and no participant in the seminar could have imagined that so much delay, so many obstacles, would have intervened between the seminar and the publication of the results. One participant found that he was unable to complete his commission, to deal with "time under communism," and this task was taken over and fulfilled by Kenneth Jowitt, who served as research assistant and student participant during the seminar. All other participants were able to complete their essays but, in several cases, only after substantial delay. Without question all the essays reflect the mutual stimulation of the seminar experience, but also without question the passage of time has served to accentuate the diversity that the essays display. Not that the results of the delay must be construed as "bad": one essay reports on research undertaken after the seminar, and one has become an earnest of a book-length treatment of its theme.

Since any harried technical assistance officer who examines this volume may judge it academic, it may be appropriate to emphasize that it is grounded in experience as well as in the world of ideas. Most of the contributors have lived and worked abroad. In fact, the amount and variety of "development" experience of the contributors (as can be seen from the biographical sketches) are impressive. Individually and collectively we speak to a real world, to problems practical and profound in development administration as we have perceived it. The "moment of truth" in my own overseas experience came—with shattering impact—when the responsible host said in effect that I might as well cool it. He felt that his culture was old before my country was born and that at least a generation must pass before results, if any, might be expected from the enterprise from which my American superiors expected an immediate "pay-off" in improved administration.

I acknowledge gratefully the assistance that has made the book possible. The Ford Foundation, through the American Society for Public Administration, provided the basic financing through which the Comparative Administration Group funded its summer seminars. For the "time" seminar, the University of California, Berkeley, provided additional support through the Institute of Governmental Studies and the Department of Political Science, which were formally co-sponsors of the seminar. The Albert Schweitzer Professorship in the Humanities at Syracuse University has supported the completion of the project. Personally, I wish to thank Dorothy Pollard, Hazel Karns, and Verna Osborn of the Institute of Governmental Studies for their efficient assistance to me as seminar organizer and director; my research assistant, Howard Magnas, for his assistance in checking references; and especially my secretary, Mary Braundel, who deftly co-ordinated as well as typed the final manuscript with incredible speed and accuracy.

Syracuse University   Dwight Waldo

September, 1968

Contributors

Dwight Waldo, born in Nebraska in 1913, received the Ph.D. in political science at Yale University in 1942. His academic career has included service at Yale University (instructor, 1941–42), the University of California at Berkeley (successively assistant professor, associate professor, and professor of political science, 1946–67), and various part-time or temporary positions in both domestic and foreign universities. In 1967 he became Albert Schweitzer Professor in the Humanities in the Maxwell School, Syracuse University. From 1942 to 1946 Waldo held various positions in the Office of Price Administration and the United States Bureau of the Budget. In 1956–57 and again in 1961–62 he was in Italy as representative of the University of California in an interuniversity program designed to establish a curriculum in administrative science at the University of Bologna. From 1958 to 1967 he was director of the Institute of Governmental Studies at the University of California, Berkeley. Since 1966 he has been editor-in-chief of *Public Administration Review*. His professional writings include *The Administrative State* (1948), *The Study of Public Administration* (1955), *Perspectives on Administration* (1956), and *The Novelist on Organization and Administration* (1968).

Peter Savage was born in London in 1933 and received his doctorate from Cornell University in 1966. From 1951 to 1961 he served in the Southern Rhodesian Civil Service. During this time he held posts in the Ministry of Economic Affairs and the Civil Service Commission and later became private secretary to the minister of the treasury and then to the prime minister. In 1961 he served as consultant to the Cabinet on the creation of a multiracial civil service and on the economic implications of the dissolution of the Federation of Rhodesia and Nyasaland.

From 1964 to 1967 he was assistant professor of political science, Indiana University, and was concurrently executive secretary of the

Comparative Administration Group. He is currently associate professor of political science, University of New Hampshire. He has contributed several articles in the field of comparative and development administration and has edited a special issue of *Comparative Political Studies* devoted to comparative administration. He is on the editorial board of *Comparative Political Studies* and is co-editor of the *Journal of Comparative Administration.*

John G. Gunnell was born in Waltham, Massachusetts, in 1933. He received his bachelor's degree (1955) from Tufts University and his master's (1961) and doctorate (1964) in political science from the University of California at Berkeley, where he was also a teaching fellow and university fellow. He served in the United States Navy (Lt. j.g.) from 1955 to 1958 and later worked as a consultant to the California Legislative Advisory Commission from 1959 to 1960. During 1960–61 he participated in the California Legislative Internship Program and was later director of that program (1963–64). In 1964 he joined the faculty of the State University of New York at Albany where he is now associate professor and chairman of the Department of Political Science. His publications include *Political Philosophy and Time* (1968) and "Social Science and Political Reality: The Problem of Explanation," *Social Research*, XXXV (Spring, 1968), 159–201.

Alfred Diamant was born in Vienna, Austria, in 1917 and received his doctorate in political science from Yale University in 1957. During World War II he served in the United States Army in Europe. He has served on the faculties of the University of Florida, 1950–60, Haverford College, 1960–67, and is currently professor of government at Indiana University. He was a visiting professor at Yale University, 1958–59, Columbia University, summer, 1961, and Ruhr-Universitaet Bochum, 1966–67. He was associate managing editor, *Journal of Politics*, 1950–55, and serves now on that journal's editorial board. He has been active in the Comparative Administration Group since its inception, has served as a member of its program committee, and has participated in its summer seminars at Indiana University (1963), University of Michigan (1964), and University of California, Berkeley (1965). As a member of the Europe Committee, CAG, he has assisted in developing more permanent ties between European and American, as well as among European, scholars of comparative administration. He is the author of works in political philosophy and comparative administration. Among the former is *Austrian Catholics and the First*

Republic: Democracy, Capitalism, and the Social Order, 1918–1934 (1960), which also appeared in German and Italian translations (1964). In the latter field are *Modellbetrachtung der Entwicklungsverwaltung* (1967), articles in various journals, and essays in the following volumes: William J. Siffin, ed., *Towards the Comparative Study of Public Administration* (1957); Ferrel Heady and Sybil Stokes, eds., *Papers in Comparative Public Administration* (1962); and John D. Montgomery and William J. Siffin, eds., *Approaches to Development: Politics, Administration and Change* (1966).

Warren F. Ilchman, born in Denver, Colorado, in 1934, received the doctor of philosophy degree at Cambridge University where he was a Marshall Scholar. He has taught at Magdalene College, Cambridge, Williams College, the Center for Development Economics, and is presently associate professor of political science at the University of California at Berkeley. He has been a visiting lecturer at the International Center for Advanced Management Education at Stanford University and at training programs of the Peace Corps and the United States Agency for International Development. A member of the executive committee of the Comparative Administration Group and co-editor of Comparative Administration Studies, Professor Ilchman is also a consultant on technical personnel for the United Nations. In 1962 and 1963 he did field research under the auspices of the Rockefeller Foundation in India and the Middle East on political problems of social and economic change. He is the author or co-author of *Professional Diplomacy in the United States* (1961), *The New Men of Knowledge and Developing Nations* (1968), and *The Political Economy of Change* (1968), and articles in various learned journals. Professor Ilchman is presently completing a book on *Comparative Public Organizations.* Essays by Professor Ilchman appear in two other Duke University Press-Comparative Administration Group volumes: *Political and Administrative Development,* ed. Ralph Braibanti, and *Frontiers of Development Administration,* ed. Fred W. Riggs.

Hahn-Been Lee was born in Korea in 1921 and received his education in humanities at Seoul National University. He received the degree of master in business administration from Harvard University in 1951 and his doctor's degree in philosophy from Seoul National University in 1967. Upon graduation from Harvard Business School, he entered the Korean Ministry of Finance and worked up the ladder of the Korean bureaucracy for ten years. Between 1958 and 1961 he was the national budget director, serving four changing regimes at this pivotal post. During all these years of civil service, he was visiting lecturer at Yonsei University and Seoul National University. After the military takeover in his country in May, 1961, he was promoted to the post of vice-minister of finance and six months later was appointed minister plenipotentiary in Geneva, representing his government to the international organization there. From 1963 to 1965 he was Korea's ambassador to Switzerland with concurrent ambassadorial assignments to Austria and the European Economic Community and ministerial duty to the Vatican. After his diplomatic tour of duty in Europe he left the government service and entered academia. After the CAG seminar in Berkeley in the summer of 1965 and during the academic year 1966–67, he stayed at the East-West Center of the University of Hawaii as senior specialist. Since October, 1966, he has been professor and dean at the Graduate School of Public Administration, Seoul National University. Dean Lee is chairman of the Development Administration Group of the Eastern Regional Organization for Public Administration and also vice-chairman of the executive council of that regional organization. Professor Lee is the author of *The Way a Small Country Lives: The Case of Switzerland* (1965); *Korea: Time, Change, and Administration* (1968); and *A Handbook on Development Administration Curriculum* (IIAS, in press). He is editing, with Abelardo Samonte, a symposium on administrative reforms in Asia. He has contributed articles to the *International Review of Administrative Sciences* and *Die Verwaltung*.

Frank P. Sherwood, who was born in Georgia in 1920, holds the doctorate in political science from the University of Southern California, awarded in 1952. In 1968 he became the first director of the Federal Executive Institute, which was established to provide for the development of top-level career officials. Before his appointment, he was director of the School of Public Administration, University of Southern California, where he served on the faculty from 1951 and from which he is on leave. He is a member of the national council of the American Society for Public Administration and serves on the Board of Editors of the *Public Administration Review*. In addition to several shorter foreign assignments, Sherwood was chief of a technical assistance mission to Brazil in 1962–63; its objective was to advise on the improvement of education for the public service in that country. He is author of *Institutionalizing the Grass Roots in Brazil* (1967) and co-author of *The California System of Governments* (1968) and *Administrative Organization* (1960). He has contributed to various professional journals and received the Burchfield award in 1963 for the outstanding essay–book review in the *Public Administration Review*.

Kenneth T. Jowitt, born in Ossining, New York, in 1941, received his bachelor's degree from Columbia College, June, 1962, and his master's from the University of California, Berkeley, 1963. In July, 1968, he became acting assistant professor of political science at the University of California, Berkeley, and he received his doctorate in June, 1969.

Edwin A. Bock was born in New York City in 1922. He received a bachelor's degree from Dartmouth College in 1943. During World War II he served with the Army in Europe and Asia and, as a civilian, directed a small research unit on governmental affairs during the first year of the American occupation of Japan. From 1947 to 1952 he was a graduate student in political science and sociology at the University of London and conducted research on the administrative class of the home civil service. He served as assistant to the director of the Public Administration Clearing House in New York from 1953 to 1954, dealing with international and technical assistance administration. In 1955 he became staff director of the Inter-University Case Program and in 1962 its president. Since 1963 he has also been professor of political science at the Maxwell School, Syracuse University. He is the author of *Fifty Years of Technical Assistance* (1954); *NGO Representation at the United Nations* (1955); editor and contributing author of *Essays on the Case Method* (1961); *State and Local Government: A Casebook* (1963); *Government Regulation of Business* (1965); and *The Politics of Federal Science Administration*, which will appear early in 1970.

Contents

Charts

Temporal Dimensions of Development Administration

Chapter 1

Introduction: On Problems, Perspectives, and Hypotheses

Dwight Waldo

Time, which is the author of authors.

Francis Bacon

The model I have taken for this Introduction is Mason Haire's Introduction to his symposium volume, *Modern Organization Theory*. This has impressed me both as a useful preview of the individual contributions and as a skillful presentation of a frame of reference in which the individual contribution could be viewed. But unfortunately, Haire's introduction cannot serve as model in any strict sense, and to set forth *why* it cannot may be a useful introduction to the introduction.

The essays presented in the Haire volume are so diverse that it might appear that some of them have been included in error. However, the collection is introduced by: "Introduction—Recurrent Themes and General Issues in Organization Theory." Nor is this a false statement, an unsupported boast. Haire was able not only to find recurrent themes in the essays, but (even in 1959) to assert convincingly that organization theory is an authentic subject, worthy of attention and presenting general issues that can be usefully addressed.

This collection of essays presents a different situation. Although it certainly is possible to draw attention to some recurrent themes, and although it is not unreasonable to speak of some general issues that are presented, this is more difficult and more problematical than in the case of the Haire symposium. What is impressive here is the diversity of the themes and, indeed, the divergences, even contradictions, in orienting perspectives. In fact, the essays which follow are not about the same subject in a way that the Haire symposium concerns organization theory—ill-defined as that phrase was in the late fifties and disparate as were the essays. Hence, it seemed appropriate to speak in this Introduction more to "Problems, Perspectives, and Hypotheses" than to recurrent themes and general issues. What follows is an attempt to explain, and in a sense to justify, this situation.

The Sources of Diversity and Divergence

The diversity and divergence manifested in the essays have their source both in the history of the enterprise responsible for their presentation and in the matters to which they are addressed. These two sources are related, as will appear, yet neither is simply a function of the other. Some words about each and their interrelations are necessary.

The decision of the program and executive committees of the Comparative Administration Group to hold two summer seminars, one focusing on space and one on time, was made in 1963. The twin ventures were conceived as probing, exploratory. That is, at that time no practical objectives were stated, and no hypotheses were set forth for testing. There was simply a presumption—or act of faith—that since all administration takes place in space and in time an enterprise that seeks to study administration comparatively should attempt to view administration, consciously and explicitly, within these grand frameworks. This was done to see what insights might be yielded, what hypotheses might be projected, what theories might be developed, and what wisdom might be gained.

With no more specific intent or instructions than this indicates, the two seminar directors were left free to develop seminar "approaches" and plans for their respective enterprises. My own prospectus or schema, used in soliciting interest and briefing possible participants, was as follows. (In further explanation I preface that although the prospectus speaks of six participants, the number of participants who wrote papers was raised to eight; and that when the participants increased in number I sought—vainly—to get at least one to discuss time in relation to some function or area, e.g., agriculture or education.)

Administration and Development: The Temporal Dimension

I. Time, Change, and Development: Some Philosophical, Ideological, and Cultural Perspectives.

My thought is that the conference is going to be dealing with very large intangibles that interrelate in the most subtle and maddening way and that it should properly open, therefore, at this level. Of all the things that might be said about these large intangibles, the writers of these papers will be guided by the general orientation and purpose of the meeting, and what they say will be designed to "put a frame around the enterprise." I have in mind here someone who has written in a general way about Time, but who is oriented toward "social science" instead of (or in addition to) philosophy.

II. Time in Bureaucratic Rational Administration: Implications of the Models and Evidence of the Data.

What I have in mind here is that since there is an assumption that the range of desirable possibilities for "developed" countries runs between, say, Weber and Simon, it would be well to have this close scrutiny of what is said and implied about Time in these models, and a further look at ways in which the evidence is or is not in accord with the models.

III. Temporal Correlations and Strategies in National Development: Problems of Synchronization, Sequences, and Rates in the Interrelations of Subsystems of Society.

A. Communist Experience.

B. Non-Communist Experience.

What is in my mind here is the broad perspective on development: interrelations among the administrative system, the political system, the educational system, the class system, the religious order, the ideological commitments, and so forth. Since this is a subject large enough for a library, presumably it should claim at least two of the presumptive six assignments. The problem then is: how to divide it. I can think of a dozen ways, but the Communist-non-Communist approach is the one which appeals to me the most. For one thing, I think we have paid too little attention to Communist experience (in the Comparative Public Administration movement, and even in Development Administration, so far as it is a separate focus). This is partly a function of access, of course; but I think we need to compare as carefully as we can, *when* we can, "their" experience as against "our" experience. Let me quickly add that I realize that the world is not divided between two qualitatively different "Communist" and "non-Communist" parts: that there is both a wide range within each of these *and* that there is a large area of the world in which these two labels make little sense. However, I return to the point that I want to achieve comparison between two (or more) different approaches to "development," with specific reference to Time.

IV. Temporal Correlations and Strategies in Development Administration: Synchronization, Sequences, and Rates in Inducing and Controlling Development.

    A. In Relatively Developed Countries.

    B. In Relatively Underdeveloped Countries.

This follows on III, but is an attempt to narrow the focus to administration, properly speaking. Again, I think it should claim two spaces out of six, but the question is how to divide meaningfully. And again I can think of a dozen alternatives, but a distinction between more and less well-developed countries strikes me as perhaps the most useful.

Probably the items designated with capital letters can and should be narrowed somewhat and suggestions are welcome. On the other hand, I want to avoid monographs on the experience of Ruritania and keep the focus as broad as possible without making the picture so fuzzy that it is useless. (I add, as stated earlier, that I realize that the dichotomy of developed-underdeveloped is in some ways unrealistic, distorting. However, I am anxious to get *comparison.*)

Now when the papers which follow are viewed in light of the prospectus, it is apparent that certain "intents" were realized: Time *is* treated generally, philosophically in one essay (Gunnell), the "models" *are* systematically examined for their time component (Diamant), and a Communist country's time treatment *is* analyzed (Jowitt). But over-all, there is considerable divergence, an air of haphazardness. In fact, in presenting the essays I prudently decided not to try to group them by subject, though I believe there is a certain logic in the order of presentation.

Certainly some of the diversity and disparateness can be attributed to the prospectus. Obviously, it is firmer and more explicit in its earlier than in its later parts. Here the categories (Communist-non-Communist, etc.) may or may not have been well chosen, but it is certain that they were very large and very general, leaving open to negotiation and even to chance the exact subjects to be addressed and the style of the addressing. Further explanation runs to the mores of academia and to beliefs about how useful or original thinking is brought about. An organizer of a faculty seminar is at most *primus inter pares,* and only in the most general way can he tell his colleagues what to do. And particularly when an area of inquiry is new and inchoate, it is presumed that there is more to be gained by speculative probing than by an imposition of a rigid research design. Nor is a summer faculty seminar a research project. Not only is each participant an independent force, but the seminar itself—if worthy of the name— has a creative power of its own that moves its members into new channels of thinking.

It is clear that the exploratory, open-ended nature of the inquiry interacted with the faculty-seminar setting in which it was pursued to produce diversity. But something more needs to be said about the orienting concepts. These made a semblance of unity and common direction even harder to attain.

As one of the epigraphs which follows has it, "time is a riddling thing." It is at once real and illusory, concrete and ephemeral, absolute and relative. It can be measured with a precision that baffles the untrained mind, but it does not "exist." It is a universal category of human experience, but it is *not* a universal category of human experience. No need to elaborate further. The point for present purposes is that if one were to search for a subject that is difficult to understand and about which there is a diversity of respectable views he could not do better. Because time *is* such a riddling thing, the mind (and the emotions) resist sustained attention. To suggest a metaphor: it is like mounting a cone of ice. One progresses only with the greatest exertion and is likely, nevertheless, to find himself back at his starting point, looking for something easier to attempt. Certainly members of the seminar found themselves wondering occasionally whether it had been wise to focus a seminar on "time." Was it parameter or variable? Both or neither? Which interpretation, which aspect, is most likely to have a pay-off for research? Is that aspect, that type of research, which is most interesting also of any potential significance? For what? If one chooses only subjects dealing with time that can be researched by existing theories and technologies of the West is he thereby enclosing himself within cultural barriers that the study of *comparative* administration must seek to transcend? Anyhow, are Western time views and technologies "truer"?

With the wisdom of hindsight one can say that perhaps certain arbitrary, limiting, and defining decisions should have been made at the outset. This would not have been obviously unreasonable. After all, the study of administration is rooted deeply in time-and-motion studies; and time measurement—or the measuring of various things by or against time—is central to much of our most advanced administrative technology. (It is an integral part of the Planning, Programming, and Budgeting System.) At another (but related) level one might have said: For the purposes of this seminar, we shall assume that the view of time as linear and progressive is, if not true, the most important in the present and proximate future; and all proceedings will take place within this assumption. Or again, one might have posited as a working base: Time is objective and linear, and we will limit ourselves to addressing its social-administrative aspects, using as major tools the concepts and technologies associated with synchronization, sequence, and rate.

The results of the seminar must of course speak for themselves. With good luck the diversity and divergence will prove useful in exposing familiar assumptions to more careful scrutiny, in suggesting new lines of inquiry, and in giving greater relevance or precision to some present studies. Whatever else, we cannot be charged with narrow orthodoxies or premature closure—granted always that we cannot jump out of our own cultural skins and that this will be evident.

But the elusive and baffling nature of time is not the only conceptual difficulty responsible for the diversity and divergence in the product of the seminar. *There was also "written into" the seminar both an ambivalence and an uncertainty as to what time should be related to.* Each of these deserves a word.

As to the ambivalence, the historical situation, so to speak, required of the seminar a dual focus, one theoretical and scientific, the other applied and practical. This dual focus, this ambivalence, is a problem for the Comparative Administration Group that sponsored the seminar; written deeply into the context of affairs, it cannot be escaped. The monies that have largely supported the Group's activities have been, in the donor's view, to promote *development*. With this objective, the university professors (who constitute most of the membership) have no quarrel, quite the contrary. But their training and locus dispose them to a different point of view (and scale of time!) than the hard-pressed technical assistance officer. Their professional values legitimate the pursuit of knowledge for its own sake; and with reason and evidence they can argue that reliable knowledge must precede effective action—and nowhere more so than in the complex business of national development.

Within the complex of study and activity of the Comparative Administration Group, these two points of view compete for primacy. Sometimes one, sometimes the other, predominates; characteristically, they appear in some "mix." Conscious of this problem and seeking to balance the scale (or to avoid trouble?), I proposed in the prospectus to treat the temporal dimension in relation to "Administration and Development." That is, my wording was intended to legitimate and accommodate both a "pure science" and an "applied science" interest. For this reason—perhaps—there was in the seminar no significant discussion or controversy along this line. In result—or for whatever reason—the essays reflect both points of view and do so, on the whole, unselfconsciously. That is, since the issue was not sharply posed and debated, and since participants were so largely free to "do their own thing," they did so without feeling the need to refute an opposing view or justify their own emphasis.

Finally, some words on the uncertainty of what time should be related to: development. Development is one of the major legitimating words of the day, and an American is as little likely to oppose it as his father was to oppose progress. But it is multi-faceted, protean, cloudy, and baffling. To be sure, some branches of social science are well aware of the difficulties the word presents and are struggling mightily to clarify and justify. Certainly there is a high level of awareness of the problem and of sophistication in dealing with it in the seminar essays. In one essay (Gunnell), indeed, a powerful thesis thereon is subtly developed. But this did not become a "seminar line"; each essayist, on this as on all subjects, was his own philosopher and his own methodologist.

The Development and Interrelation of Themes

I wish now to indicate the major themes developed in the essays and comment on their interrelations. The aim is to provide a synoptic view and to call attention to some thematic relationships that might escape the notice of the cursory or selective reader.

I

The collection is introduced by Peter Savage's "Of Time and Change: Temporal Perspectives in Development Administration," which is the most general and synoptic of the essays. In it one is introduced to most of the major subjects and problems that, one way or another, are treated in more detail in the following essays. In it the main "varieties" of time are introduced, and they are introduced in context, that is, in the context of development. At the center is a "developer" who must balance and mediate disparate and even conflicting perceptions of time.

Savage presents a classification of the differing times with which the developer must deal. To do this he uses as his perspective or tool the notion of the "ecology of administration," which has been prominent in the literature of comparative administration in this decade. "Environmental time" contains, first of all, cultural time, i.e., the indigenous and traditional ideas of time that (by definition and hypothesis) must be accommodated or changed if development is to occur. Environmental time contains also political time, which is conceived as composed of two "times," time as history and time as the political present. Political time is pre-eminently the time of the political leaders, the mobilizers. These two times are, often or essentially, "imports." But they are a part of the extra-national environment; and to the extent that they are adopted and used by political leaders they become environmental for the administrator.

The characteristic Western perception of time as linear and progressive is a part of the larger environment; it underlies and is entwined with time as history and time as political present even though it often—at a particular time and in a sense—conflicts with them. It is matrix also for what is to the administrator *his* most important time. This is rational time, the perspectives and technologies of "synchronization, sequence, rate, duration, succession, recurrence, and continuity." In planning, which is both technology and ideology in developing countries, rational time is central; but its co-ordination with cultural and political times is difficult, always incomplete and problematical.

Though Savage explicitly states that he does not wish to present the administrators as the "good guys" of the drama, they nevertheless are the center of his sympathetic attention. Their arduous and thankless task is to try to reconcile the diverse times with which they must perforce deal. They must cope with extra burdens imposed by the inadequacies of political leadership, with an extreme "politicizing" of administration. They must mediate, proselytize, strategize, and do so effectively if development, not chaos, is to be forthcoming.

II

Savage is aware that development is a complex and troublesome concept, as various observations indicate; but it is not his business to deal with the problem. In the following essay, "Development, Social Change, and Time," John Gunnell chooses to confront the problem frontally. Indeed, this is a radical confrontation—one dealing with roots. We are presented with a critique of some of the basic philosophical premises and major methodological constructs of contemporary social science. If the critique were to be accepted as valid, then the implications for much contemporary social science—including the other essays in this collection—are far reaching.

It is difficult in a few sentences even to suggest the main lines of so lengthy an essay and so subtle an argument. The essence of the matter (this is bold, but brevity necessitates boldness) is that to understand what development means one must understand what social change means, and to understand this one must introduce concepts of time. Time, then, is not something that may or may not be left out of a social science construct: A concept of time is a basic, informing element in all social science. Nor can we objectively choose a uniquely "correct" time for our use: "There are as many 'times' as there are differentiating activities and modes of thought." Time is symbolic and social: "All conceptions of time, even those of natural science, may be understood as social in the sense that they are related to the needs and activities of society."

Gunnell begins, as his title indicates, with development. He finds the attempts at definition futile exercises, displaying circularity or infinite regression. To speak meaningfully of it, he asserts, it is necessary to address the wider perspective of social change in general. To this he turns, in an analysis ranging from Aristotle to current major figures in social science, and the conclusion is that the key to the understanding of change has not been found. Or at least it has not been found or used in major theories and models. What is needed is a new view, a fresh start: "It is not a question of developing more sophisticated theories [for reconciling statics and dynamics] but a question of the epistemological foundations of social science."

In examining, criticizing, and seeking to alter these epistemological foundations, Gunnell works his way through the intricacies of social theory beginning with Max Weber. He concludes that we need a new paradigm of the process of inquiry itself. This new paradigm must recognize, in a way the older positivist ones did not, the functions of symbols in mediating, understanding, and even shaping the world. For the present inquiry the significance of this is that an understanding of social change (and hence of development) necessitates an understanding (from the inside, or empathically) of the understandings of time with which they are intimately joined.

A summary—at least my summary—does not do justice to the argument. No doubt the argument, so out of keeping with the predominant scientific spirit of contemporary social science, will be unacceptable to many. But at bare minimum it deserves to be pondered by any student who prizes his open-mindedness and honesty.

III

The title of Alfred Diamant's "The Temporal Dimension in Models of Administration and Organization" indicates well enough what one will find in the essay. But it does not adequately suggest the scope and depth of the presentation. Only half the essay is given directly to classification and analysis of the "models"; the other half is given to exploration and interpretation that make the classification relevant for the basic concerns of the seminar.

The task set is to inquire "whether the intellectual foundations of the discipline and the presently available theories and models of administration and organization . . . provide efficient instruments for conceptualizing rapid social, political, and economic change." To perform this task, Diamant deems it necessary first to "examine briefly the concept of time, especially the notion of social time, and the manner in which it relates to problems of social change."

Here there begins to be, necessarily and (I should argue) desirably, a weaving back through concepts and themes set forth in the first two essays. Sometimes—here as in later essays—there is repetition and reinforcement; but there is also the statement of new "time" categories and a reshaping of previously enunciated concepts. Especially valuable is the presentation of the central ideas of three works which probably were the most influential works on time for the seminar as a whole: George Gurvitch, *The Spectrum of Social Time,* Wilbert E. Moore, *Man, Time, and Society,* and Mircea Eliade, *Cosmos and History: The Myth of the Eternal Return.* Moore's triad of synchronization, sequence, and rate, especially, is a recurring motif.

Diamant finds it necessary, secondly, to discuss "models and theories in the social sciences" generally, before setting himself to the task of surveying the temporal dimensions of administrative-organization theories: thoroughness, honesty, and accuracy will not permit less. The discussion begins with a review of the nature of theories and models (after all, what are we talking about?), proceeds to a discussion of "hard" versus "soft" social science theory (are we talking about suggestiveness, prediction, or what?), and then turns to a consideration of types of models —steady state, equilibrium, non-equilibrium, input-output, cybernetic, and so forth. Still not content and ready for the classificatory task, Diamant turns then to a discussion of "categories of the social system."

Finally, the "temporal dimension" in theories of administration and organization—theories of more than a score of writers, ranging from Follett to Parsons, from Fayol to Riggs—are presented schematically. The presentation is in the form of a six-celled matrix; one axis being Nature of Social System, the other Nature of Organizational Change. Diamant does not then leave us to wonder why he classified writers as he did; his rationale for each classification is given, together with his reservations and puzzlements. This is followed by six observations—to me acute, even profound—on the implications of his categorization. He concludes with rueful observations on a double-standard in the values of academia: "Mobilization systems" (of indubitable Western inspiration) are Good, but "administrative systems" (because they are Western) are Bad. "Why is a mobilization administrative system not appropriate for a mobilization political system?"

IV

"New Time in Old Clocks: Productivity, Development, and Comparative Public Administration" ranges, in space, to the far reaches of the world and, in time, from the origins of civilization to the present moment. It is an attempt to understand what the major time conceptions and metaphors in the human experience have meant *for* that experience, or more precisely, for matters of concern to the seminar, such as change, productivity, development, and alternative modes of administration. The author's own statement of aim is more modest: "to understand, in a preliminary fashion, the concern with time as a part of the intellectual, industrial, and urban development of western Europe and especially to examine the administrative systems of non-Western nations in terms of their hospitality to Western time-oriented institutions and values." Nevertheless, my description will stand.

Ilchman's essay is built upon a point of view, a thesis, or series of related theses: Time beliefs and values constitute or are part of a "metaphor," which codifies and simplifies reality for its believers and guides individual and collective actions. In the modern West, a time metaphor new in human history arose and became predominate. This is linear, progressive time, time as "an arrow pointing 'upward.'" " 'Progressive time,' as a metaphor, conceived of time as pushing *forward* toward expanding productivity, *through* human co-ordination and the exploitation of advancing technology, *for* a better collective life." Much of the history of the modern West can be written in terms of the development and power of the metaphor, and much of what is now happening in non-Western lands is related to the diffusion and impact of the "arrow" time-metaphor.

Perhaps because a thesis needs a counter-thesis to gain force, Ilchman does not simply begin with the development of the "arrow" metaphor, though in his treatment of "The Rise of Progressive Time" we are given a succinct and insightful discussion of this development. Rather, he sketches the time metaphors typical of archaic man and traditional cultures. From ancient civilizations, we are led through the development of Greek, Roman, Muslim, and Christian time concepts—developments which prepared the way for the emergence of the arrow metaphor. (There are stimulating observations, also, on the interrelations of time and space metaphors.)

Ilchman presents the rise of his metaphor in the West in terms of interaction with both ideas and institutions—with religious and ideological developments, with the rise of nationalism, urbanism, and industrialism, and with history in the sense of major change and conflict. He then turns his attention to the worldwide diffusion of the metaphor, and discusses such matters as progressive time conceptions in the nationalism of the newer states and the inevitable friction and confusion arising when the progressive time of new national elites comes face to face with time perspectives of ancient cultures—whether primitive or highly civilized.

In the second half of the essay the focus is progressively narrowed. Perhaps more accurately, there is increasing refinement in the analysis and more attention to the details of development and administration without, however, the loss of a world-encircling concern. We are led through a discussion of growth and development as these are viewed in the lenses of various social sciences, and into a discussion of time and timing with respect to management processes. The essay closes with an exercise in specifics and a statement of four hypotheses: Data from fourteen developing countries are correlated in an attempt to find the factors or variables significant for productivity.

V

The essay "Developmentalist Time, Development Entrepreneurs, and Leadership in Developing Countries" presents at once a development of now-familiar themes, a variation on familiar themes, and a change of themes. Most important, it presents a distinct change in perspective of the author; alone among the essays it represents a view from the "inside," a view informed by contemporary social science, to be sure, but also by the personal experience of a "developer."

Hahn-Been Lee's main objective is "to identify the optimum time orientation for development and to specify the incidence of such an optimum time orientation among potential elites—this with a view to integration of resources toward the goal of national development." The essay opens with a discussion of time perspectives in which a distinction is made between "external time" and "internal time," and of the associated changes which are brought with the reception of the former. Typical and important reactions are perceived as falling into three categories: escapist, exploitationist, and developmentalist. These three are presented schematically in a matrix in which one axis is Time Perspective (past, present, and future) and the other is Attitude toward Change (negative, ambivalent, and positive). These are, of course, explained and related to the populations of developing countries, in a discussion that takes account of subtleties and in a second schematic presentation that presents "residual" as well as dominant time orientations.

The essay then proceeds boldly to relate time orientations to types of elites (there is, of course, a large literature on elites in the developing countries) and to "program orientations for different administrative systems." Again, we are given two schematic presentations and interpretative comment, but these do not lend themselves to summary. But we are not merely given sets of categories; Lee is interested in a very real world. He focuses on political and administrative elites, and discusses as "potential development administrators" the intellectuals, the military, and businessmen. Without losing sight of time orientations, the essay passes in its concluding pages into a discussion of the nature and sources of innovation, the finding and developing of creative leaders, and a delineation of the task of the creative leader in resolving conflict and integrating time perspectives.

VI

With "Leadership, Organizations, and Time" we reach, for this endeavor, what is perhaps the narrowest theoretical focus and the clearest claim to field research (as against experience and observation in the field). But the theoretical focus is, nevertheless, very broad, embracing and interrelating various concepts any of which alone presents serious problems. And the field research, as the author emphasizes, is only a promising beginning, however intriguing and suggestive the results.

The three major concepts—or conceptual fields—are given by the title, leadership, organizations, and time. It is Sherwood's wish and intent to relate leadership and time, and in that sense organization is a subordinate concern. More specifically, he seeks to relate the perceptions of time of an "administrative leader," and his *use* of time in performing his administrative-leadership functions, to various factors in the environment (organizational and extra-organizational) and to "organizational success," or goal achievement.

He addresses himself first to leadership which, as the informed know, is one of the slipperiest words in the social science lexicon. We are of the opinion that we have advanced notably in a generation of conceptual refinement and research, and Sherwood sketches the advances in our sophistication. But he properly notes the central problem of defining the "success" which must be the scale on which leadership is measured and concludes with the restrained observation that "even the seminal writers have left us with a great deal of uncertainty."

The proposal he advances in the next sentence has a certain boldness, considering the chameleon and controversial nature of time: it is no less than probing the riddles of leadership through the use of time technologies and time concepts. There are faint echoes of early time-and-motion studies in what follows. But there are also a theoretical sophistication and an inter-cultural comparative dimension that are thoroughly contemporary.

Sherwood reports at some length on a United States-Brazil comparative study executed as a doctoral dissertation under his direction, and briefly upon his personal research at Westlab (pseudonym for a large government R & D organization). The former involved the collection of a considerable amount of data, from interviews and observation, in the Brazilian and American bureaucracies, and the testing thereby of various assumptions and hypotheses concerning the transferability of administrative technology and effective modes of administrative reform. Given my own interests, the findings—or perhaps more modestly, speculations and hypotheses—are fascinating. This is true also for the Westlab report, which lends itself to replication on an intra-cultural basis as well as extension into inter-cultural dimensions. A very promising line of research, I judge, has been opened up.

VII

With "Time and Development Under Communism: The Case of the Soviet Union" the lens of time is turned in a still different direction. This essay represents an attempt to bring together for examination of their interrelations events of great complexity and ideas of great diversity. It is perhaps conceptually the most complex of the essays, adding to many of the ideas and problems of the preceding essays the convolutions of Communist-Soviet studies and certain methodological concerns of the author (bearing on the relation of a "*general* set of problems" to the "*distinctive* form and content" they may assume).

The formal objective (as noted earlier) "is to consider the matter of time and development with special reference to communism," taking the Soviet Union as the case study. This objective is pursued through use of (1) elite theory and study of the ideas and behavior of the communist elite, (2) Wilbert Moore's tripart schema, rate, sequence, and synchronization, as the most apt instrument for taking the "temporal dimension," and (3) distinctions developed by Philip Selznick in *Leadership in Administration* between routine-efficiency factors on the one hand and change-institutional development factors on the other.

The analysis begins with Lenin's "reversal" of Marx, the development of Party doctrines, the evolution of Stalinism; and it proceeds through a summary review of Party doctrine and actions in the development—economic, social, and political—of the Soviet Union. It is clear from the analysis that beliefs about time were of central importance in Communist ideology and were of "operative" importance at various levels—from the Kremlin to factory floor—in the events of recent decades. No explicit resemblances or correlations between Soviet events, problems and ideas and those of other developing countries are noted by Jowitt, but anyone who has read the preceding essays will be struck by the relevance of what has been said before for the Soviet experience and vice versa. It is clear that Communist doctrine and apparatus "make a difference." It is also clear that there are many similarities between Communist and non-Communist situations. It is this complex relationship between the general and the specific—I take it —that is the center of what were referred to above as the author's "methodological concerns."

Despite the conceptual complexity, nevertheless, the presentation is essentially *narrative*. That is, we are given the chronological "story" of the development of Communist doctrine, of Russian development under communism, and of party organizational problems—all as related to "objective" and "subjective" time. Main themes are the early perception of "relative backwardness," the achievement of "diminishing backwardness," Khrushchev's "exploitationist time," and the "retreat to technology" of Brezhnev and Kosygin. The essay focuses in its concluding pages on the dilemmas of the Party arising from the fact that an instrument forged for and adapted to achieving a high rate of development is not easily adapted (for example) to purposes of synchronization in a contemporary complex setting. The final section on the adaptive Party is given even more relevance by events in the Soviet Union and its satellites since its writing, and raises interesting questions (which might be designated by the term "objectivity") concerning methodology in social science.

VIII

Appropriately, the final essay, "Governmental Problems Arising from the Use and Abuse of the Future—the Last Colonialism?" turns attention to the future. Here we have a speculative probing of the relationships between present and future, or more precisely of the question whether "the growing capability to shape the future, and the rising disposition to use this power . . . [is] best understood in terms of a benevolent colonialism." This presents itself to Bock as an appropriate question to pose with respect to the so-called developing countries. But it strikes him as especially relevant for countries that have attained "strong scientific, technological, and industrial capabilities." The center of attention is, in fact, the United States. It is hypothesized that present people, institutions, and government in the United States and those a few decades hence are "two separate and rightfully sovereign states."

Certainly the inquiry is an appropriate and timely one, presenting—and mingling—scientific and moral questions, as well as those more immediately germane, i.e., constitutional, political, and administrative questions. The capability to affect the future constantly rises, and indeed the scope and magnitude of present actions affects the future in unprecedented ways quite apart from conscious (or at least self-conscious and intelligent) intent. There is also a growing concern with the future, in various activities that, for instance, center about the term "planning" and in the study and projecting that is indicated by the term "futuristics."

The inquiry is pursued—using a mixture of sophisticated concepts and mother wit—by analyzing the "usefulness" of the future both for individuals and for the government, with the conclusion that these are highly important in both cases but only vaguely understood and capable of highly consequential conflict. To the extent the future is predicted, planned, and controlled it loses its present need-satisfying, safety-valve function, which depends upon its amorphous and multi-potentialed quality. Bock speculates on the consequences of—presumably—greater and greater effort to control the future; what this means, for example, with respect to the strategic importance for both politics and administration of "access to points of prevision," i.e., to the data and technologies that constitute "computerized crystal balls." He concludes with observations on the relevance of the accentuated generation-gap of our day, and reflections on the problem of securing "representation" of the future in the present.

This is, in brief, how the editor sees the enterprise as a whole and what, in rough, he sees in each essay. To the extent he is correct, the reader has been facilitated in his understanding. To the extent he is incorrect, the authors deserve a better understanding. The reader is now urged to examine the essays himself. Even in the unlikely case that the editor's summary view could not be faulted, the essays contain a richness that no introduction can do more than suggest.

Chapter 2

Of Time and Change: Temporal Perspectives in Development Administration

Peter Savage

Watching the clash of cultures and the attendant release of primordial emotions stripped of their usual niceties, I could not help observing that man is only superficially a reasoning animal. Basically he is a desiring, suffering, death-conscious and hence, a time-conscious creature.

J. T. Fraser, *The Voices of Time*

We fret over improving things, in order that posterity may be happy; but posterity will say as usual: "In the past things were better, the present is worse than the past."

Chekhov

The systematic association of time and development is a hard one to make. Yet curiosity, the one sufficient reason for comparative study, prompts one to ask whether the temporal dimension of politics and administration has anything to reveal about the process of development. If the other dimension or parameter of human existence, space, can be obviously and profitably juxtaposed against development, why not time?

The problems of where to begin are formidable. Philosophers, sociologists, and anthropologists provide no overarching criteria of relevance for relating time to politics and administration. Writers on development and development administration do little better in agreeing upon what *these* particular terms denote. So this essay starts with the stipulation that in many non-Western countries there is a range of concerns about large-scale changes in the terms of human and social existence, that these concerns become reflected in the aims and commitments of political regimes, that the pursuit of these aims becomes in large part the business of administrative organizations of government, and that time is inescapably a relevant factor in these matters.

In the traditional Western perspective, with its implicit and explicit commitment to rationality and its related concern with differentiating things—and hence classifying them—two primary categorizing devices are used as lenses for looking at many kinds of phenomena. One is "space." The other is "time." But there is only one premise inherent in the use of these two classifying or ordering concepts, namely, that all phenomena have spatial and temporal qualities. When further differentiation and definition, application and measurement, are undertaken, then numerous and vexing problems arise. Both concepts are used in many different ways, given many different meanings, and ascribed many different values.

From this point, one might proceed in any of several directions, the choice of a focus being a function of one's aims and the criteria they provide. The aim here is to examine time in the context of a concern with development. This involves two crucial questions: What are the significant temporal characteristics of a developed nation? And are there differences between developed and developing nations as far as these temporal characteristics are concerned?

From the literature of cultural anthropology, one can get a sharp awareness of how culture-bound are time premises and perspectives. To catalogue the differences between the time perspectives of traditional and modern societies can be a useful preliminary effort to making significant statements about relevance of time to development and its administration. But, unless one is prepared to espouse the holistic view that development entails the transformation of time perspectives from whatever they are to those of a developed society, it is difficult to get down to narrower, more concrete statements about time and development by following this particular line any further. What is needed at this point is a classifying scheme of some sort to help in grasping some of the aspects of time in relation to the goals, problems, and requisites of development. Thus, there follows a simple taxonomy of the time perspectives relevant to administration in developing countries. Given these, it is possible to identify a few of the more critical temporal problems of development administration.

The Varieties of Administrative Time

Administrative systems do not function in a vacuum; the environmental realities playing upon administration are crucial to both its structure and operation. The idiosyncratic features of individual societies and cultures are reflected in some fashion or other in the administrative system and constitute the environment with which the system interacts. The writings of Fred W. Riggs, especially, remind one to search for such "ecological" factors in understanding and explaining the behavior of administrative systems.[1]

Among the political, social, and economic realities at play in the administrative environment are time premises and perspectives. "Environmental time" may be said for analytic purposes to have two main elements, cultural time and political time.

Cultural Time

Cultural time comprises the time orientations and time horizons common in society or common among those groups affected by the goals and programs of development. Thus, the environment may be marked by a predominant cultural understanding of time as linear and directed, or cyclical and eternally returning, or eternal and uniform, or an admixture of all three.[2] The following assessment of the Indian conception of time is an example of cultural time in this sense:

1. See, for instance, *Administration in Developing Countries: The Theory of Prismatic Society* (Boston, 1964).
2. Julius T. Fraser, "Comments on Time, Process and Achievement," in Fraser, ed., *The Voices of Time* (New York, 1966), p. 136.

The Indian conception of time is very different from what the western mind regards as intuitively obvious. In Indian thought, time, like other phenomena, is conceived statically rather than dynamically. . . . This static conception of time permeates Indian thought.

The persistent Indian conception of a transcendent reality as more important than the phenomenal world it underlies and sustains results in a kind of paralysis of the individuals' sensitivity to time. . . . This paralysis manifests itself in a characteristic lack of time concepts which non-Indians regard as common sense.[3]

Cultural time is often reflected in attitudes toward and uses of the past, present, and future and in manifestations of everyday, commonplace social behavior. For instance, J. L. Sadie observes:

A characteristic which more than anything else distinguishes the tribal people from technologically developed communities is the absence of a regard for and concern about the future. "The lobotomised personality"—in the phraseology of the psychologists—would not be an inappropriate term in this connection. The future as a concept which elicits action is not part of their culture. The "sufficient unto the day" approach does not make for an inclination to accumulate for the sake of sustaining life at some future time.[4]

In *The Silent Language,* Edward T. Hall provides numerous illustrations of the impact of different views of time on social behavior in different cultures. Of special pertinence are examples of misunderstandings and conflicts that have arisen when, in technical assistance operations, indigenous ideas of time have been quite different from those of the foreign "experts."

Attitudes toward the past, present, and future have an important influence on a receptivity to progress and on the activities which engineer change. A predominant regard for the past rather than the future can make an administrative environment regressive and existence-oriented instead of progressive and improvement-oriented. This is well portrayed in Jack E. Weller's *Yesterday's People: Life in Contemporary Appalachia* which, though concerned with an area or subculture of the United States, con-

3. Hajime Nakamura, "Time in Indian and Japanese Thought," *ibid.,* pp. 77–80.
4. "The Social Anthropology of Economic Underdevelopment," in David E. Novak and Robert Lekachman, eds., *Development and Society: The Dynamics of Economic Change* (New York, 1964), p. 215.

tains obvious parallels to traditional cultures in developing countries.

Much of the mountain music is nostalgic and melancholy. . . . Mountain ballads often refer to friends, family, or situations of a time now past. Much of mountain literature is backward looking. Folk stories paint the picture of the hero going back home, either to find the old security again around the fireplace or front porch, or else to find it gone, while memories flood in. Much of mountain talk and gossip is backward oriented: how things used to be, how much better things were, what fun people used to have, how "everybody" went to church then—as if the "good old days" held the only joy. Too often the tomorrows of life have held only sorrows, fears, frustrations, or disappointments. The outlook of the mountain man's culture is "regressive."[5]

It is well recorded and noted that an appreciation and use of linear, progressive time appears to have been critically important to the history of development in the West. Thus, it seems plausible to hold that the laggardly development in non-Western areas is linked with different notions and uses of time. It seems reasonable to suspect that cultural understandings and attitudes toward time affect the process of development and that what, in part, impedes this process, however one wishes to define it, is the absence of the array and paraphernalia of Western time and timing techniques in the culture.

However, cultural time is not the only kind of time, and the relation of cultural time perspectives to politics and administration is not necessarily simple. Thus one must ask: What do cultural understandings of time have to do with the politics and administration of development?

This question prompts several related ones. One wonders whether there is in fact a series of culturally idiosyncratic understandings and uses of time which are duly reflected in the politics and administration of development so that time and timing in the context of development mean different things to different societies. Are timing problems of rate, sequence, and synchronization posed and handled differently depending upon predominant or

5. Lexington, Ky., 1965, p. 34.

particular cultural norms about time? How and to what extent do cultural norms and perceptions about time generally permeate the process of development in most countries? Do they occur uniformly throughout the developmental process so that politicians, administrators, and the administered share the same orientation to time and function with similar time concepts because they are mutually involved in the development process? At what points in the translation of aims into implementation do cultural norms about time become important in the process of development administration generally, and are there differences in the way time is viewed and used at different points in the political and administrative chain involved in development?

Amid all the diversity and complexity of differing cultural understandings of time and their behavioral manifestations, one fact seems clear in outline: The contemporary development process in non-Western countries is not permeated from top to bottom by a coherent cultural attitude toward time.

The administrative environment of development is not marked by a common attitude toward time. A significant part of the process of development administration is generally unaffected by cultural understandings of time. In the first place, such understandings have little relevance in the political realm, where, as suggested below, the process of policy formulation is premised upon a general use of time as history and time as the political present. Nor are they often relevant to that part of the administrative realm which, as again this essay will later suggest, is required to exercise the time techniques and time technology needed to implement goals of development adopted with Western assumptions about time.

There is characteristically a fundamental inconsistency between cultural and political time perspectives in developing nations. In the political realm where arguments over development policy tend to be about how time can be bought, saved, and spent in relation to comprehensive national goals, the various modes of indigenous cultural time frequently are unimportant. One would be hard put, for example, to trace "the static conception of time which permeates Indian thought" in the rhetoric and rich detail of Indian five-year plans. Nor at this level is there recognition of the unpalatable fact that the transfer of Western technology is seriously hampered by indigenous attitudes toward time and timing. It is later, and at the lower levels of implementation that problems and conflict will arise. "Culture" often seems to be ignored in frenzied drives toward the outward manifestations of development, only to reappear as the reason for the failure of policies that cannot possibly be implemented.

Cultural understandings of time as part of the administrative environment of time perspectives are most significant at the lowest administrative levels. (My own brief experience as an administrator made clear that progression up the hierarchy is very much a question of expanding time horizons: As a voucher clerk I had to insure that vouchers were paid within five days so that the government could take advantage of a discount for prompt payment; as secretary to a Prime Minister, I was more concerned with such questions as whether ten years was the period which we could reasonably expect a new constitution to last, given violent political and social movements.) This is where the intimate human connection between time and development occurs. Here development administrators are acting within an administrative environment set by the calendrical and clock time of months, weeks, days, hours, and minutes. Here this time perspective comes into contact and conflict with time perspectives rooted in myth or natural rhythms.

Thus, much of the significance of cultural time for development administration exists at the lowest, most operational level of the administrative hierarchy, the point at which policy touches people. Here it is often necessary to handle the problems which arise from the incongruence of thrusting the policy products of Western time perceptions and time technologies onto a culture which may be premised on different assumptions about time. Here social attitudes and behavior premised on a traditional view of time as cyclical and eternally returning have a direct and marked impact on the process of development administration.

Political Time: Time as History and Time as the Political Present

From the point of view of administration, political time is another element of environmental time. Political time is important as a source of premises affecting development administration, but these premises are not necessarily reflections of either cultural time or the time perspectives which underlie rational administration of developmental goals. Political time has two aspects: the time perspectives and premises of history manifest in political doctrine and those of the political present. Although these two aspects are often empirically intertwined, they can be analytically isolated for the purposes of discussion.

In the realm of political doctrine there is usually a particular consciousness and appreciation of "time as history." By this is meant a consciousness of and a concern with the past, present, and future as parts of a historical stream of national development. This is the realm of ideology, of ideals and utopias, and of grand designs and militant slogans, where a sense for the past is the necessary foundation for an appreciation of the present and a vision of the future. The sweep of history in this sense is a dominant part of the temporal context of contemporary development politics.

Language is revealing, and it is in the political rhetoric of development that this temporal theme is unmistakable. The language of those who lead the movements and formulate the policies which, with luck, go on to become "national destinies" clearly reflects a preoccupation with time as history. Consistently, political leaders and elites in the developing areas hark back to the national past, on the one hand glorifying its indigenous content, and on the other condemning its colonial element. One way or another it is a depository from which to draw ringing slogans of political action and development. To be sure there are varying attitudes toward the past from country to country, but whether at any particular moment it is condemned, negated, or glorified, the past is used as a means to give a new shape to the future.

Similarly leaders and elites commandeer the future. But it is generally a telescoped future, as the rhetoric of development amply testifies. This rhetoric is dominated generally by a fore-shortened utopianism in which the potentialities of the nation are not limited by time, nor, it often seems, by much else. Certainly the time-forward component of utopianism seems to disappear in a rhetoric in which both the time necessary and the time available for development are undervalued.

Although the end results of most development policies may be marginal, they do not start out this way. In their conception, at least, the politically formulated goals of development represent social, economic, and political changes of considerable range and impact. The wish to catch up to the "yesterdays" of the West appears to demand rapid change in nearly every facet of society. In such circumstances, it becomes difficult for elites and leaders to discriminate among priorities. Moreover, goals are frequently perceived as carrying heavy penalties for delay; therefore, they cannot be subjected to long and hard scrutiny before adoption. The imperatives of development give rise to a logic of haste.

Thus, there is a second mode or aspect of time of great importance in the political realm. The temporal concerns of development policy frequently lie in a middle ground between the sweep of history and the temporal ordering in the form of synchronization, sequences, and rates which implementation requires.[6] This middle ground generally comprises immediate or urgent temporal concerns about the goals of development, which are, in short, concerns about the political present. In this context of temporality which is below the level of ideology and doctrine, a logic and rhetoric of "instant development" tends to predominate, crowding out precise judgment and careful decision. In the political realm the temporal aspects of issues of development policy are assuredly debated, but the temporal yardsticks frequently turn out to be simple notions of relative priority and urgency rather than quantified facts and estimates of synchronization, sequences, and rates. National planning is often a case in point.

6. Wilbert E. Moore, *Man, Time, and Society* (New York, 1963) posits synchronization, sequence, and rate as the three prominent temporal features of administrative organizations.

Although development in nearly all countries involves national planning of one sort or another, a common obstacle to its success is the clash of the political present and its peculiar logic of haste with the temporal ordering prerequisites for rational planning formulation and implementation.

One can search the political rhetoric of development in vain for acknowledgments of the rational, pragmatic requirements of a temporal ordering to development; there is rarely any reference to elementary notions of synchronization, sequences, and rates. Taking an obvious and fairly well-documented problem such as education, it is quickly apparent that there is characteristically a sort of "battering ram" approach which envisages a multiplicity of simultaneous goals: a vast building program; an expansion in primary, secondary, post-secondary, professional, technological, and scientific education; the achievement of mass literacy; the creation of the skilled manpower requirements of a complex economy; and a realizing of political-ideological goals, such as equalizing opportunities and recruiting elites.[7] In one sense this is a synchronized approach—everything at once. But there tends to be scant attention to the careful temporal ordering needed for the complex interweaving of policies which often conflict and carry with them different rates of implementation.

There is a growing body of literature on the theory of economic development available to provide "models" for political decision-making. Whether the theory espouses the cause of balanced or unbalanced growth, it is based on quantified notions of the proper synchronization, sequences, and rates to be applied to a range of economic variables. What is interesting about the normative aspects of this literature is that they seldom provide the operating premises of the political present.

In summary, political time, with its dual aspects, stands between cultural time and the time perspectives implicit in "rational" administration. On the one hand, there is not much cultural time in political time. On the other hand, political time

7. See the various essays contained in James S. Coleman, ed., *Education and Political Development* (Princeton, 1965).

makes little acknowledgment of the time perspectives necessary to the temporal strategies of implementation.

Environmental Time and Development Administration

Time as history and time as the political present predominate in the political realm of development, and leaders and elites clearly tend to premise issues of public policy on such modes of time. Cultural time and the two modes of political time together comprise the environmental time premises and perspectives facing administration. The characteristics of this environmental time are generally of a kind which create critical problems for development administration.

The relative absence of indigenous cultural understandings of time in the political realm, combined with a propensity to view time as history, leaves the way open for imitating the ends of Western development. In fact, there is a remarkable imitative quality about the development goals of non-Western leaders and elites. Certainly the strategy and tactics of development vary from country to country, but the ultimate goals of development tend to look alike: industrialization, urban accretion, material and social welfare, widespread education, the spread of technological and scientific expertise, and all the varied accoutrements for international stature.

Although the goals of development are by no means restricted to the economic realm, it is there that the imitative tendency can most clearly be seen. Leaders and elites assume or assert that to be developed is to be economically progressive in the way that the West is. Western industrialized economies, or at least their hardware and output capabilities, are taken as a model. Non-Western leaders aspire to emulate this model without necessarily emulating the political and social means by which it was attained. One must admit, of course, that the choice of different means may in the long run lead to different, distinct ends; however, in the short term, i.e., between 1945 and now, the weight of the evidence indicates a fairly faithful transference of the Western model of economic development. The model not only specifies roads, railways, airlines, dams, bridges, factories, plants, armies, embassies, and universities, but also the whole gamut of such facilitating mechanisms as banking, currency, exchange and import controls, tariffs, planning, and public enterprises; all of which, in turn, require the support of the myriad and diverse elements of an underlying technology.

It is difficult in describing this tendency not to exaggerate. Nonetheless, there does seem to be something of a "follow-my-leader" process at work between the Western and non-Western world. In this process, there is a clear tendency for the imitation of Western goals to carry with it Western assumptions about time and temporal ordering—assumptions, moreover, which are often quite at variance with indigenous cultural attitudes toward time. With the imitation of ends comes the positing (often implicitly or unconsciously) of Western time and timing assumptions which underlie these ends. It is relatively easy for non-Western governments to adopt, politically, objectives of development which come from the Western world and then to frame rough political priorities for their implementation. The distinct temporal context of development politics, in which the predominant use of time as history leads to an ideology of instant development, results in the formulation of development objectives that are all encompassing and invested with urgency. Elites and leaders frequently take as national objectives of development all that is desirable rather than just what is possible. There is no time, as there appears to have been in the history of Western development, for reasonable political debate which can attune development goals to social realities. Instead there is a doctrine of "everything by yesterday."

So far this essay has argued that environmental time is composed of two distinct sets of time perspectives. But there is a third set of perspectives which is an important source of premises for development administration.

Rational Time

In addition to environmental time, there is a set of time premises and perspectives which belongs particularly to administrative organizations. This is a set of what might be termed rational time perspectives. These perspectives are the requisites of a time technology needed to achieve limited, ordered objectives, through co-ordinated specialization. They are time perspectives and premises reflected in a whole range of administrative techniques concerned with temporal co-ordination; techniques such as plans, timetables, deadlines, rates, routines, cycles, budgets, logistics, and lead-in and tool-up activities. The variety of administrative activities dependent on rational time perspectives is very great, of course, but they can be conveniently designated as activities concerned with synchronization, sequence, rate, duration, succession, recurrence, and continuity as strategies of temporal ordering.

In developing countries, the administrative system is called upon to exercise the time techniques and time technology needed to achieve goals of development adopted with Western assumptions about time. In the formulation of development policy and in the subsequent translation of development objectives into administrative actions, administrators are concerned with the quantified aspects of temporal ordering, and with the reduction of development objectives to specific, phased activities. All the varied conceptual and operational paraphernalia of Western time technology become important to the process of development administration.

The spread of planning, inherently a technique of temporal ordering and allocation, is indicative of the importance of time technology as an input in the calculus of development. Indeed, planning in the sense of the realistic and quantified application of temporal strategies to the imperatives of political policy is frequently equated with development administration. Similarly, the myriad structural and operational alterations stemming from administrative reform, which are designated to engineer co-ordination, all emphasize the predominantly rational character of the time perspectives and premises relevant to this phase of development administration; for co-ordination implies the application of synchronization, sequences, and rates, particularly in a quantified way. Even in carrying out basic functions concerning law and order and revenue collecting, administration operates in a context of rational time, for such functions are expressions of a government's different temporal concerns, not for synchronization, sequences, and rates this time, but rather for duration, continuity, succession, and recurrence.

Additional evidence of the growing importance of rational time is to be found in the pressures which planning and co-ordination, as elements of a time technology crucial to development, exert on administrators to forsake the limitations and the assumptions of their own compartmentalization, functional specialization, or technical expertise. Instead of being confined to questions of temporal ordering within a relatively specific functional area of development policy, they are increasingly required to apply their time technology to the programming of various projects which go beyond their own particular expertise.

All this is not to say that administrators are the "good men" of development. They are frequently far from rational, sophisticated calculators and logicians of efficiency. The notions of synchronization, sequences, and rates which they apply are frequently very rudimentary. Planning in most non-Western areas is not at all a matter of mathematical precision. The various co-ordinative devices spring not, as they frequently do in the West, from the complexity of what has to be done, but from the general air of urgency or the sheer necessity of keeping minimum essential state services going. More often than not synchronization and sequence turn out not to be a matter of phasing various objectives, but a question of deciding whether to pursue educational development, *or* reform land tenure, *or* nationalization of public transportation, *or* development of community health services, *or* the securing of national integrity by increasing defense activities.

Temporal Problems of Development Administration

Environmental time, with its component parts of cultural time, political time as history and the political present, together with rational time, provides a convenient initial way for reducing the perplexities of time from the point of view of administration. It is now possible to identify more precisely some of the critical temporal problems of development administration.

The Shift from Formulation to Implementation

The characteristics of the environmental time perspectives and premises of administration are associated with the doctrine of urgent and comprehensive development on the Western model. This, in turn, results in a shift of the main responsibility for success in development from those who formulate policy to those who implement it—a shift from those who act under the influence of political time to those who must act under the impetus of rational time.

Warren Ilchman (in a following essay) argues cogently that Western development depended in large measure on a pervasive belief in progressive time; and that significant elites in the non-Western world have now committed themselves to this belief. The political rhetoric of development demonstrates this. What it fails to demonstrate is that these elites have absorbed also the critical time and timing implications of a belief in progressive time as an ideological component of development. In this sense, their commitment often appears to have been incomplete.

On the other side, the political formulation of development goals inadequately reflects indigenous cultural understandings of time, owing to the politicians' predominant use of time as history or time as the political present. In result, the strong impulse to development is not realistically related to the possibilities of achieving development. The assumption behind many ambitious development goals is simply that they will be achieved by the very fact of their rightness—through the means of an application of Western technology, when the time for implementation comes. What tends then to become important is not accommodating to, or changing cultural attitudes toward, time but insuring that the right time technologies are built into the administrative process. That is, the preferred solution is neither to modify the urgency and simultaneity of development objectives nor to adjust for cultural attitudes toward time, but simply to improve time technology within administration. But administration alone cannot bear such a burden. The temporal perspectives of haste, immediacy, and expediency often cause a great many of the politically formulated goals of development to remain out of phase with the environment.

In these ways the political half of the development process tends to default on important temporal premises of public policy. This default places a great burden on development administration, for success now depends on implementation rather than formulation. It is administration which must come to grips with the fact that timing assumptions behind development goals are not related to indigenous social realities. It is administration which must somehow deal with temporal concerns which were submerged or ignored in the formulation of policy. Administration must increasingly seek to translate into accomplished development an essentially atemporal ideology of development and a political predisposition to haste and simultaneity.

Administrators are expanding the scope and extent of their activities in non-Western nations: their roles are expanding beyond the merely instrumental. It has long been accepted that important, durable, and often dominant aspects of an administrator's responsibilities are to offer advice in the formulation of policy, to implement agreed policy, and to administer the daily business of public management.[8] To these aspects, plainly administrative, are now being added responsibilities to act as key agents of economic, social, cultural, and even political development in new nations. Indeed, the evidence of scholarly attention itself suggests that while administrators are becoming the new men of development, elites and leaders are becoming the forgotten men. In shifting the burden of achievement from formulation to implementation, however, few stop to question whether development goals are reasonably conceived. We seem no longer prepared to admit that the defects of development policy can be of

8. This characterization of the role of administration is contained in Fritz Morstein Marx, "The Higher Civil Service as an Action Group in Western Political Development," in Joseph LaPalombara, ed., *Bureaucracy and Political Development* (Princeton, 1963), pp. 62–95.

two kinds: the nature of the goals as well as the adequacy of the implementative machinery.

Much of the interest and work of students of comparative administration and the very emergence of the field of "development administration" testify eloquently to the assumption that what is wrong with development lies not in its formulation but in its implementation. But this is in some ways an inadequate and unenlightening assumption. Submerged in the shift of attention is evidence of the striking failure of elites and leaders concerned with development to appreciate the main currents and social realities of their time. There is no doubt about the accumulating evidence of administrative inadequacies. However, there is much to suggest that "development" is often a case of failing to recognize problems; followed by an exacerbation of the problems; followed by events which force things to a head; and finally followed by a political decision to remedy the problems under circumstances in which not even the finest cadre of administrators could succeed. This pattern of political response often seems more significant than the deficiencies of the implementative machinery.

Nonetheless, this movement of scholarly attention from the realm of politics to administration is doubtless a reflection of development circumstances as they are, i.e., a shift of the weight of responsibility for success from the one realm to the other. This essay suggests that the shift is associated with the characteristics of the time perspectives of the administrative environment in developing countries. These perspectives result in a political policy of simultaneity and haste for development in all phases and this, in turn, requires that the administrative system rather than any other element in the political process wrestle with the fundamental temporal problems.

The Impetus Toward Politics

With our advancing knowledge of administrative behavior, it has seemed appropriate to dispense with the once fashionable "politics-administration dichotomy" and to fuse the boundaries between politics and administration. This predisposition has served to play down an administrative system's strictly executive role in development, emphasizing instead its independent power or political role. The recent literature on comparative and development administration leaves little doubt that many administrative systems fulfil what is generally considered to be a political role in society. For example, Riggs states flatly, "in the developing countries the extent of bureaucratic involvement in politics is exceptionally high."[9] And LaPalombara writes:

Among other things, we know that some policy implications are implicit in all significant administrative behavior and that the power and influence-seeking groups of a society, sensing this, will cluster about administrative decision points, hoping in this way to exert some leverage over the quite clearly political decisions that emanate from the bureaucracy. What is true of the more advanced countries is probably accentuated in developing nations where the bureaucracy may be the most coherent power center and where, in addition, the major decisions regarding national development are likely to involve authoritative rule-making and rule application by government structures.[10]

The "quite clearly political decisions which emanate from the bureaucracy" are in part associated with the characteristic environmental time perspectives confronting development administration. Through the default of the political realm over important temporal issues of public policy, the administrative system is impelled, in its application of temporal strategies, to make normative as well as technical judgments about issues of development policy. In fact, one can hypothesize that much of what appears to be political policy-making by administrators in non-Western countries is decision-making about some temporal aspects of public policy normally assumed to be part of the political realm in more developed countries.

In order to remedy the temporal inadequacies of "simultaneous and instant development" emanating from the political realm,

9. Fred W. Riggs, "Bureaucrats and Political Development: A Paradoxical View," in LaPalombara, *op. cit.*, p. 121.
10. Joseph LaPalombara, "An Overview of Bureaucracy and Political Development," in LaPalombara, *op. cit.*, p. 14.

there is considerable pressure upon high level administrators to abandon any pretense of exercising an apolitical function. Such administrators increasingly find that where *everything* is desirable, the task of relating possibilities to scarce resources involves political as well as technical decisions about temporal ordering. The primary choices of action, to which other choices, involving the application of quantified notions of synchronization, sequences, and rates are subordinate, frequently turn out to be political decisions. They are political not in the sense of having an ostensible ideological component but rather in the sense that deciding who gets what, when, and how, when resources are scarce and goals are multiple, is essentially a political act. Where, for instance, the goals of education are as amorphous and competitive as they are in most non-Western countries, the administrator acts politically when he makes preliminary choices about the desired relationship of various educational possibilities to developments in the economy and in political institutions. He also acts politically when he makes choices about the phasing and speed of primary, secondary, and higher education in terms of the application of resources, the kinds of knowledge required, and the outlets for variously educated manpower.

To recapitulate: the "normal" assumption behind the application of rational time is that the objectives for administrative action will come down from the political realm in an ordered way. The characteristics of political time premises, however, make a virtue of the logic of haste—everything at once. Thus, the necessary ordering of objectives prior to the application of rational time techniques has to be done by the administration, and in many cases it is a political ordering.

Thus, part of being a development administrator is to be preoccupied with the specific and practical aspects of timing, in a way which involves qualitative and thus normative judgments. There is, for such an administrator, a temporal context in which the doctrine of instant development has to be translated into gross development policies; a context in which the qualitative aspects of synchronization, sequences, rates, duration, succession, continuity, and recurrence have to be applied to policies and priorities before they are broken down into the complex web of operations requiring quantified aspects of these temporal notions.

Again, this is not to say that since, in this sense, administrators are the *new* men of development they are also the *good* men. It may well be that an administrator will act to block, subvert, or thwart development, that he will act to preserve the status quo, to conserve rather than innovate. What is significant is that however he does act and for whatever reason, his ability to be effective is increasingly a function of the temporal context in which he finds himself; a context in which he is bequeathed the qualitative as well as the quantitative implications of a temporal ordering to development.

The Mediation of Time Perspectives

Cultural understandings of time are a part of the environmental time perspectives of administration. But, this essay suggests, they are largely ignored in much of the development process. Political time premises owe little to variations in cultural time. Similarly, rational time perspectives are likely to be technologically not culturally centered. For these reasons one of the significant problems of development administration at the lowest levels becomes the need to mediate the cultural understandings of time which have been ignored or violated in the formulation of development policy.

The weight of the evidence from ventures in administrative reform suggests that administration is not improved very much simply by building in better rational time techniques. This is because such reforms do not really attack the prior problems posed by the absence of cultural time in the doctrine of development, and in the logic of haste. Increasingly, the lower reaches of development administration must mediate the inevitable confrontation between the time premises of the government and the time premises of the people. The community development officer, the irrigation engineer, the health inspector, the postal clerk, the customs official, and the policeman, all engaged in development in their fashion, have to confront cultural time as a mode of temporal awareness that may have had almost nothing to do with setting the policies they administer.

The resolution of this problem is not simple. It requires at least three things from those involved as development administrators in the confrontation.[11] First, they must try to achieve policies within the limits of cultural understandings of time. They must translate and amend instructions to administrative action in the light of cultural norms and attitudes toward time. They must ameliorate the specificity and mathematics of development policies when these confront the people they are intended to change. They have to break down the quantified formulas of synchronization, sequences, and rates drawn from a largely alien technology into vaguer, less stringent sets capable of achieving at least some results. Although some aspects of administrative technology have unyielding time requirements inherent in the process, not all aspects do. To summate, such administrators have to try to do for people what *can* be done by way of changes premised on Western time technology, given the prevailing cultural understandings of time. In this they must be more than administrators in the usual Western bureaucratic sense; innovation and variance from Western rational time premises are both important and possible in this kind of administrative role.

Second, as the new men of development, and thus committed to Western time technology themselves, they are required to proselytize; to persuade the people they administer that the new time conceptions and assumptions on which policies for their betterment are based are the true paths to progress. In trying to change the temporal limitations of the indigenous culture, administrators must seek to create new and different needs which can then be fulfilled by the adopted time technology. Thus, administrators are involved in the consumption aspects of time as well as in the strictly productive aspects, and one of their objectives must

11. In this part of the essay Walter C. Neale's stimulating chapter, "The Economy and Public Administration in Developing Countries," in Fred W. Riggs, ed., *Frontiers of Development Administration* (Durham, N.C., forthcoming), proved of great help.

be to establish the conditions for an increased consumption of the products of the new time technology.

Finally, administrators, as temporal brokers between government and the people, have to convey the environmental clues about cultural understandings of time up to the level at which, hopefully, someone will take them into account when policies are made and resources are allocated. In doing this they are giving their judgments of the local conditions to those who apply temporal strategies to the desired ends of development, in the hope that such judgments will point up the defects of strategies which are too precise.

The confrontation between different attitudes toward the proper use of time is a prominent and repeated theme. The use of Western time techniques may, for example, violate cultural norms about proper division of an individual's time between personal ends and family obligations. The field of education can be cited in illustration. Here cultural norms about the proper length of time which should be spent in becoming educated may conflict sharply with those represented by a newly established educational system based on Western assumptions. The confrontation of Western time technology with cultural understandings of time is an especially acute one in development administration for it is, above all else, a process which makes decisions about the time budgets of people, about how much time individuals undergoing change are to allocate to various activities, in a word, about the proper use of time.

Of course, the extent to which problems of temporal mediation and translation are significant in development administration depends on the presence of alternative political, social, or economic structures for dealing with them. The evidence from the literature of development suggests that the general absence or, in cases where they do exist, the malfunctioning of such structures as political parties, interest groups, market mechanisms, and elements of the mass media results in the administrative system's becoming the only reliable instrument for dealing with the temporal problems of a government deep into development.

Conclusion

This essay started with two assumptions: that the association of time and development was a hard one to make, and that making it might not be very revealing about the process of development administration. As the literature of development already displays a wide range of imponderables, there is danger in adding yet another which might turn out in the final analysis to be a non-problem of development. The use of a simple taxonomy, such as the one developed in this essay, makes it easier to grasp some of the aspects of time and to demonstrate why they are crucial in the context of an interest in development administration.

As seems always the case, the initial phase of trying to cast new light on old problems is a matter of too much speculation chasing too little empirical evidence, the end result of which usually is no more than an agenda for research. So it is with this essay. Only three of the critical temporal problems of development administration have been outlined. The stipulated characteristics of environmental and rational time reveal a range of fundamental problems confronting administration in developing countries. There are, for instance, the difficulties which development administration encounters in having to act under the pressure of haste and simultaneity inspired by the time premises of the political present. Administrators in this situation must make decisions with less knowledge, less participation of other people, less opportunity to use their "rational time" premises, and less ability to seek indigenous solutions as opposed to available Western alternatives, than if the logic of haste did not apply. Another range of problems emerges when one considers that the premises of rational time assume that there is an ability to know enough about achievements to assess means-ends relations. However, in development administration, where the ends, the settings, and the means available all have some degree of novelty, this assumption does not hold—or holds even less well. Thus, the utility of rational time to administrative effort in development frequently becomes suspect.

There seems, therefore, some utility in pursuing the temporal dimension of development administration, particularly with respect to the different time premises and perspectives which are relevant to administration. Time is far from being the only imponderable in development administration, but it does emerge as a significant dimension in the study of the goals, requisites, and problems of development and efforts at its administration.

Chapter 3

Development, Social Change, and Time

John G. Gunnell

Ah, time is a riddling thing, and hard it is to expound its
essence.

Thomas Mann

In seeking to circumscribe and illuminate the temporal dimension of development administration, we are confronted at the
outset with concepts that seem to lack any substantive meaning.
There is general agreement that it is useful to distinguish development administration from other types of administration "as a
separate focus for research,"[1] but although recently ". . . the term
'development administration' has become a fashionable expression . . . it is somewhat artificial. Its meaning is unexplored and
deceptively vague, and it is in danger of becoming merely a slick
expression for 'good public administration' that adds nothing to
professional vocabulary or to thinking about problems of public
administration."[2] The ambiguity surrounding the term certainly
derives in part from the fact that administration, though a relatively differentiated activity in modern Western society, is entwined in developing countries with what in terms of much
recent thought would be understood as non-administrative phenomena.[3] The traditional study of administration and bureaucracy

1. Ferrel Heady, *Public Administration: A Comparative Perspective* (Englewood Cliffs, N.J., 1966), p. 10.
2. Irving Swerdlow, ed., *Development Administration* (Syracuse, N.Y., 1963), p.
ix.
3. Fred W. Riggs, *Administration in Developing Countries* (Boston, 1964), pp.
51–54. See also his "Administrative Development: An Elusive Concept" in John
D. Montgomery and William J. Siffin, eds., *Approaches to Development* (New
York, 1966), pp. 225–256.

presupposed a particular social context and tended to universal-
ize its concepts. But the "relativity" of administration has become
one of the premises of contemporary studies. This shift in perspective has been accompanied by the rise to prominence of the
ideal of "development" and of development administration. However, for these we lack clear and acceptable definitions.

Development and Development Administration:
A Search for Meaning

To assert that "development administration is the process of
guiding an organization toward the achievement of development
objectives"[4] tells us little more than that development administration is the administration of development. The designation of an
activity or class of activities as an instance of development administration should involve more than arbitrary classification; it
should indicate, at least to some extent, an explanation of that
activity. Also, a definition may be so broad that it loses meaning.
The suggestion that development administration or the pursuit or
attainment of development objectives involves innovation and
creativity or that it is "the public management of economic and
social change in terms of deliberate public policy"[5] does not carry
us very far toward isolating the activity in question. It is unlikely
that we shall succeed in clarifying our ideas about development
administration until we arrive at a more meaningful concept or
theoretical definition of development.

Despite the burgeoning literature on development—social,
economic, political, administrative, and other—there remains
considerable confusion about the meaning of the term and the
appropriateness of the diverse models which have been recommended for ordering the elusive phenomena the word suggests.
In discussions of development there is often either an immediate
redefinition in terms of another concept such as "modernization,"

4. Edward W. Weidner, *Technical Assistance in Public Administration Overseas: The Case for Development Administration* (Chicago, 1965), p. 200.
5. Paul Meadows, "Motivation for Change and Development Administration," in
Swerdlow, *op. cit.*, pp. 86, 98.

"industrialization," "Westernization," "self-sustained growth," "structural differentiation," and/or a shift to a consideration of the requisite conditions, causes, goals, or impact of development. Although this *may* be quite relevant, "development" in the end seems to connote much, whereas its denotation is vague and its defining characteristics tend to remain unspecified. Lucian Pye, for example, after analyzing several current definitions of "political development," concludes that "in the last analysis the problems of political development revolve around the relationships between political culture, the authoritative structures, and the general political process."[6]

Sometimes the problem of conceptualization of development is overcome by ignoring it and concentrating on specific case studies in which the meaning of the term is assumed to be self-evident. Indeed, there may be some justification for such a procedure, since development as understood by most social scientists is a relatively circumscribed historical event, both in terms of its impact on the material conditions of social existence and the extent to which it permeates the consciousness of modern society; it can be "empirically investigated." But no mere accumulation of case studies will in itself lead to an adequate understanding of development or produce a viable concept.

If the concept of development is to be adequately delineated, it must be supplied with substantive content yet apply in cross-cultural contexts and encompass diverse goals and areas of endeavor, both in the public and private realms. However, the solution does not lie, at least in the first instance, in a concerted effort on the part of the community of scholars to establish operational definitions and agreement on models. Apparent semantic difficulties are only manifestations of deeper theoretical problems; the need for restatement and re-theorization is of a more fundamental nature. To speak meaningfully about development, it is necessary to make some decisions about the wider perspec-

6. Lucian W. Pye, "The Concept of Political Development," *The Annals of the American Academy of Political and Social Science*, 358 (Mar., 1965), 13. There is no need to undertake a systematic review of the literature to demonstrate the existence of these problems since both self-criticism and awareness are prevalent. Cf. Joseph LaPalombara, ed., *Bureaucracy and Political Development* (Princeton, 1963).

tive within which any notion of development must inevitably be conceived—the idea of social change. Any statement about development presupposes, at least implicitly, a conception of social change, for if development is anything, it is an aspect of social change. But if development and development administration are to become substantive concepts, they must be defined narrowly enough to include certain instances of social change and exclude others. This is why, for example, the equation of "development" and "structural differentiation" is ultimately unsatisfactory; differentiation and integration may be attributes, indicators, or accompanying characteristics of development, but they do not meaningfully distinguish it from other forms of social change.[7] Such conceptual reduplication begs the question.

Time and Social Change: Explication of the Problem

The principal focus of contemporary social science is on the problem of social change, and it is in this focus, especially as it relates to development and reflects the concern of the modern age, that the social sciences gain their relevancy. If it is true "that the correct basic model, the underlying pattern (in terms of which we do and should think about society), is a specific transition, a metamorphosis,"[8] then it is principally the social sciences that are addressing themselves to this emerging paradigm. Despite the contemporary concern with social change, social science evidently feels itself ill-equipped to deal with this dimension; or at least it is acutely self-conscious of what some have charged is its methodologically, and even ideologically, static or conservative bias and its inability to conceptualize change adequately. It is well recognized that in the study of both comparative administration and comparative politics "one of the limitations of most

7. Cf. S. N. Eisenstadt, "Modernization and Conditions of Sustained Growth," *World Politics*, XVI (July, 1964), 576–594; also Talcott Parsons, "Some Considerations on the Theory of Social Change," *Rural Sociology*, XXVI (Sept., 1961), 219–239.
8. Ernest Gellner, *Thought and Change* (London, 1964), p. 73.

existing models lies in their handling of social change."[9] However, this limitation merely reflects a theoretical impasse that is apparent in the social sciences in general in their attempt to deal with the element of change in the human condition or what C. A. O. van Nieuwenhuijze has aptly termed the "inconstancy complex."[10] Nowhere is this problem more evident than in the current critiques, justifications, and modifications of functionalism and systems analysis.

Attacks levied against functionalism and systems theory for their failure to account adequately for change—especially the rapid change associated with political development—have been numerous; and the active responses of the advocates, both in defending such approaches and in offering qualifications, would seem to imply that the criticisms are not irrelevant.[11] Yet much of the literature growing out of the debate over whether an approach such as structural functionalism is inherently defective in terms of conceptualizing social change centers, for the most part, on a superficial issue which tends to obscure the substantive problems underlying this controversy. It is evident that "despite its emphasis upon the conditions for stability, structural functionalism does not lead necessarily to a defense of the *status quo* or to a disregard for processes of change."[12] The main problem presented by structural functionalism becomes unintelligible when it

9. Edward W. Weidner, "Development Administration: A New Focus for Research," in Ferrel Heady and Sybil Stokes, eds., *Papers in Comparative Public Administration* (Ann Arbor, Mich., 1962), p. 104. For a review of contemporary theorizing on the problem, see Robert A. Packenham, "Approaches to the Study of Political Development," *World Politics*, XVII (Oct., 1964), 108–120. See also Alfred Diamant, "Political Development: Approaches to Theory and Strategy," in Montgomery and Siffin, *op. cit.*

10. *Society as Process* (The Hague, 1962), p. 40.

11. For recent representative attempts to restate systems theory and structural-functional approaches in order to produce suitable conceptual frameworks for dealing with social and political change see Gabriel A. Almond, "A Developmental Approach to Political Systems," *World Politics*, XVII (Jan., 1965), 183–214; Alvin Boskoff, "Functional Analysis as a Source of a Theoretical Repertory and Research Tasks in the Study of Social Change," in George K. Zollschan and Walter Hirsch, eds., *Explorations in Social Change* (Boston, 1964); Don Martindale, ed., *Functionalism in the Social Sciences: The Strength and Limits of Functionalism in Anthropology, Economics, Political Science, and Sociology* (Philadelphia, 1965). For further literature on this debate, see Werner J. Cahnman and Alvin Boskoff, "Sociology and History: Reunion and Rapprochement," p. 16, n. 28, in Cahnman and Boskoff, eds., *Sociology and History* (Glencoe, Ill., 1964).

12. William Flanigan and Edwin Fogelman, "Functionalism in Political Science," in Martindale, *op. cit.*, p. 119.

is couched in terms of "dynamic" versus "static" models or "process" theories versus "structural" theories. Dynamic elements and explanations of change can conceivably be introduced into any approach, and "equilibrium" models may be supplemented by mechanisms of change or transformed by the introduction of notions such as that of a moving equilibrium.[13] Although it is not always apparent, what underlies the debate over structural functionalism is not the question of dynamic elements in the theory but the problem of reconciling two different philosophical positions on the study of social phenomena.

Dahrendorf, in his well-known critique of structural-functional analysis in contemporary sociology, argues that concentration upon the "social system" is part of a utopian heritage which has led to a neglect of the problem of change and urges that sociologists adopt a conflict model and begin to look at society as a process of continuous change as well as an equilibrium. Interwoven with, or at least latent in, this demand for a different way of viewing society is the suggestion that investigators direct their attention toward "familiar reality," become "problem-conscious," and concern themselves with "historical change" rather than building a "huge and allegedly all-embracing superstructure of concepts."[14]

Dahrendorf not only explicitly identifies the conflict model with the non-utopian open society but equates it with the unique, concrete, and historical. But on its face the concept of "conflict" is no more empirically grounded or closer to historical reality than "system" or "equilibrium"; as a model, conflict remains in the realm of the abstract and merely provides an alternate, or as Dahrendorf seems to suggest, a complementary mode of describing social relations or a different distribution of emphasis.

Such model refinements may be salutary, and a considerable amount of interesting theorizing, especially that revolving around the concept of "institutionalization," has worked toward a rap-

13. Cf. Francesca Cancia, "Functional Analysis of Change," *Am. Soc. Rev.*, XXV (1960), 818–827; Gideon Sjoberg, "Contradictory Functional Requirements and Social Systems," *Jour. Conf. Res.*, IV (June, 1960), 198–208.

14. Ralf Dahrendorf, "Out of Utopia: Toward a Reorientation of Sociological Analysis," *Am. Jour. Soc.*, LXIV (Sept., 1958), 115–127. Also "Toward a Theory of Social Conflict," *Jour. Conf. Res.*, XI (1958), 170–183.

prochement between structural-functional and conflict models.[15] Yet the problem implicitly raised by Dahrendorf, the problem of relating a conceptual model of society to society as a concrete historical process, remains unsolved. Dahrendorf prefaces his article with a quote from Plato's *Timaeus* in which Socrates, referring to the *polis* described in the *Republic*, states that he wishes the city could be viewed in action. It is interesting to note that subsequently in the *Timaeus* and *Critias* this is accomplished, not by adding dynamic or conflict elements to the model in the *Republic*—these were there already—but by recalling an ancient tale relating the history of a similar society in the past. Myron Weiner, discussing the inadequacy of functional analysis for the formulation of a "theory of political change" suggests "linking historical studies of political development with the systematic study of existing political systems," but this suggestion seems to be more an evasion of the problem than a solution.[16]

In a consideration of social change, as with development, we are immediately confronted with the problem of *time* which is generally understood as "intrinsic to the very concept of change."[17] But precisely why and in what manner it is "intrinsic" is problematical.[18] In our tradition of thought, "change" and "time" are closely linked, nearly synonymous, and to account for one is in some sense to account for the other. Also we find that time and change ultimately appear to refer to the historical dimension of society, and we are cautioned that "if we abstract from time, we kill society, because it is in itself a process, it is life, it is moving."[19] Wilbert Moore suggests that the predominance of static models is part of the natural development of an analytic science which preoccupies itself initially with description before explaining change through time and developing process con-

15. See Zollschan and Hirsch, *op. cit.*, Sec. II, "Working Papers in the Theory of Institutionalization."

16. Myron Weiner, "Political Modernization and Evolutionary Theory," in Herbert R. Barringer, George I. Blanksten, and Raymond W. Mack, eds., *Social Change in Developing Areas* (Cambridge, Mass., 1965), pp. 108, 111.

17. Wilbert E. Moore, *Social Change* (Englewood Cliffs, N.J., 1963), p. 23.

18. Max Heirich has offered an interesting analysis of the idea of time in several theories of social change in "The Use of Time in the Study of Social Change," *Am. Soc. Rev.*, XXIX (June, 1964), 386–397.

19. J. A. Ponsionen, *The Analysis of Social Change Reconsidered* (The Hague, 1962), p. 16.

cepts.[20] But the problem of the relation between statics and dynamics in social theory is not a problem of models as such but a problem of reconciling models with reality; it is not a question of developing more sophisticated theories but a question of the epistemological foundations of social science. The attempt to create so-called dynamic models may be largely a misdirected enterprise, and certainly the mere introduction of dynamic elements into a model does not automatically account for the temporal or historical dimension of social reality.

E. R. Leach has argued that the terminology and models of functionally oriented social science are fictional structures and abstractions from reality, and thus social structures necessarily appear as static equilibriums while "real societies exist in time and space" and "every society is a process in time."[21] Although the occasionally tortuous path which Leach suggests for seeking a remedy to the inevitable tension between concept and reality may not be entirely satisfactory,[22] his work deserves special attention since it directly confronts a major problem of conceptualization in the social sciences in general and especially the difficulty that sociology has encountered in dealing with social change. Leach maintains that sociology and anthropology have tended to derive their concepts from Durkheim rather than Weber and consequently have formulated their generalizations for the purpose of comparison, have valued stable societies and viewed change as pathological, and have neglected the explanation of social action on the level of participant meaning.

When the concept of social structure is utilized as a category of comparison there may be an emphasis on synchronic studies and an attending supposition of stable equilibrium which distorts the dynamic character of social reality; however, the real danger is in social structures becoming reifications of "models which exist only as logical constructions" in the mind of the investigator and the stress on external organization leads to a disregard of the

20. Wilbert E. Moore, *Man, Time, and Society* (New York, 1963), p. v.
21. *Political Systems of Highland Burma* (Cambridge, Mass., 1954), p. 5.
22. Cf. Ernest Gellner, "Time and Theory in Social Anthropology," *Mind*, LXVII (Apr., 1958), 182–202, esp. 191–192, 203. Also E. R. Leach, *Rethinking Anthropology* (London, 1961), chap. i.

historical context and the cultural symbols which distinguish one society from another. Descriptions of social structure tend then to be in terms of categories which claim universality but which are in fact derived from ethnocentric hypotheses about how a social system works or should work. Leach contends that in order to understand social structure and social action the investigator must not look primarily at functional or technical relations which have been determined a priori but at the ritual patterns or aesthetic and ethical symbols, both verbal and non-verbal, which express the existential structure of society and the meaning of action for the participants. When these are specified, social structure, as understood and articulated by the actors, will not appear as the precise coherent whole reflected in the functionalist's model but as an imprecise and often inconsistent, and even conflicting, set of ideas about the system. Leach further contends that these inherent conflicts and ambiguities in ritual expression are both a necessity for the effective operation of a social system and the vehicle of change; and that once the different operative ideas are understood, social structure and social change can be explained.

Leach's analysis is obviously not more free from difficulties than Dahrendorf's. But his argument serves to demonstrate again that at the root of the problem of accounting for social change and the temporal or historical dimension of social reality lies the problem of the relation between typological comparison and particular explanations of "how things work," and that explanation of social phenomena must proceed in the direction of penetrating the symbols and meanings which are manifest in interpersonal communication and constitute the actor's view of reality. Leach correctly emphasizes the neglect of historical studies in functional analysis and the need for grounding explanation in the historico-cultural situation, and above all that comparison and explanatory generalizations are not necessary equivalent.

Another aspect of the same problem appears in the common assertion that since structural analysis leads to a static or synchronic approach, it is necessary to develop diachronic theory to account for change through time. Or, phrased in a different manner, structural models must be complemented by process models. Nadel suggests that "the greater facility with which [structural analysis] can employ geometrical, spatial models, the less, it seems, must be its capacity to take account of events *in time* affecting and varying social structure." However, in opposition to Firth, who believes that structure must be augmented by another concept to express variance and change, Nadel argues that this problem is the result of a misunderstanding and that the notion of structure does not exclude "recognition of events and processes in time."[23] Thus far Nadel is perfectly correct, for simply to utter the word "structure," despite some of its static and spatial connotations, does not mean a neglect of the temporal or historical dimension.

To a large extent what Nadel means by time is what may be termed implied or implicit time, i.e., the fact that the performance of social roles or the maintenance of a social structure indicates continuity and takes place over time or in particular sequences. The mere introduction of temporal language such as continuity, duration, sequence, and process does not automatically account for what many individuals mean when they refer to the temporal dimension of social reality. It is not that the study of structure excludes recognition of time, but that time does not necessarily constitute a significant variable in such studies.[24] As Fortes has demonstrated, structural studies *can* include time as a significant variable,[25] but this may require looking at structure as the result of a particular historical process rather than as a configuration of groups or role alignments. Social action over time gives rise to forms and structure or relatively stable entities which become the context of further action which in the end may create new forms. Obviously these two aspects are not entirely separable. We can fruitfully investigate social structure either as a particular configuration of relations at a particular time or as an entity that has evolved over a certain period, but it may not be

23. S. F. Nadel, *The Theory of Social Structure* (Glencoe, Ill., 1957), pp. 126, 128. Emphasis in original.

24. Raymond Firth, *Essays on Social Organization and Values* (London, 1964), p. 13.

25. Meyer Fortes, "Time and Social Structure: An Ashanti Case Study," in Fortes, ed., *Social Structure* (New York, 1963), p. 58.

possible to account satisfactorily for both aspects simultaneously.

What is at issue here is not merely whether time appears as a significant variable. When Leach and Firth challenge structural analysis, they are challenging a mode of explanation not only in regard to its ability to deal with social change but in its adequacy for producing a meaningful understanding of social relationships in general. The problem is not one of supplementing a structural model with a process model; the problem revolves around the relationship between models and social reality. When Firth suggests that notions of structure must be complemented by the concept of "organization," like Leach he is advocating not so much an alternate or supplementary model as a different explanatory approach that looks at the particular working arrangements through which a society orients itself and posits and pursues its goals[26] rather than isolating and reintegrating variables in terms of some formal analytic schema designed for purposes of generalization and comparison. What we are confronted with is a problem which has plagued social science from its inception; it is a problem which was strikingly manifest during the nineteenth century in what may be loosely (and perhaps misleadingly) described as the conflict between history and sociology, a conflict which was to a great extent concerned with the attempt to solve the problem of understanding social change.

Time and Social Change: Perspective on the Problem

It was precisely the tension between generalization on the one hand and the unique, changing, and historical character of society on the other which formed the focal point of much of Weber's work, and it might well be argued that social science has not been able to advance far beyond Weber in terms of a solution to this problem. Today we are faced, in the work of Parsons and others, with the drive for a systematic sociology and the development of general abstract conceptual frameworks which are con-

26. Firth, *op. cit.*, pp. 35, 45, 49–50, chap. iii.

ceived as universal in scope and which are basically comparative in orientation. This approach tends toward conceptual reification and the objectification of models such as the "social system" which operate at the expense of the identity of the phenomena which they are designed to illuminate. And despite the current emphasis on making these approaches dynamic and the recent attention to evolution and social change,[27] they continue to fail to provide satisfactory explanations of particular instances of social change. Too often those who criticize and distrust model-building and nomothetic analysis, which they feel ultimately leads to an equilibrium view of society and to a neglect of how actual societies operate, leave us with an alternative which amounts to little more than the idiographic descriptive narrative of the traditional historian.

What is interesting is that "both functionalism and historicism have arisen in reaction to 'unilinear' theories of progress and evolution."[28] The sociology typified by Comte and the early evolutionists purported to be an historical science of society, but the universe with which they were concerned was centered outside concrete history, and social change was viewed in terms of organic analogies and laws of uniform development which facilitated comparison. Functionalism was in part a reaction to such obvious deficiencies of evolutionism as the neglect of internal social arrangements, the attempt to fit observations into an a priori philosophy of history, and the assumption that putting events into a historical series somehow serves as an explanation either of the sequence or the result. But the functionalist alternative was not based so much on a remedy for these deficiencies as on the recurring idea in the Western intellectual tradition that an explanation of change is predicated on an understanding of the essence of that which changes, and this meant an understanding of structure and function. In attempting to explain social change in these terms, the functionalist, like the evolutionist, tended to subordinate empirical investigation to the development of ab-

27. See, for example, Talcott Parsons, "Evolutionary Universals in Society," *Am. Soc. Rev.*, XXIX (June, 1964), 339–357.
28. Cahnman and Boskoff, *op. cit.*, p. 9.

stract categories of analysis which would supposedly be applicable to the description and explanation of all social systems.[29] In addition, although functionalism did not ignore the problem of social change, the concern with the conditions of stability led to a rejection not only of evolutionism, which assumed change to be a natural fact, but of historical considerations in general. A distribution of emphasis which favored synchronic analysis tended to disadvantage the approach in its formulation of explanations of change, which became understood as a derivative and even pathological phenomenon. But even more importantly, the emphasis on the relation between reconstructed formal elements in a social system was, and continues to be, conducive to a sociology based on a new kind of comparative anatomy which, like evolutionism in its search for universal categories, again does violence to the explanation of particular processes and events. The historical school also opposed the naturalistic sociology represented by Comte, Spencer, and Mill and the implication of the unity of mankind contained in the search for laws of uniform social development. Rather than turning toward the creation of a new science of society, they stressed the pluralistic character of social phenomena and attempted to raise narrative history to the approach to the study of man. With Croce, the absolute autonomy and universality of historical thought were proclaimed.

This is not the place to attempt to disentangle the intricate threads of nineteenth-century intellectual history but it was here, in the midst of this controversy about historical knowledge and the methodology of the social sciences, that Weber placed himself. It is precisely because he sought to mediate this controversy that he has been viewed both as one of the fathers of modern systematic sociology and the child of historicism. For some, "Weber's sociology is the most coherent expression of the historiography of an epoch which has ceased to believe in history" and the culmination of an intellectual tradition which constituted "the transition or decline of German thought from historicism to typo-

29. See Kenneth Bock, *The Acceptance of Histories* (Berkeley, 1956) and "Evolution, Function, and Change," *Am. Soc. Rev.*, XXVIII (Apr., 1963), 229–237.

logical sociologism."[30] Others maintain that in Weber's work the "formal aspect remains subordinated to the historical one" and that "in replacing typological conceptualization as a means with systematic sociology as an end" contemporary sociology has reversed Weber's emphasis.[31] However, Weber sought in the construction of the ideal-type a mode of conceptualization which could serve the need of sociological explanation and generalization and yet preserve the identity, meaning, and fluidity of social phenomena: "We do not wish to force schematically the infinite and multivarious historical life, but simply to create concepts useful for special purposes and for orientations."[32] This is not to assert that Weber definitively "solved" the problems, only that the issues with which he grappled remain the ones we confront when attempting to grasp the dimension of social change. As Serges Hughes points out, "there are grounds for believing that if there is any dialogue possible between Croce and a good part of modern sociology, it would have to be done through the mediation of Weber."[33]

The problem of conceptualizing social change and grasping the temporal dimension of social reality does not necessitate an abandonment of generalization in favor of historical description. The accumulation of historical material is not sufficient for adequate explanation, but attention to such material is necessary both for understanding how a society works and how it changes. Above all, the problem is not one of introducing more sophisticated mechanisms of change into existing models or producing new ones; the problem revolves around the correspondence between concepts and sociocultural reality. What is required is a reconsideration of the nature of concept formation in the social sciences, and this is essentially an epistemological rather than a methodo-

30. Carlo Antoni, *From History to Sociology*, trans. Hayden V. White (Detroit, 1959), pp. 167, vii.

31. Werner J. Cahnman, "Max Weber and the Methodological Controversy in the Social Sciences," in Cahnman and Boskoff, *op. cit.*, pp. 85–103.

32. Max Weber in Talcott Parsons, ed., *Max Weber: The Theory of Social and Economic Organization* (New York, 1947), p. 300.

33. "The Evaluation of Sociology in Croce's Theory of History," in Cahnman and Boskoff, *op. cit.*, pp. 137–138.

logical question. And this is why Weber's work becomes the starting point of any such reconsideration.[34]

Unlike the systematic sociology of Parsons in which concepts are derived from a theoretical system which is nearly accorded an ontological independence and validity of its own and from which concepts gain meaning by participation in the system, Weber's theoretical construct, the ideal-type, finds its origin, meaning, justification, and application in the realm of the explanation of concrete social events. The ideal-type is an *ad hoc* construction emerging from a confrontation between the theorist and reality. Like any construct it is not itself a part of the world it attempts to capture in the sense that it is a symbolic medium, a way of seeing and organizing phenomena. The purpose of the ideal-type is explanatory; it aims exclusively at making the encountered world intelligible. The universe with which Weber was concerned was not a universe of abstractions in which the unique and historical entity or event was isolated as an instance of a general category and integrated with other categories in a formal system. An ideal-type is essentially a construct designed to reflect a system of historically expressed symbols and to make the structure and meaning of social action accessible. Even concepts such as society and history represented not so much structural forms of interaction as historical tendencies toward particular symbolic patterns of behavior.[35] As Cahnman points out, Weber's "theoretical con-

34. For a contrary interpretation see Talcott Parsons, "Evaluation and Objectivity in Social Science: An Interpretation of Max Weber's Contribution," *Int. Soc. Sci. Jour.*, XVII (1965), 46–63. Parsons maintains that Weber believed that he had found in science or the "generality of theoretical conceptualization and the canons of empirical validity" a standard of relevance which freed the investigator from the particularism of the historical school (p. 54). But Parsons fails to distinguish in Weber's thought between concept formation and the testing of concepts. In the formation of concepts Weber never divorced himself from history. Parsons makes the incredible and unsubstantiated assertion that "Weber is not concerned with the problem of the grounds on which valid empirical science in the field of human meaning and motivated action is or is not possible. . . . He was no more concerned with the epistemological problem than is the modern physicist with the question of whether the physical world 'really exists'. . . ." (P. 57.) Such a statement can only derive from a view which insists on interpreting Weber's thought as part of an historical development culminating in Parsonian sociology.

35. Nathan Rotenstreich, *Between Past and Present* (New Haven, 1958), p. 177. See also H. Stuart Hughes, *Consciousness and Society* (New York, 1961), p. 325.

struct summarizes a historical process; 'formal' sociology is transformed into 'cultural,' or historical sociology."[36]

What separates Weber's formulations from much of contemporary sociological theory is the extent to which his concepts preserved the historicity or identity of social reality by referring to the subjective meaning structure of human activity. Much of contemporary sociology has become disengaged from its subject matter and is marked by an increasing formalism; and it is *this* tendency which underlies the problem of social change. "The search for categories that apply without reference to time or place easily produces a static bias unless we are extremely careful to notice the historical limits of our generalizations."[37] For Weber there could be no closed system of concepts both because of the changing perspective of the investigator and because of the fact that reality continually manifested itself in new forms. This meant that the focus of sociological investigation was not typological classification and comparison but the maintenance of relevance between construct and reality. Weber's neglect of social structure and institutional framework was the inevitable consequence of an approach which took intentional action and subjective meaning as the fundamental datum. What distinguishes this orientation from an approach such as that of Durkheim, with its concern for structure, is not so much the emphasis on action as one on prior decisions about the ultimate nature of social reality and the relation between theory and object.

The perspectives of Weber and Durkheim may be taken as representing two modes of theorizing which are grounded in the very nature of sociation. "The first presents us with a view of society as a network of human meanings and embodiments of human activity. The second, on the other hand, presents us with society conceived of as a thing-like facticity, standing over against its individual members with coercive controls and molding them in its sociological processes."[38] Neither view can be

36. *Op. cit.*, p. 110.
37. Barrington Moore, Jr., *Political Power and Social Theory* (Cambridge, Mass., 1958), p. 136.
38. Peter Berger and Stanley Pullberg, "Reification and the Sociological Critique of Consciousness," *History and Theory*, IV (1965), 196.

complete in itself; both relate to a process in which intentional action creates social objects which in turn become the context of action. The social order is both the creation and creator of action. But the fact of "objectivation" or the externalization of action in institutions and other social artifacts becomes the starting point for a mode of theorizing which may end in "reification" or a process whereby *"the characteristic of thing-hood becomes the standard of objective reality."*[39] The processional and integrated character of social phenomena begins to recede as the world breaks down into a universe of things and of changes between one thing and another—statics and dynamics.

Although the anti-historical character of Durkheim's thought has probably been exaggerated,[40] social change nevertheless appears in his formulations as a kind of comparative statics, the change from one abstract set of relationships or pattern of society to another; here "description of change seems impossible as description breaks the film down into static pictures," which in the end are inseparable from formal concepts.[41] To argue that these concepts are historically grounded does not solve the problem. Concepts derived from the analysis of concrete social events are raised to the level of universality and then re-introduced as categories for organizing data; this insures the ultimate alienation of concept and reality. Here we reach the problem of the extent to which sociological concepts and theoretical variables which are abstracted from the experience of Western societies can be meaningfully applied as either descriptive or explanatory categories in radically different cultural contexts.

For Weber, sociological concepts, although indicating forms of social relations, served essentially to illuminate historical occurrences and human choice, whereas formal sociology, such as that typified by Parsons, tends to destroy the historicity of the data by subsumption in archetypes, such as roles and systems of action (in a way similar to that by which primitive man overcame historical uniqueness by enveloping it in the primordial myth).

39. *Ibid.*, pp. 199–200.
40. See Robert N. Bellah, "Durkheim and History," in Cahnman and Boskoff, *op. cit.*, pp. 85–103.
41. Ponsionen, *op. cit.*, p. 26.

These archetypes, although originally grounded in historical experience, are restated as timeless, placeless, and universal categories of description. Here both action and the product of action are lifted from the temporal or historical dimension; the present as the scene of meaningful action and change becomes the space of an abstract process of interaction between equally abstract entities. For Weber social change did not present itself as a particular conceptual problem because it was presupposed; his concern was not man and society as reified abstractions or objects defined by a limited a priori vocabulary, but "man as a concrete reality in historically changing society."[42] Yet for contemporary social science, social change and accounting for the temporal dimension does present itself as a problem, or more precisely as an anomaly —and necessarily so.

It is relevant to note that this difficulty is hardly of recent origin, as our discussion may have implied; it has been a persistent aspect of Western thought from the time of Aristotle. For Aristotle, as for modern sociology, change and time are basically devoid of ontological status. Aristotle's political sociology could not grasp change as reality, for what was real was a thing which at any moment or "now" was in a particular state with a particular form, and this form was in the end a logical category of definition. Social reality could be conceptualized only insofar as it could be subsumed under one of the definitive categories that described the universe. These categories had no transcendental existence as they had in Plato's system. Reality referred to the immanent world, which to a large extent was a world of uniqueness and change; but only that which existed within a present, without change, and conformed to one of the categories, could be said to "be." For example, Aristotle well recognized the *polis* as an entity with an historical existence, e.g., Athens existing in the past, present, and future and performing unique actions. Yet on the level of science or political sociology only to the extent that the form or the constitution remained the same was Athens the same *polis*. Thus, there was an irreducible gap between the logi-

42. Karl Jaspers, *Three Essays*, trans. Ralph Manheim (New York, 1964), p. 230.

cal and the empirical, sociology and history, and statics and dynamics. In terms of Aristotle's philosophy the problem was insolvable. Social reality manifested itself as a series of successive forms or structures, and change was that nebulous dimension which somehow interceded between successive structures. Aristotle could conceptualize changes in time, i.e., a series of discrete constitutions, but not change through time. It might not be an exaggeration to say that subsequent sociology has to a large extent occupied itself with attempting to solve a problem which does not admit solution in terms of its own logic.

Time and Social Change: Toward Solution of the Problem

In the last analysis, the problem of conceptualizing social change is the problem of reconciling the quest for generality with the demand for empirical relevance. We experience sociocultural reality in its uniqueness or historicity which means that "we remain aware of its being bound up with the time dimension of the mode of human existence, or with the time as such."[43] Yet the rationalizing mind in its encounter with the world distinguishes, abstracts, and compares in its desire to order and encompass the complexity of reality. The drive to name and qualitatively distinguish the components of the phenomenal world is complemented by the drive to reintegrate what has been abstracted into a conceptual system; as with Aristotle, the search for the social system is the search for a definitive vocabulary. But this process destroys the historicity of the data and obscures the existential relation between the data. To a certain extent this is inevitable, for the symbol-object dichotomy is the price paid for discursive thought. Yet there may be, nevertheless, viable alternatives to a mode of theorizing which is marked by the search for universal categories and renders unintelligible what at present we most wish to understand.

As van Nieuwenhuijze has pointed out, "Social science theory

43. Van Nieuwenhuijze, *Society as Process*, p. 23.

has not been successful in developing notions meant to conceive of reality exclusively in terms of inconstancy—notions like 'process,' 'action' or activity."[44] This is so because the mode of conceptualization which predominates is basically one of qualitative distinction between observed entities with constancy presupposed, and change must be dragged in by the back door as simply that which takes place where constancy is absent.

Even those theories which attempt to complement "structure" with "process" or argue that we must look at both "statics" and "dynamics" do not actually accord change or time an equal place. This is not simply a normative preference for stability. In a pattern of thought that divides the world up into "things" and states of a system, change loses any real meaning. Change is relegated to a position not unlike that of chaos in classical thought; it is chaotic essentially because it cannot fit the categories that define the elements of the universe. From Aristotle to the present, change is basically coming-to-be and degeneration or, in contemporary terminology, integration and differentiation. There is no need to enter into a detailed survey of theories of social change; suffice it to say that many of the major theories from the nineteenth century to the present are basically variations of one logical scheme where qualitative difference between entities is equated with time lapse and change. In terms of such theories, "what is empirically perceived as changes can but conceptually feature as change from one thing or state of affairs to another. Never can it feature as the dynamics of reality, in the sense of an equivalent complement to statics."[45]

Even cybernetic models, which claim to conform to the modern vision of the universe as an open-ended process by providing a means for "mapping the performance of some thing or process over time,"[46] are in fact only highly sophisticated, or complicated, versions of the basic construction in which change appears as that which occurs between different "things" or states of a system. The

44. *Ibid.*, p. 79.
45. C. A. O. van Nieuwenhuijze, "Social Scientist in Pursuit of Social Change," revised version of a paper presented at the International Seminar on Interdisciplinary Approach to Social Change in Developing Countries, New Delhi, 1964, p. 25.
46. Karl Deutsch, *The Nerves of Government* (Glencoe, Ill., 1963), p. 25.

premises of many of the proponents of some version of systems theory demonstrate two of the basic fallacies of social science in its approach to social change: The idea that scientific theory evolves naturally from statics to dynamics and that the basic problem in conceptualizing social change is to inject dynamic elements into equilibrium models or otherwise make them relevant for specifying a time series. But there is no logical order of theoretical development, and we cannot equate the so-called dynamism of models with the time dimension of social reality or history. The introduction of such notions as "moving equilibrium" and distinctions between "macro" and "micro" time do not solve the problem. So-called dynamic theories tend to be not so much dynamic as complex.

To view the position of the social sciences as caught between the poles of grand theory and hyperfactualism is an oversimplification, and to advocate middle-range theory is too easy a solution if it does not entail some fundamental changes in epistemological assumptions. Nor is the current theoretical impasse to be solved by turning social science into a policy science, as has been the tendency in the study of political development, which in some cases has become synonymous with technical assistance. Since some of the most important questions which social science faces have become problematical in terms of the predominant mode of theorizing, the way forward must lie in the direction of a new, or at least modified, view of the relation between theory and reality. Van Nieuwenhuijze, like Leach, has at least provided an indication of the path along which a meaningful attempt at re-theorization might proceed.

Van Nieuwenhuijze contends that social science must begin by focusing not on "what a thing is but how it works." This means that the search for definitive and universal categories must be relinquished in order to allow the constant interaction and mutual determination of constructs and instances of reality. To accomplish this, "conceptualization in categorical terms would have to be replaced by conceptualization in *ad hoc* terms" which would mean that concepts and theories would be limited in their inclusiveness, both historically and in terms of the present. This vertical complementarity between concept and instance of reality must be supplemented by a horizontal complementarity both between concepts and between particular elements of social reality. Here the traditional relation between concepts—that of logical opposition and qualitative distinction—would be replaced by "*ad hoc* mutual relevance," whereby concepts would derive their meaning from their relation with other concepts in "an encompassing process of endlessly interwoven operational relationships." With this complementarity between instances of reality and between concepts on the one hand and between conceptual patterns or theories and observed patterns of reality on the other hand, change would not present itself as a problem; it would appear as an a priori assumption. From this perspective statics and dynamics or structure and change would not constitute different ontological dimensions but complementary aspects of the same order of reality.[47]

Nowhere has this need for mutual relevance been more evident than in the cultural shock social science has suffered in its encounter with other societies in its study of development; here the frustration of trying to work with formal categories derived from Western experience has been most poignant. And this frustration has been assuaged largely by moving to still higher levels of conceptual abstraction and substituting universal description for explanation.

But as should now be clear, the problem of conceptualizing social change is not one of simply creating "better" theories and models in the sense of more complex, formal analytical frameworks. Social science involves more than arbitrarily ordering data; like physical science "it is also a way of thinking about the world, a way of forming conceptions."[48] In other words, it is impossible to justify any theory, model, or methodology except in terms of a commitment to prior decisions about the nature of the universe which they are designed to explore. There is an inevita-

47. Van Nieuwenhuijze, "Social Scientist in Pursuit of Social Change," pp. 27–29; *Society as Process*, pp. 33, 53–57, 133, 137, 141, 149, 151. For further discussion see his *Intelligible Fields in the Social Sciences* (The Hague, 1967), esp. chap. vii.
48. Norwood Russell Hanson, *Patterns of Discovery* (Cambridge, 1958), p. 30.

ble circularity involved in any attempt to justify our procedures for approaching the study of either the social or physical world. But once this circularity is admitted we are in a position to view our difficulties more candidly and re-evaluate our distribution of emphasis. Sometimes we seem to think that our conceptual problems may be solved by purging our language, operationalizing our concepts, and consolidating our theories, but these difficulties are for the most part only symptomatic of deeper theoretical questions concerning our choice of basic assumptions.[49]

The time has come to become self-conscious about these assumptions. As long as the debate about how to deal with social change continues on the level of technique and method without reference to the philosophical positions and visions which justify and determine these approaches, there can be no serious or meaningful choice between them. When the premises of a science no longer meet the needs of experience, no refinement of methods, models, or techniques will solve the problem. What is called for is a re-evaluation of what Kuhn has termed the "paradigm" of scientific activity or the consensus on the regulative principles which support research. In the present state of the social sciences this may be not so much a question of taking a second look at an operative paradigm as choosing between emerging ones; social science may be still basically pre-paradigmatic, or at least many of its fundamental premises remain unexamined. But in any case, to recommend a new paradigm, or the making of an option between competing ones, means new ways of theorizing.

The failure of social science to comprehend social change may indicate that "the profession can no longer evade anomalies that subvert the existing tradition of scientific practice" and that it should consider "a new set of commitments, a new basis for the practice of science."[50] A new paradigm would involve a new view of social reality or at least one significantly different or more explicit than that implied in the predominant trends in social scientific research, but "paradigms differ in more than substance,

49. Maurice Natanson, *Philosophy of the Social Sciences* (New York, 1963), p. 14.
50. Thomas S. Kuhn, *The Structure of Scientific Revolutions* (Chicago, 1962), p. 6.

for they are directed not only to nature but also back upon the science that produced them. They are the source of the methods, problem-field, and standards of solution accepted by any mature scientific community at any given time. As a result, the reception of a new paradigm often necessitates a re-definition of the corresponding science."[51]

The crisis manifest in the proliferation of theories designed to capture the current problematical dimension of social change would seem to signal a need to examine the other half of the circle, to reconsider our assumptions about sociocultural reality rather than occupying ourselves with revising our conceptual apparatus in an attempt to account for embarrassing aporias. If the problem of social change cannot be solved within the framework of contemporary social science, and if a solution is to emerge in line with some of the suggestions discussed above, it is necessary to consider in more detail the assumptions about social reality and the attending manner of concept formation and explanation which might be entailed by such a view. The scope of this essay will allow neither a complete presentation of the perspective from which the following remarks derive nor a systematic account of the sources on which they rest, but some summary statements are necessary to provide a foundation for the subsequent analysis of time and development.

Symbols, Social Change, and Development

Man's encounter with the world is mediated by symbolic forms ranging from myth to discursive reason. Although language or speech in the strict sense is the most fundamental mode of symbolization, non-discursive or presentational symbols such as those embodied in art as well as the action and gestures associated with ritual and other forms of meaningful behavior must be understood as modes of significant expression. Through these symbolic forms man creates a virtual reality which can never be definitive

51. *Ibid.*, p. 102.

but rather changes in response to the demands of experience. It is through the creation of these forms that man orders his experience, orients himself in the world, and organizes for action; action and the products of action can only be understood and explained in terms of these conceptions of reality by which society both explains and justifies itself. The convergence of symbolic forms gives rise to a system of social relations and a form or style of life; social reality presents itself to us as a symbolic crystal.

This is not the place to set forth in detail the various aspects of a theory of symbolic forms or to inquire fully into the implications of such a theory for social science, but the assumption here is that symbols are the principal data of social inquiry.[52] This perspective involves a rejection of a dominant trend in sociological theory which is based on the assumption that social relations can be explained and understood apart from the conceptions of reality of the participants. Rather, the point of view is that social interaction is conceptually informed, and thus in social science explanation is most essentially a process of making intelligible the conceptual basis of action. Accordingly, one of the central tasks of social-scientific analysis must be to understand how these conceptions are formed and how they change; in other words, since social behavior is integrally related to the process of the symbolic transformation of experience and the communication of significant symbols, epistemology and the study of sociocultural phenomena must be closely allied.

From this point of view, models of society would appear at least in part as forms of symbolic interaction; and in explanations of action relevance would not be determined solely with reference to a first-order theoretical system through which the investigator approaches the phenomena, as is the case in physical science. The constructs of the social scientist must be continually formed with regard for the second-order concepts already operative in society; the meaning of the data and the connections

52. For a more detailed presentation of this perspective see John Gunnell, *Political Philosophy and Time* (Middletown, Conn., 1968), chap. i; and Gunnell, "Social Science and Political Reality: The Problem of Explanation," *Social Research*, XXXV (1968), 159–201.

between data must be derived not from a system imposed from without but from symbols manifest in particular configurations of social relations.

His observational world, the social world, is not essentially structureless. It has a particular meaning and relevance structure for human beings living, thinking, and acting therein. They have preselected and preinterpreted this world by a series of common-sense constructs of the reality of everyday life, and it is these thought objects which determine their behavior, define the goal of their action, the means available for attaining them—in brief, which help them to find their bearings within their natural and socio-cultural environment and to come to terms with it.[53]

Thus, the concepts of social science cannot be definitive ones, and we should not assume them to be so. The assumption which must inform concept formation dictates that we must understand that "the description of reality is essentially inexhaustible."[54]

For too long social scientists, especially those concerned with the problem of ideology, have asked basically inappropriate questions such as "what types of belief are produced by particular systems of social relations" or "what systems of social relations are produced by particular beliefs." Ideas or beliefs and forms of social action are not free-floating variables which can be fruitfully distinguished and then brought back together in terms of causal and semi-causal relationships. Social action and social relations *express* ideas or beliefs or conceptions of reality; they relate to one another in somewhat the same way as words to meanings. We cannot explain action apart from the participants' conceptions of reality; our explanations of social action must proceed from concepts which refer to the "rules of a particular social order." Consequently,

Explaining action is explaining choices; and explaining choices is exhibiting why certain criteria define rational behavior for a given society. . . . Thus in any society we shall be only able to identify what

53. Alfred Schutz, *Collected Papers I: The Problem of Social Reality* (The Hague, 1962), pp. 5–6.
54. Stuart Hampshire, *Thought and Action* (New York, 1960), p. 21.

is going on if we have identified and assessed the established methods of reasoning and criticism in that society.[55]

To understand social action and the structure of social relations, it is necessary to penetrate the configuration of shared symbols that define a society and make it possible, and to realize that when these symbols change the character and significance of social action and social relationships change accordingly. As long as we persist in working within a pattern of thought that allows debate about idea and action or belief and institution in terms of cause and effect, there can be little progress in understanding either; until we begin to approach social reality as essentially a world of meaningful symbols cast in significant forms, social action will continue to appear enigmatic.

From this perspective, social change presents itself as a special conceptual problem. Social science tends to treat social change as if it were some timeless and placeless problem; but there is no problem of social change as such apart from the difficulty of conceptualizing a certain class of phenomena. The literature of social science persists in speaking of the explanation of social change and theories of social change; but there can be no explanation or theory of social change in the abstract any more than there can be a general explanation or theory of physical change in the natural sciences. Such misconceptions are the heritage of evolutionism and functionalism. Understanding social change is merely one aspect of understanding the relation between social action and the symbolic transformation of experience. Above all, in proper perspective, the idea of social change would signify neither an element of a general or universal theory of society— there can no more be a unitary theory of social change than a unitary theory of society—nor a chaotic gap between qualitatively different entities. Instead, social change would serve to indicate or focus attention on instances where patterns of thought and action *tend* either toward dissolution or emergence, where an

55. Alastair MacIntyre, "A Mistake About Causality in Social Science," in P. Laslett and W. G. Runciman, eds., *Philosophy, Politics, and Society*, 2nd Series (New York, 1962), pp. 51, 57, 59, 60. Cf. Peter Winch, "Understanding a Primitive Society," *Am. Phil. Quart.*, I (1964), 307–324.

historically limited image or orientation is in the process either of crystallization or disintegration.

The term "image" as used here approximates Boulding's concept.[56] However, there is no need to subscribe to his mechanistic model of image formation, maintenance and change. Although the use of the cybernetic model is not without utility, it might be better understood as a metaphor to convey the idea of symbolic transformation rather than as an analogical representation of the process that is involved. But Boulding's stress on communication, including message content as well as network, on the symbolic character of the image, its relation to social behavior and its importance on all levels of human activity—these are useful.

The notion of social change, then, would refer to significant transformations of the social image and the corresponding alterations in behavior. Here we may once more refer to Kuhn's study of the nature of scientific revolutions which, although it presents an analysis of a limited area, might be helpful in indicating what is involved here or what is characteristic of social change in general. Just as the theory and practice of "normal science" change when anomalies call into question the operative paradigms or assumptions about the physical world, social behavior changes when the image of reality that orients and justifies it no longer fits the needs of experience or when creative individuals introduce new ideas that subvert the image. Image, paradigm, or form of life signify sets of assumptions from which follow rules that govern behavior and institutions that embody these rules.

As with all rules, there may be cumulative developments in meaning and operation; and at some point they may cease to be relevant or become too restrictive and no longer satisfy the needs of those who follow them. Since rules necessarily limit the scope of activity, they foreclose possibilities which remain open to discovery and in this sense create their own alternatives; any view of reality or image of society claims a greater comprehensiveness than can possibly be maintained. This does not mean that images or paradigms supersede one another in well-defined stages, but the appearance of anomalies may eventually create the need for a

56. Kenneth Boulding, *The Image* (Ann Arbor, Mich., 1961).

choice which in the end proves to be a choice between different views of reality and consequently "between incompatible modes of community life."[57]

This specification of the general nature of symbolic transformation dictates that analysis proceed not in the direction of creating what is often referred to as general conceptual or analytical frameworks, but toward an illumination of historically limited instances of social change. When change occurs, it occurs because of something which happens at a particular time and place. This does not mean an abdication of generalization or comparative studies in favor of historical analysis, but it does mean that explanatory concepts and categories must emerge from a confrontation and interaction with the data. To approach social reality on the level of symbols means that concepts must to a certain extent be formed in an *ad hoc* manner, that their relevance must be defined not in terms of an extrinsic theoretical framework but in terms of the extent to which they reflect the symbolic world which confronts the observer. In regard to social change, what is necessary is a penetration of a society's symbolization of the experience of change. Social change cannot be meaningfully investigated apart from an understanding of change as an awareness on the part of those involved.

Thus approached, the concept of development would signify a historically limited instance of social change. Development as a limited generalization can be a meaningful concept because it is empirically grounded and conforms to a set of relatively well-articulated experiences in the modern age. But if this is so, we might well ask why social scientists continue to debate about what development is. I submit that the answer can be found only in the premises that lie behind a pattern of thought which insists on fitting development into one or another a priori conceptual framework. Thus, we get continual assertion that development really is "differentiation," or "rapid social change," or whatever; if it is not something that fits into one of the categories of a definitive system, it cannot be anything. If understood in this manner, development might apply to the rise of the Mycenaean civiliza-

57. Kuhn, *op. cit.*, p. 93.

tion in pre-classical Greece; but at the same time it would lose any substantive meaning—and this is precisely what has happened. What we are confronted with is a rather vulgar Platonism —the belief that all social phenomena must somehow fit into the universal categories of a synthetic conceptual system if there is to be any systematic empirical inquiry.

Many of the things that development is said to be might well be understood as indicators or aspects of development, but *development is not primarily a set of diverse characteristics to be recorded, but a pattern of thought and action to be understood.* As a pattern of action, it involves a particular configuration of symbols and a mode of self-interpretation on the part of society. We must understand that "the state of a people's politico-economic development, together with its rate and direction, depends largely upon what is in the minds of its members, and above all upon the content of the minds of its elites, which reflects in part, as do civilizations, the conceptions men form of the universe."[58] As Spengler implies in this passage, any ecological approach to the study of development cannot proceed merely on the basis of environmental factors, for man does not act in relation to his environment as such, but to his image—his symbolization—of it. This image shapes his questions as well as his answers, and any assessment of a society entails an apprehension of its symbolic world.

The problem of defining development is not merely a semantic difficulty; the lack of agreement about the concept is the result of the deeper theoretical problem in social science. In terms of the approach suggested here, development would appear as a limited and somewhat self-defining generalization which would take its meaning largely from its articulation as an operative set of symbols. As it is now employed, the concept connotes a wide range of experiences including such notions as purposeful action, innovation, and creativity; but it obviously cannot fruitfully cover *all*

58. Joseph J. Spengler, "Theory, Ideology, Non-Economic Values, and Politico-Economic Development," in Ralph Braibanti and Joseph J. Spengler, eds., *Tradition, Values, and Socio-Economic Development* (Durham, N.C., 1961), pp. 4–5.

change, innovation, and creativity.[59] The purpose here is not to offer a complete analysis of the defining characteristics of a relevant concept of development, but only to penetrate one aspect of this configuration of symbols in the hope of clarifying some of the aspects of behavior which the term denotes.

Time and Development

Thus far, our consideration of time has been solely in terms of the social scientist's confrontation with the temporal dimension of social phenomena, i.e., social change. The argument has been that the so-called problem of social change stems from a conceptual impasse which can be overcome by adopting a particular theoretical posture, one which assumes that concept formation must proceed on the premise that social reality or the principal datum of sociation is symbolic in character. Consequently, an understanding of the concept of development, as an instance of social change, entails an analysis of the symbols associated with this phenomenon which distinguish it as a view of the world and a pattern of behavior. This once more brings us to the question of time, time now conceived as an element of the social image, especially the awareness of change, articulated by the participants in a society.

It is the thesis here that to a large extent development is characterized by the emergence of a particular image of time and change. This means, for example, that the principal criteria for defining development will not constitute the presence of any particular set of institutional arrangements or the successful attainment of certain goals, although these might be understood as indicators of development. To define development in terms of the success of the goals or the achievement of factors pre-determined by the investigator may be too restrictive in some cases and too broad in others. We will not find development a very useful concept if we merely utilize it as a short-hand expression for "a

59. Weidner, "Development Administration," p. 100.

political process which, in fact, will accomplish its political goal."[60] Huntington has argued that development should not be equated with a narrow notion such as "modernization," since modernization might well lead to something quite the converse of what is usually understood as development.[61] However, if modernization is too narrow, certainly his alternative of "institutionalization" is too broad. Again, the whole dilemma stems from the curious propensity to define development in terms of something else—the belief that underlying development is an essence which, if only we can grasp it, will suddenly illuminate the phenomena.

Development as a mode of thought and action involves the emergence of an orientation toward time and change which has found its paradigmatic expression in modern Western society. In general, this means a perspective in which society as well as the life of the individual is perceived as moving along a unilinear plane from the past, through the present, and toward the future; and in which the future is understood not only as a dimension of existence and a boundary of life but as an object of intentional action which can be anticipated, appropriated, controlled, and made to conform to goals devised in the present. Implied is the idea that life and its activities can be measured and defined by precise temporal co-ordinates; and time itself is perceived as a resource to be inventoried, conserved, and allocated. Time is viewed as a *scarce* resource, imposing constraints on action which is concentrated in, and segregated by, time. This temporal ordering or "timing" of life becomes "at once the symbol of man's attempt to order and control time and a symbol of time's fateful mastery over the human enterprise."[62] This scheduling or organization of life according to temporal units—the introduction of a range of symbols which Wilbert Moore summarizes in the notions of rate, synchronization, and sequence—along with the general image of social existence as historical and the future viewed as

60. Karl von Vorys, "Toward a Concept of Political Development," *Annals Amer. Acad. Pol. and Soc. Sci.* (Mar., 1965), pp. 14–19, 19.

61. Samuel P. Huntington, "Political Development and Political Decay," *World Politics*, XVII (Apr., 1965), 386–430.

62. Moore, *Man, Time, and Society*, pp. 7, 8, 11.

something to be calculated and valued as possibility are fundamental to the experiences we attempt to denote by the concept of
development.

An understanding of development involves an understanding
of the process through which old symbolic patterns break down
and give way to a new vision of the universe embodying the
temporal perspective characterized previously. Although we
must guard against reducing the meaning of development to a
particular temporal orientation, the range of experiences we associate with development and the values manifest in these experiences presuppose a particular conception of, and attitude toward,
time and the relation between society and history. We must be
careful not to ask such improper and unanswerable questions as
whether a certain time imagery *causes* development or whether
development *causes* a particular time perspective, or whether
time is an independent or dependent variable.[63] But when one
refers to development in terms of such attributes as modernization, Westernization, industrialization, or the decline of traditional society, we must presuppose a process of reorientation in
temporal awareness or at least a reconciliation between different
time perspectives and attitudes toward history.

This becomes clear when we consider the depth to which temporal
regularities are embedded in the ideology of industrialization which
arises out of the fact that for industrial processes to be effective,
it is essential that time be measured accurately and schedules
adhered to with rigor. This has its semantic reflection, since in an
industrial society such as our own, time is something we "make" or
"save" or otherwise cherish. . . . From one point of view, then, technological change is to be thought of as a process of adjustment
between two time systems, one exact and demanding, and the other
imprecise and relaxed. Hence it would seem logical to assume that a
primary requirement in bringing about economic and technological
change, or "development" in the current sense of the word, would be
to effect an adjustment on the part of the peoples who have a less
demanding time-system to one under which they must become contin-

63. Cf. Robert Jay Lifton, "Individual Patterns in Historical Change: Imagery of
Japanese Youth," *Comp. Studies in Soc. and Hist.*, VI (July, 1964), 369–383;
Frederick Wyatt, "In Quest of Change: Comments on Robert Jay Lifton's
Individual Patterns in Historical Change," *ibid.*, pp. 384–392.

uously more aware of the passage of time, and revise their habits accordingly.[64]

To argue that development is a meaningful concept only in the context of a particular time perspective, that it is largely defined by this perspective, and that the appearance of development implies the formation of new attitudes toward time that may conflict with more traditional ones, demands some discussion of the question of time in general and especially the problem of social time.[65]

The "Idea" of Time

We, like Alice, find the notion of time perplexing and continually seek its meaning, but "time" is not the name of some entity. It is a symbolic form for organizing our experience of change and conceiving the relation between things. In its concrete manifestations it ranges from the formal metric of science to the succession of historical events to the psychological sense of duration and passage. The language of formal time, with its categories such as duration and succession, which allow us to analyze and classify the various instances of temporal symbolization is deceptive; for an abstract concept of time is a relatively late development in both the individual consciousness and in a culture. It is the diversity of empirical instances of temporal ordering and the attendant values which create the complexities involved in attempting to sort out the meanings of time. There is in fact a multiplicity of temporal realms and activities and a multiplicity of time languages, and most of our problems about time are created either by confusing different levels of discourse, such as those belonging to the experience of the physical and social world, or by failing to differentiate clearly temporal and, for example, spatial symbols.

64. Melville J. Herskovits, "Economic Change and Cultural Dynamics," in Braibanti and Spengler, *op. cit.,* pp. 127–128.
65. For a detailed discussion of the perception and conception of time, the origin and development of this concept in Western culture, and the literature bearing on this subject see Gunnell, *Political Philosophy and Time,* esp. chap. ii.

Time, even in the physical world, is a conventional order and not an intrinsic structure; whether time is to be considered a necessary attribute of nature is largely a decision of the scientist and his assumptions about and explanation of the universe. Social time is also a created realm, but in relation to the social scientist it is not a function of his theory but given in the conception or image of the social world which informs the behavior of the actors. Although physical time may be said to be a first-order structure in the sense that there is no going beyond the scientist's theory to a deeper reality, social time is a second-order structure in the sense that it is independent of the temporal perspective of the social scientist to which, as with clock time, it may, however, conform in varying degrees. *The most radical point to be made is that time is not a necessary category of experience, and differences in the symbolization of time in different cultural contexts may be so diverse that attempts to find similarities may be very tenuous.* In children, as well as in the mythic vision of primitive and ancient cultures, time consciousness and temporally organized action is virtually absent or sublimited in spatial categories.

The scope of this discussion does not permit a detailed examination of the vast, but unfortunately diverse and unsystematic, body of research touching upon the cross-cultural and intra-cultural differences in time conception and attitudes toward time and history. But perceiving the differences between these various conceptions and attitudes is crucial for understanding social change and the mode of behavior which we associate with development. Development implies a certain focus in regard to the experience of change—a focus which could not exist in a non-historical society or in a society whose image of the future was not one of promise and possibility.[66] We need not argue that images of time cause social change, but an analysis of temporal images is an essential aspect of any explanation of social change on the level of meaningful action. To explain any particular instance of "devel-

66. For an exhaustive treatment of the vision of the future in Western culture see F. L. Polak, *The Image of the Future* (2 vols.; New York, 1961). The considerable body of literature which has appeared in recent years concerning the "end of ideology" in the West revolves largely around whether the modern age has abandoned or should abandon a substantive vision of the future and whether, with the rise of modern industrial democracy, such a vision is needed at all.

opment" behavior requires an understanding not only of the temporal focus immediately involved but the pre-developmental images of time and history which may or may not facilitate the introduction of "development" symbols. Resistance to innovation may come, for example, from a view of history which entails a belief that "everything that happens has happened before."[67] Thus, studies of pre-developmental orientations are indispensable as well as an understanding of how temporal categories arise in a society and how one temporal perspective gives way to another.[68]

If one pole of social time could be considered as a situation in which the experience of time is virtually absent, as in mythic thought, then the other pole might be understood as modern industrial society, in which temporal experience becomes almost totally absorbed in the highly rationalized and structured orders of formal and quantitative time. The phenomenon of development involves not only an awareness of historical existence, and especially a positive image of the future, but the beginning of a mode of social organization adapted to quantitative time. Possibly one of the factors which separates a "developing" from a "developed" society is the attainment of a point at which the future seems no longer truly problematical, at which society begins to lose its historical character as the gap between present and future narrows, and begins to appear more like the four-dimensional world of the physicist. Mumford has brilliantly portrayed the process through which Western society began to orient itself toward clock-time or machine-time before and during the industrial revolution, when "time-keeping passed into time-serving and time-accounting and time-rationing" and "abstract time became the new medium of existence."[69] The formalization of social time not only provides a method of controlling human

67. Agehanaanda Bharati, "Cultural Hurdles in Development Administration," in Swerdlow, *op. cit.*, p. 71. See also Walter Firey, "Conditions for the Realization of Values Remote in Time," in Edward Tiryakian, ed., *Sociological Theory, Values and Sociocultural Change: Essays in Honor of Pitirim A. Sorokin* (Glencoe, Ill., 1965).

68. See for example Daryll Forde, *African Worlds, Studies in the Cosmological Ideas and Social Values of African Peoples* (London, 1954).

69. Lewis Mumford, *Technics and Civilization* (New York, 1934), pp. 14, 17. Also Wilbert E. Moore, "The Temporal Structure of Organizations," in Tiryakian, *op. cit.*, p. 163.

behavior but negates historical or lived time in the sense that it leads to a spatialization of time.[70] It was precisely this compression of social and organic life that occasioned Bergson's revolt in the nineteenth century, as well as the humanistic response to existentialism in the contemporary age, with its affirmation of the primacy of human, experienced, or "lived" time.

The time perspective of the modern industrial society is eminently displayed in the general drive toward organization where "timing" appears as the negation of "time."[71] The close relation between organization theory, the reduction of uncertainty, the rationalization of experience, and the management of time was apparent in the work of Taylor and continues to be important. "This *time-binding* character of strategies deserves the greatest emphasis, for it makes possible at least a modicum of rationality in behavior, where, without it, this would be impossible."[72] Bell suggests that "utilitarianism provided a new definition of rationality: not the role of reason, but the role of measurement" whereby lived time was transformed into chronological or spatial time for measuring out the life of the individual.[73] But the alliance between rationality and measurement and the relation between organization, timing, and the spatial ordering of human activity is at least as old as Plato.[74] It is not merely that "time rules the work economy, its very rhythms and motions,"[75] but that time as measurement is central to many aspects of organized human activity.

In modern industrial society, time becomes not only a mode of control but the central commodity; resources, both natural and human, are measured in temporal units which become the crite-

70. Sebastian de Grazia, *Of Time, Work, and Leisure* (New York, 1964), pp. 299, 306.

71. See the interesting speculations of Roderick Seidenberg, *Posthistoric Man* (Chapel Hill, N.C., 1950). Also Lewis Mumford, *The Transformations of Man* (New York, 1956): If the trend of "New World Man" continues "a new creation, post-historic man, would come into existence" (p. 155). Post-historic man has been the dream of some (Plato, Hobbes, Rousseau, Marx) and the fear of others (Weber, Bergson, Orwell).

72. Herbert A. Simon, *Administrative Behavior* (New York, 1957), p. 68. Emphasis added.

73. Daniel Bell, *The End of Ideology* (Glencoe, Ill., 1960), p. 224.

74. See Hannah Arendt, *Between Past and Future* (New York, 1961), pp. 109–112.

75. Bell, *op. cit.*, p. 226.

rion of scarcity. In a world of advanced technology and optimum productivity, the organization, co-ordination, and allocation of time, rather than increases in labor and capital, become the main problems.[76] Here the future begins to lose its elusiveness. The image of the future becomes less determinative because the future is, in a sense, given; it is no longer so much probability as certainty, or at least its achievement becomes basically a technical problem. Again, time is reduced to space as the dimensions of time appear like gradations on a ruler; the future already exists, the goals and values are agreed on, and attainment involves traversing the distance from one "place" to another. The idea of future tends to imply choice and uncertainty, but these attributes lose their significance in a situation where the values to be realized are agreed upon and achievement presents itself as assured.[77] The so-called end of ideology argument and the corresponding revolt against utopianism represented by such thinkers as Daniel Bell do not mean that the future is not a matter of concern, but rather that with the rise of modern industrial democracy and the welfare state the future is something to be planned and administered—a technocratic, non-ideological or supra-ideological future to be won through social science and social engineering.[78] However, in developing countries, planning itself becomes an ideology and the idea of a "planned future" is decisive in combating traditional values. Here the future is not given; it is still a dimension to be attained.

All conceptions of time, even those of natural science, may be

76. Moore, *Man, Time, and Society,* pp. 4, 18, 32; Mumford, *Technics and Civilization,* p. 270; Egbert De Vries, "Unbalanced Development and Technical Change," *Essays on Unbalanced Growth* (The Hague, 1962), p. 24.

77. For example, Seymour Martin Lipset, *Political Man* (New York, 1963), argues that modern industrial democracy "is not only or even primarily a means through which different groups can attain their ends or seek the good society; it is the good society itself in operation" (p. 439). G. L. S. Shackle, *Decision, Order and Time in Human Affairs* (Cambridge, 1961), points to the emptiness of choice in the rationality model of conventional economic theory, but this may be more a reflection of society than a failing of the model.

78. See Daniel Bell, "The Study of the Future," *Public Interest,* I (Fall, 1965), 119–130. The character of modern communications media may contribute to this contraction of the temporal dimension. The work of Marshall McLuhan should be noted: *The Gutenberg Galaxy* (Toronto, 1962); *Understanding Media* (New York, 1964). See also Harold A. Innes, *A Plea for Time* (Frederickton, N.B., 1950); *The Bias of Communication* (Toronto, 1951).

understood as social in the sense that they are related to the needs and activities of society. The week, for example, is a product of convention—it is not given in nature—and even the divisions of year, month, hour, minute, and second are largely arbitrary. Even in extremely rationalized social orders where formal time may become highly internalized, it is useful to distinguish analytically the dimension of social time. In many cultures a concept of formal time is not operative, and even in modern Western society, abstract quantitative time does not supersede, but tends to exist side by side with other socially relevant aspects of temporal experience. Social action is often oriented in terms of cyclical time or significant recurring events or dates such as holidays and elections; ritualistic time is not destroyed in modern society. Since action has an external aspect, it can always be understood objectively in the context of chronological time, but the subjective or internal aspect of action, where meaning inheres, is governed by a perception of time that may be radically different from its formal or cosmic context.

[The] standardized space and time of natural science is not the basis for typifications of spatial and temporal location utilized by men in daily life. Indeed, the reverse is the case: the primary grounding of our being in the world is in subjective space and time. . . . But . . . this is only half the story. Although the individual defines his world from his own perspective, he is nevertheless a social being, rooted in intersubjective reality.[79]

Social time, like individual or psychological time, tends to be qualitative, discontinuous, and heterogeneous; it is grounded in the values attached to the events which make up its content. If the past, present, and future are viewed in terms of the clock or calendar, they lose their significance and appear as homogeneous, spatial, and perfectly graduated like railroad tracks fading off in either direction. But even in Western culture, with its highly rationalized temporal structure, individual and social action remains organized largely in terms of a subjective time, the dimensions of which are neither qualitatively similar nor infinitely divisible. Although Aristotle attempted to sustain a general definition

79. Schutz, *op. cit.*, p. xxx.

of time as the number of motion, the more specifically he tried to define time the more he found it necessary to draw on analogies from human experience and finally to admit that "becoming" and the ideas of past, present, and future have relevance only in terms of such experience, especially the experience of history and human finitude. Although Augustine concluded that the past and future existed primarily in memory and anticipation, it still seemed possible to assign them a certain objectivity in the sense of "that which has been" and "that which will be"; but the present or "that which is" was impossible to grasp except as the range of the soul's immediate subjective experience, an idea not unlike James's "specious present."[80]

Oswald Spengler may have exaggerated the importance of time imagery when he stated that "it is by the meaning that it intuitively attaches to time that one culture is differentiated from another,"[81] but social action is incomprehensible apart from an understanding of this imagery. Social time and space provide the matrix of social action, the symbolic context circumscribing the values which define rational action within a given society.[82] In highly complex societies, social time is the product of the interaction of multiple "times" including formal, historical, biological, psychological, religious and metaphysical, and cosmic or chronological. There are as many "times" as there are differentiated activities and modes of thought. In the same manner as the convergence of symbolic forms creates the totality of the social image, the levels of time imagery enter into what Gurvitch has termed the "spectrum of social time." Each social activity moves to some extent within its own time perspective and "difficult as it may be, every society must attempt to unify, even if only relatively, these multiple manifestations of time and arrange them in a hierarchy."[83]

80. See George Mead, *The Philosophy of the Present* (Chicago, 1932).
81. *The Decline of the West* (New York, 1926), p. 130.
82. The best treatment of social time remains Pitirim A. Sorokin, *Socio-cultural Causality, Space, Time* (Durham, N.C., 1943). Also P. Sorokin and R. Merton, "Social Time: A Mathematical and Functional Analysis," *Am. Jour. Soc.*, XLII (Mar., 1937), 615–629.
83. Georges Gurvitch, *The Spectrum of Social Time* (Dordrecht, Netherlands, 1964), p. 13. Also see Georges Gurvitch, "Social Structure and the Multiplicity of Times," in Tiryakian, *op. cit.*

Groups and organizations not only compete for the control and allocation of the time of the individual, but compete for the authority to prescribe the total time perspective of society. In societies in the process of development, this reconciliation of temporal perspectives may become an acute problem, one which permeates all elements of society. For example, in regard to bureaucracy, Eisenstadt has emphasized the multilayered character of administration in the new nations.[84] Here we may assume that conflicts between elements of the bureaucracy rooted in the traditional culture and elements embracing an ideology of modernization must be explained, at least in part, in terms of differences in attitudes toward time and history. And in post-colonial states there may exist a middle bureaucratic stratum which, although highly rationalized or "Westernized" in its temporal orientation in the sense of the values of scheduling, organization, and efficiency, may, in its commitment to "law and order," conflict with a more recent stratum which is highly ideological, entrepreneurial, and future-regarding.

Even in relatively stable industrialized societies, the integration of the diverse temporal perspectives of various groups, organizations, and interests, the compatibility of different attitudes toward time and history, and the relationship between private and public or qualitative and formal time, all present continuing problems of adjustment.[85] But it is the problem of cross-cultural communication and the adaptation of old patterns of culture to new modes of thought and forms of social organization such as those entailed by the process of development which most strikingly presents the dilemma of divergent time perspectives. Dif-

84. S. N. Eisenstadt, "Problems of Emerging Bureaucracies in Developing Areas and New States," in Bert F. Hoselitz and Wilbert E. Moore, eds., *Industrialization and Society* (UNESCO, 1963), p. 160.

85. See for example, Jules Henry, "White People's Time, Colored People's Time: Of Hope, Achievement, and Time in the Lower Classes," *Trans-action*, II (Mar.–Apr., 1965), 31–34; J. D. Ketchum, "Time Values and Social Organization," *Canad. Jour. Psych.*, V (Sept., 1951), 97–109; J. E. Hulett, Jr., "The Person's Time Perspective and the Social Role," *Social Forces*, XXIII (Dec., 1944), 155–159; Lawrence K. Frank, "Time Perspectives," *Jour. Soc. Phil.*, IV (July, 1939), 293–312. See also Margaret Mead, ed., *Cultural Patterns and Technological Change* (UNESCO, 1953); Robert J. Smith, "Cultural Differences in the Life Cycle and the Concept of Time," in Robert W. Kleemeir, *Aging and Leisure* (New York, 1961); Marian W. Smith, "Different Cultural Concepts of Past, Present, and Future," *Psychiatry*, XV (1952), 395–400.

ferent cultures, and various societies within a culture, possess different rhythms of life which are closely tied to their time imagery. Perhaps we can extract a remark of Wiener's from its context to metaphorically illuminate this point: "*Within any world with which we can communicate, the direction of time is uniform.*"[86] Even within what we understand as the continuity of the Western tradition, the disparity between temporal orientations in different historical periods is sufficiently pronounced to dispel any easy assumptions about the uniformity of social time; and changes in temporal orientation may be virtually constitutive of a new form of life. But like Gurvitch, "all that we wish to emphasize here is the great multiplicity of social times"[87] and the implications of this fact for explaining social action.

Probably no one has succeeded in capturing the character of these problems better than Edward T. Hall in his study of temporal symbols in different cultural patterns.[88] Hall offers numerous examples of the problems of cross-cultural communication raised by different orientations toward time and history and differing attitudes relating to the past, present, and future, punctuality, planning, etc. Such differences in attitude are significant even within different sections of one country such as the United States, and quite pronounced contrasts are evident between countries within the West. But the gap between temporal images in Western and non-Western cultures may be so great, the categories for ordering experience so divergent, that meaningful communication becomes nearly impossible. One anecdote related by Hall is especially significant in pointing to the difficulty of reconciling traditional views of time and history with the future-regarding modes of thought and action associated with develop-

86. Norbert Wiener, *Cybernetics* (Cambridge, Mass., 1961), p. 35. Italics in original.
87. Gurvitch has attempted to present, in some detail, a typology of different "times" (enduring, deceptive, erratic, cyclical, retarded, alternating, pushing forward, and explosive) and the social organizations with which they tend to be associated. He also considers the temporal orientations of different social elements as well as the time scales and time perspectives of various global and historical societies. His treatment is useful mainly because it serves to draw attention to the "relativity" of temporal orientations. Cf. both the book and the article cited in n. 83.
88. *The Silent Language* (Garden City, N.Y., 1959).

ment. An American agriculturist, questioning an Arab farmer about his expectations for his crop yield, received an angry and hostile response. The American later learned that the Arab had understood his apparently harmless question as an insult: any mortal who inquires into the future is either presumptuous or unbalanced; the future is the province of God.[89]

89. *Ibid.*, p. 16.

Chapter 4

The Temporal Dimension in Models of Administration and Organization

Alfred Diamant

> I returned and saw under the sun, that the race is not to
> the swift, nor the battle to the strong, neither yet bread to
> the wise, nor yet riches to men of understanding, nor yet
> favor to men of skill; but time and chance happeneth to all.
> For man also knoweth not his time: as the fishes that are
> taken in an evil net, and as the birds that are caught in the
> snare; so are the sons of men snared in an evil time, when
> it falleth suddenly upon them.
>
> Ecclesiastes, IX, 11–12

In a variety of ways the Comparative Administration Group
which sponsored the Berkeley seminar in 1965 and thus made
possible the present set of essays has attempted to assess the
significance of administrative organization and processes, and of
administrative behavior for development and modernization. All
too often in the past it has been assumed and/or asserted that
public administration is essential to successful development and
modernization, without a prior investigation as to (1) whether
the intellectual foundations of the discipline and the presently
available theories and models of administration and organization
do indeed provide efficient instruments for conceptualizing rapid
social, political, and economic change; (2) how to make these
concepts operational for research; and (3) how to translate the
results of this research into prescriptions for change. This paper is
addressed to the first of these three tasks.

Questions concerning "time" and "change" (particularly social change) are central to any discussion of development and modernization. At the same time, social science methodology continues to be troubled by unresolved issues concerning the nature and utility of "models" and "theories." Thus, to lay a proper foundation for the examination of problems of "time" and "change" in "theories" and "models" of public administration it will be necessary to take two preliminary steps: (1) In the first section, I propose to examine briefly the concept of time, especially the notion of social time, and the manner in which it relates to problems of social change; (2) in the second section, I shall explore certain vexing issues concerning the role of theories and models in social science methodology. Special attention will be given to the presence or absence of dynamic elements in social science models and theories, for it would appear that only those thories and models of administration and organization which possess these dynamic elements will prove to be useful in conceptualizing change, making the concepts operational, and translating the findings of theory and research into action.

Time in the Social System

Time and Modernization

There is a wide range of demands for change placed on a society attempting to adopt the principal features of Western industrial civilization. Of these, the demands for change in the timing of human activities, because they involve altering the pace of fundamental political, economic, and social processes, seem to meet the strongest resistance. Reporting a discussion with an African textile mill manager, Douglas Steere paints a vivid picture of the way "certain African values interfered with the production of a really committed labor force and with the smooth operation of the mill." Labor turnover at the plant was nearly 100 per cent, and workers, after earning enough for what they considered their legitimate needs, left the mill to go back to their villages: "they felt completely justified in leaving the grim, whistle-controlled interminable routine of the mill to go home."[1] The laborers rebelled against two basic aspects of industrial civilization: an increasing specialization which imposes on the individual a number of conflicting roles whose demands, including time demands, create tensions he seems to be unable to resolve; and the need for the co-ordination of manpower and resources to fit into a carefully timed schedule based on astronomical cycles.[2]

Not all members of modernizing societies treat Western time demands like the African mill workers; quite the contrary. Especially among the leadership groups of such modernizing societies there is a conviction, often reinforced by strongly held ideology, that development is not proceeding fast enough. They attempt to mobilize the entire society for the tasks of modernization,[3] and reject any suggestion that for effective development there are inevitable stages through which the system must pass. There is strong insistence on "accelerating" the modernizing process and on introducing the most sophisticated features of an industrialized system, including those that impose rigid demands on timing, both short-range and long-range. Planning, after all, is a system for managing time on a long-range basis, and the verbal commitment to planning is a well-known feature of modernizing systems—as is the consistently poor record of plan fulfilment, resulting from a failure to marshal the necessary material and human resources, in space as well as time.[4]

One notes here almost a reversal of roles and attitudes concerning time, between the highly industrialized societies and those engaged in modernization. It is now the leaders of the new states who urge their societies on with an achievement ethic (but not

1. "Development: For What?" in John H. Hallowell, ed., *Development: For What?* (Durham, N.C., 1964), pp. 226, 227.

2. Wilbert E. Moore, *Man, Time, and Society* (New York, 1963), pp. 18–19.

3. See Alfred Diamant, "Bureaucracy in Developmental Movement Regimes: A Bureaucratic Model for Developing Societies," *CAG Occasional Papers* (Bloomington, Ind., 1964), for a discussion of the concept of mobilization and for citations of the relevant literature.

4. This has been fully explored by the 1964 Syracuse University Comparative Administration Group Seminar on comparative national planning administration. A summary volume reporting the findings of this seminar is Bertram M. Gross, ed., *Action Under Planning* (New York, 1966).

necessarily a Protestant one) and who attempt to teach them the values of thrift, saving, and investment, whereas the people of the affluent industrialized societies devote themselves increasingly to questions about leisure in a seemingly timeless stage of high mass consumption. In some senses, it is thus no longer the West which is running on "urgent time" but the new states; it is no longer the West which is urgently concerned with savings and investment, but the societies in rapid transformation.

Physical and Biological Time

The definition and measurement of time has always presented greater difficulties than that of the other major dimension of our existence—space. This has troubled scientists as well as philosophers. As G. J. Whitrow points out, our judgments about time and about events in time "appear themselves to be 'in' time, whereas our judgments concerning space do not appear in any obvious sense to be in space." Physicists, he goes on to say, seem to be deeply influenced by the fact that space is "presented to us all of a piece, whereas time comes to us only bit by bit." Furthermore, the past can be recalled only with the dubious aid of memory, whereas the future is hidden from us almost entirely. Whitrow suggests that this piecemeal character of time, as compared with space, makes for profound difficulties in measurement: "Free mobility in space leads to the idea of the transportable unit of length and the rigid measuring rod. The absence of free mobility in time makes it more difficult for us to be sure that a process takes the same time whenever it is repeated."[5]

Time and the measurement of time have been of concern not only to the physicists but also to the biologists. As early as 1842 clinical and physiological studies showed that almost all organs and functions of the body exhibit a daily rhythmicity: "All these rhythms are expressions of a so-called 'physiological clock' which we have to consider as a basic feature in nearly all living systems,

5. *The Natural Philosophy of Time* (New York, 1963), pp. 2–3. See also the several essays in Herbert Feigl and Grover Maxwell, eds., *Scientific Exploration, Space, and Time*, Minnesota Studies in the Philosophy of Science, Vol. III (Minneapolis, 1962).

including unicellular organisms."[6] When checked under carefully controlled conditions which denied the human subject any clues to human time and of the day-night cycle, the operation of these physiological clocks proved to be indeed independent of human clock time, though approximately oriented to a 24-hour circle; hence the term "circadian rhythm" for this phenomenon. The problem of re-synchronizing the circadian rhythm with the environment, a familiar one to all long-distance jet travelers, has not yet received much systematic attention, chiefly because the workings of the self-sustained circadian oscillator have not yet been fully explained.

Social Time

Our concern here, however, is not so much with physical or biological time as with time and timing in human organization. For "beyond bare physical necessities," the temporal order is a social order "whose workings over time cannot be explained by mechanical or physiological models."[7] Though we might think of human history as capable of being described by "difference equations of an infinite degree," yet the manner in which "today depends not only on yesterday or even the day before yesterday, but on all previous yesterdays" surely makes prediction virtually impossible even with the aid of sophisticated mathematical tools.[8] It is the peculiarity of social systems, as Boulding points out, that they are "to a considerable extent determined by the images we have of them" and that the cause of these images "must be found in our total experience."[9] Thus social systems, though they combine both mechanical and image-determined elements and exhibit patterns of image growth which resemble biological growth patterns, cannot be handled with any but social science tools and concepts.

6. Juergen Aschoff, "Circadian Rhythms in Man," *Science,* June 11, 1965, pp. 1427–1432.

7. Moore, *op. cit.,* p. 44.

8. Kenneth E. Boulding, "The Place of Image in the Dynamics of Society," in George K. Zollschan and Walter Hirsch, eds., *Explorations in Social Change* (Boston, 1964), p. 6. See also his *The Image* (Ann Arbor, Mich., 1956) for a more extended statement.

9. Boulding, "The Place of Image," pp. 10–11, 13.

The time of a social system, then, is a time constructed and fashioned for use in that particular system and in others like it. Differences in social systems, as was suggested previously, will result in different conceptions of time. Furthermore, the larger and more complex the social systems and their subsystems, the more concerns with temporal order move to the center of the stage. Conflicting demands will be placed on the time of the system's members and it is thus useful, as Wilbert Moore does, to suggest that a social system in which one power center makes and effectively enforces demands on the individual's time be called totalitarian—the individual's total time is controlled from one center.[10] Georges Gurvitch in his speculative and highly suggestive book *The Spectrum of Social Time* is quite correct when he characterizes social life as always taking place "in divergent and often contradictory manifestations of social time."[11] He also illuminates the reciprocal relations between the social system and the time created by it: "The total social phenomena both produce and are products of social time. They give birth to social time, move, and unfold in it. Thus social time cannot be defined without defining the total social phenomenon."[12]

Modern man's conception of social time must be seen, first of all, in a global perspective which reaches back before the beginning of the Christian era. The basic time conception of what Mircea Eliade calls "archaic man" was cyclical. He saw events unfold in terms of an ever recurring rhythm, an insight gained from his having to cope with the elements as they confronted him in the seemingly eternal rhythm of the seasons. The horizon of archaic man was defined by his notions of archetypes, of a golden age, and by the myth of the "eternal return."[13] Once Christian man abandoned this safely bounded world for the realm of a historic process which would lead in a "straight line" to salvation

10. *Op. cit.*, p. 10.
11. Dordrecht, Netherlands, 1964, p. 13.   12. *Ibid.*, p. 27.
13. The following argument relies very much on *Cosmos and History: The Myth of the Eternal Return* (New York, 1959). See also the several essays, especially those by Max Knoll, Adolf Portmann, and G. van der Leeuw entitled, respectively, "Transformation of Science in Our Age," "Time in the Life of Organism," and "Primordial Time and Final Time," in Joseph Campbell, ed., *Man and Time: Papers from the Eranos Yearbooks* (New York, 1957).

and redemption, he also found himself exposed to the dangers inherent in that historic process. Ever since then, according to Eliade, man has sought to overcome history, to master it, to "bring it to an end," as Marx and others have tried to do. The one act that can "save" man from the terror of history is faith: "Since the 'invention' of faith, in the Judaeo-Christian sense of the word (i.e., for God all is possible), the man who has left the horizon of archetypes and repetition can no longer defend himself against that terror except through the idea of God. . . . Any other situation of modern man leads, in the end, to despair."[14] Without necessarily accepting Eliade's particular philosophical or theological position, one can agree that modern man has sought refuge in various forms of "faith" in order to make sense of a historical process which seems to have no beginning and no end.

There are still other consequences flowing from a linear conception of time and history which are relevant to our concern. Man believes himself to be able to "make history" but finds either that "history makes itself" (as a result of acts of commission and omission in the past), or that history is made by an increasingly smaller number of men who monopolize the making of history and prevent the vast number of their contemporaries from participating in that activity.[15] It is pertinent to note at this time that our subsequent analysis of administration and organizations theory will show a strong tendency to focus on the elite in organizations and to assume that managing, mobilizing, goal-setting, etc. in organizations is the province of that elite.

It would be a dangerous oversimplification to characterize all current time conceptions as linear. Even Eliade suggests[16] that cyclical notions of time have not been entirely eliminated but have survived in a lower, material (immanent) form in the physical sciences (cycles of astronomical time), in the social sciences (trade cycles), and in a variety of industrial processes which call for steady repetition of a single action or a group of actions. Moore observes that endless repetition of short cycles is psychologically intolerable, but so is the total absence of recurrence:

14. Eliade, *op. cit.*, pp. 161–162.   15. *Ibid.*, p. 156.
16. *Ibid.*, pp. 141–147.

"The distinction between time as a boundary condition and time as a flow of events, though somewhat arbitrary, is meaningful in the patterning of social action. If events were endlessly novel, not only would predictable order in life be impossible, but so too would notions of time itself. It is the rhythmic recurrence of patterns that permits the sense of structure and . . . of temporal units."[17] Man thus continues to utilize both "cyclical" and "linear" conceptions of time in his efforts to make sense of his actions and his environment. This coexistence of two conceptions of time will prove to be a significant aspect of the time dimension of administrative and organizational models.

A troublesome aspect of the concept of time is the "distinction between moments, on the one hand, and on the other their apparent organization into *history* or an understandable drift and flow of action."[18] Phenomenologically speaking there can be only single moments or single acts, but if this is carried to its ultimate conclusion it would be impossible, for example, to conceive of such entities as melodies which require that we hear individual notes in relation to others that precede as well as follow them in order to have a complete melody. Therefore, "all representation of a direction, a passage, or a distance—in short everything which includes the comparison of several elements and expresses the relation between them—can be conceived only as the product of a temporally comprehensive act of cognition."[19] The connection between time as the momentary unit, the single act, and time as a process or flow is effectively established by Shackle: "Transformation of one moment into another is inherent in the idea of the moment. The *detached* observer can adopt the figment of a 'calendar axis' along which he supposes the viewpoint of the *engaged* observer, the time-experiencing individual, to move."[20]

17. Moore, *op. cit.*, p. 16.
18. G. L. S. Shackle, *Decision, Order and Time in Human Affairs* (Cambridge, 1961), p. 19.
19. Edmund Husserl, *The Phenomenology of Internal Time-Consciousness* (Bloomington, Ind., 1964), p. 40. Translation of a lecture delivered originally in 1904 and subsequently published in Germany.
20. Shackle, *op. cit.*, p. 43. For another phenomenological effort to get "inside" the actor and view action from the actor's point of view see Alfred Schutz, "The Social World and the Theory of Social Action," *Social Research*, XXVII (1960), 203–221, reprinted in *Philosophical Problems of the Social Sciences* (New York, 1965), pp. 53–67.

That is to say, the outside observer can conceive of a time axis, but for the individual engaged in action "the present alone is uniquely actual in total solitary exclusiveness."[21]

But if the present alone is "uniquely actual" can there be any relationship to past and future? This question, too, Shackle answers adroitly, and in the process creates a most persuasive anti-determinist concept of decision-making. As far as the past is concerned, Shackle points out, "the experiences which the decision-maker looks to in making his choice of action do not all belong to one and the same brief moment of the calendar axis but are spread along it over an interval perhaps of years."[22] There is, thus, a certain objective reality to the past. The future, however, is not something that can be found out, it is "not here to be discovered, but must be created."[23] Choices about the future are choices between "figments or imaginations," and every choice which thus creates a new future introduces "an essentially new strand into the emerging pattern of history."[24] In Shackle's view, for a decision taken in the "solitary moment-in-being" to be meaningful, it must not be fully determined; neither can it be completely random. "In a predestinate world, decision would be *illusory*; in a world of perfect foreknowledge, *empty*; in a world without natural order, *powerless*."[25] There can be no decision in a universe where the actions of man resemble those of an automatic machine; there can be no decision in Shackle's terms if the actor has perfect knowledge about all alternatives and their preferential ordering; and there can be no decision in a cosmos lacking all order. This non-illusory, non-empty, non-powerless decision is, for Shackle, "choice in the face of bounded uncertainty."[26] This notion of bounded uncertainty will prove to be of considerable

21. Shackle, *op. cit.*, p. 42.
22. *Ibid.*, p. 9. A most effective model of decision-making that avoids the trap of defining a decision as an event in a single moment is Robert E. Agger, Daniel Goldrich, and Bert E. Swanson, *The Rulers and the Ruled: Political Power and Impotence in American Communities* (New York, 1964). They define political decision-making as a process of making choices, a process being a series of related events or acts over a period of time. The total process consists of six stages and one event, as follows: (1) policy formulation; (2) policy deliberation; (3) organization of political support; (4) authoritative consideration, event—decisional outcome; (5) promulgation of the decisional outcome; and (6) policy effectuation. In this manner the "decisional outcome" is embedded in a process extending over time and can be fully understood only in its total temporal setting.
23. Shackle, *op. cit.*, p. 42.   24. *Ibid.*, pp. 19, 1.
25. *Ibid.*, p. 43. Emphasis in original.   26. *Ibid.*, p. 5.

relevance to the organization literature, in which there is a tendency to seek for complete knowledge in order to control fully the goals, structure, and functioning of the organization. Much of organization theory and writing on administration will turn out to be preoccupied with control and with the search for unbounded certainty for the decision-makers; only occasional writers will concede the possibility of definite limits on the scope of the decision-maker, and even those theorists will not want to abandon notions of a "predestinate world" and of "perfect foreknowledge."

There have been many attempts to develop categories, dimensions, and manifestations of time as an aspect of the social order. Georges Gurvitch, for example, conceives of eight manifestations of social time: enduring time (time slowed down, of long duration); deceptive time (sharp crises produce a time of surprises); erratic time (time of irregular pulsation); cyclical time (past, present, and future revolve in a cycle); retarded time (time too long awaited); alternating time (time of delay and advance); time pushing forward (future becomes the present); and explosive time (time of creation).[27] Max Heirich identifies four dimensions of time: time as a social factor, "as a resource to be used for alternative purposes and as a social meaning affecting other actions"; time as a causal link, either between time and space (setting) or as a time-time link (sequence); time as a quantitative measure; and time as a qualitative measure. These four uses of time form the basis for classifying social theorists according to the manner in which they conceive time.[28]

27. Gurvitch, *op. cit.*, pp. 30–33. Frequently the aridity of Gurvitch's conceptual schemata is broken by insights which clearly bear the mark of much sensitivity for the reality of political and organizational processes: "The awareness of time in organizations differs according to whether it is a matter of leadership, participants who benefit, conformists, or participants in revolt. The time is always too short for the first and too long for the last. Also, leaders try to master time in order to prolong it, while participants in revolt try to master the time in order to shorten it, and provoke the overthrow of the organization" (p. 44). Robert Presthus' typology of people-in-organization (upward-mobiles, indifferents, and ambivalents) which is supposedly based on very hardheaded empirical research does not, in the end, look very different from Gurvitch's scheme, which is in the best European tradition of sociology in the grand style. See Presthus, *The Organizational Society: An Analysis and a Theory* (New York, 1962), chaps. vi–viii.

28. "The Use of Time in the Study of Social Change," *Am. Soc. Rev.*, XXIX (1964), 386–397.

There would seem to be no end to the categories of social time which social scientists could invent. But even if there are no limits to the imagination of category builders, there seem to be rather narrow boundaries to the utility of such schemes. Instead of constructing elaborate categories it might be more useful and instructive to identify major components of the notion of timing or temporal ordering; this is what Moore has done most effectively:

Much of social behavior depends for its orderly qualities on common definitions, assumptions, and actions with regard to the location of events in time. Certain activities, for example, require simultaneous action by a number of persons, or at least their presence at a particular time. . . . Thus one element of temporal order is *synchronization.* Other activities require that actions follow one another in a prescribed order; thus *sequence* is a part of the temporal order. For still other activities the frequency of events during a period of time is critical; thus *rate* also is one of the ways that time impinges on social behavior. For all these elements of social coordination the term *timing* is useful. . . . Time is an intrinsic quality of personal and collective behavior. If activities have no temporal order, they have no order at all.[29]

I doubt whether Moore would want to make time an independent variable in social organization and behavior, but he is correct in suggesting that it is a crucial variable and that it is the temporal aspect of social life which constitutes its dynamic quality.

Moore's characterization of the essentially dynamic quality of social life and of the crucial nature of its temporal dimension, together with Eliade's perhaps rather too sweeping generalizations about post-primitive man's linear conception of time serve to illuminate important aspects of the theories of political development. Now that we are no longer so confident about the inevitability of certain well-defined stages in economic and political development, it becomes more plausible to define political development not as the end result of a finite set of events occurring in definite stages but as

a generic process of successfully sustaining new demands, goals, and organizations in a flexible manner. In the case of the "developing nations" it means the meeting of particular goals and demands. Cer-

29. Moore, *op. cit.,* pp. 8–9.

tain of these are given for each society. . . . Other demands and goals of a particular sort involving nation-building and socio-economic progress can be processed provided the system acquires certain system capabilities.[30]

This conception of political development implies, above all, a notion of linear time: political development is seen as a long-range linear process of meeting new goals, demands, etc. It also implies the presence of all three of Moore's dimensions of timing: sequence, synchronization, and rate.

The issues raised by Moore and Eliade, among others, are also relevant to the problems raised by the nature of existing models and theories of administration and organization—a central concern of this essay. I shall try to show, in the third section, that most of these theories and models either ignore the questions of dynamism and change or conceive of organizational change as tending toward equilibrium, that is to say, change as being kept within narrow limits. As a result, there is little concern with time (linear or cyclical), which is surely a paradoxical condition for a body of literature dealing with complex organizations which are, to say the least, the very epitome of sophisticated timing.

Models and Theories in the Social Sciences

Models and Theories

Before we can proceed to an examination of models and theories of administration and organization, it is necessary to state with as much precision as can be mustered what is meant by the terms "model" and "theory" in the present discussion.

The two terms are used interchangeably here, even though there has been some criticism of this practice. Abraham Kaplan is probably quite correct when he points out that if both models and theories are meant to be isomorphs of the "real system which provides the subject matter . . . this usage of the term 'model' is of dubious worth methodologically. If 'model' is coexistensive

30. Diamant, "Bureaucracy in Developmental Movement Regimes," pp. 14–15.

with 'theory,' why not say 'theory'?"[31] Kaplan is critical of this confusion of "model" and "theory" chiefly because he does not want to see science limited to a single cognitive strategy—model building. As far as he is concerned model building is only one of several possible cognitive strategies and is not to be "identified with the scientific enterprise as such."[32]

I am inclined to agree with Kaplan that there are indeed many ways of "going to heaven" and I, too, do not assume a single, preferred "scientific method." But for historical reasons the term "model" has been in use in studies of organization and administration for some time now, chiefly as the result of the Weberian bureaucratic ideal-type.[33] There is also the fact that a good bit of writing in this area has been heavily normative and prescriptive, and the ideal-type model—using the term in its strict methodological sense—became transformed into an "ideal" to be sought and attained. More recently there have been some attempts to purge studies of administration and organization of these normative concerns; but success has been limited, even though it might well be more tidy to distinguish between normative and empirical theories of administration and organization.

In spite of Kaplan's exhortation at least one writer uses the two terms interchangeably, or rather he uses the term "model" in his examination of a whole range of social science theories and applies it also to his own cybernetic analogue of the political system.[34] Another writer also engaged in the construction of a cybernetic model of the political system does not even have an index entry for the term "model."[35] Thus, both have constructed

31. *The Conduct of Inquiry: Methodology for Behavioral Science* (San Francisco, 1964), p. 264.

32. *Ibid.*, p. 265. In another place he warns behavioral scientists that "it is less important to draw a fine line between what is 'scientific' and what is not than to cherish every opportunity for scientific growth. There is no need for behavioral science to tighten its immigration laws against subversive aliens. Scientific institutions are not so easily overthrown" (p. 28).

33. I have surveyed the development and use of the Weberian bureaucratic ideal-type in "The Bureaucratic Model: Max Weber Rejected, Rediscovered, Reformed," in Ferrel Heady and Sybil L. Stokes, eds., *Papers in Comparative Public Administration* (Ann Arbor, Mich., 1962), pp. 59–98.

34. Karl W. Deutsch, *The Nerves of Government: Models of Political Communication and Control* (New York, 1963). See especially Part I: "The Search for Models of Society and Politics," pp. 3–72.

35. David Easton, *A Systems Analysis of Political Life* (New York, 1965). See especially Part I: "The Mode of Analysis," pp. 3–33.

feedback analogues of the political system, but one calls it a "theory," another a "model." At this point, Kaplan would suggest that "model" and "theory" are indeed the same thing when both are analogues, and that no theory is to be condemned

> as "merely an analogy" just because it makes use of one. No two things in the world are wholly alike, so that every analogy, however close, can be pushed too far; on the other hand, no two things are wholly dissimilar, so that there is always an analogy to be drawn, if we choose to do so. The question to be considered in every case is whether there is something to be learned from the analogy.[36]

The difficulty of finding a single definition, agreeable to everyone, of the term "theory" has been discussed many times, more recently by Anatol Rapoport who suggests that instead of trying for such agreement on definition it might be "more instructive to look at the genesis of various types of expositions and discussions offered as thories and to examine the role they play in the development of social science, particularly of political science."[37]

Surely the fatal blow against the attempts at definitional nicety by writers on administration and organization was struck by Herbert Simon, who in a collection of essays entitled *Models of Man* attempted to set forth "a consistent body of theory" of human behavior in organizations. In outlining the general schema of the book, Simon uses the term "theory" quite consistently, but refers to "models" of individual behavior in one of the sections without having laid a foundation for the use of the term. Thus, one gains the impression that "model" and "theory" are being used interchangeably.[38] I hope that I have now clearly established the futility of arguments "about what ought to be properly called a theory," and can go on to other aspects of the use and function of models and theories in the social sciences, and especially in political science.[39]

36. Kaplan, *op. cit.*, pp. 265–266.
37. Anatol Rapoport, "The Uses of Theory in the Study of Politics," in Edward H. Buehrig, ed., *Essays in Political Science* (Bloomington, Ind., 1966), p. 4.
38. *Models of Man: Social and Rational; Mathematical Essays on Rational Behavior in a Social Setting* (New York, 1957), pp. vii, 1–3.
39. Rapoport, *op. cit.*, p. 4. Easton defines a theory as being "any kind of generalization or proposition that asserts that two or more things, activities, or events covary under specified conditions" (*Systems Analysis*, p. 7).

There is no doubt that theory construction and model building enjoy great vogue today, and that those engaged in it often give the impression that theirs is the "only true begetter of scientific knowledge. . . . The words 'model' and 'mode' have, indeed, the same root; today model building is science a la mode."[40] In the study of administration and organization the use of idealized models has been found most fruitful. By starting with such a model it is then possible to permit "various imperfections to enter the picture. . . . For the theorist and the systematic observer the model provides both a checklist of actions to be noted and a pattern for tracing through the implications of observed 'imperfections.' "[41] Though models of this kind may "provide understanding, which may be prized for its own sake," we must remember that "to understand the world does not mean to hold in our hands the blueprints by which God created it, but some very human sketches by which we ourselves can find our way."[42] This last caveat of Kaplan's seems to be particularly appropriate to organizational studies. All too often theorists of organization, both past and present, have aspired to just such perfect blueprints on the basis of which men and resources were to be marshaled and mobilized in a thoroughly autocratic manner. In spite of the protestations to the contrary by a number of contemporary writers on organization and administration, the tendency to play God has remained an all too prominent characteristic of that literature.

Karl Deutsch has nicely categorized these instrumental as well as non-instrumental functions of models and theories: "We may think of models as serving, more or less imperfectly, four distinct functions: the organizing, the heuristic, the predictive, and the measuring (or mensurative)."[43] To these four should be added a prescriptive function, especially in modern organization theory beginning with Max Weber and Frederick Winslow Taylor. Some, like Taylor, were of course involved in administration and thus were directly concerned with prescription. But others whose con-

40. Kaplan, *op. cit.*, p. 258.
41. Moore, *op. cit.*, p. 88. On some of the problems that arise when the discrepancy between model and existence is persistently great see Alfred Diamant, "The Relevance of Comparative Politics for the Comparative Study of Public Administration," *Adm. Sci. Quart.*, V (1960), 87–112.
42. Kaplan, *op. cit.*, p. 310.   43. *Op. cit.*, p. 8.

nection with applied problems was not so clearly visible as it was in Taylor's and Urwick's cases have tended to blur the predictive and prescriptive elements of their work. There seems to be little doubt that Simon's "discovery" of limits on human rationality was intended not only to yield replicable results, but was also meant as a prescription for those engaged in constructing and directing organizations.

Having dealt with the general nature of models and theories and their uses in the social sciences, two issues which are particularly relevant to administration and political development remain to be discussed. The first of these involves the conflict over the utility of "hard" (scientific) and "soft" (belletristic) types of theories and models in political science. The second, especially relevant to our concern for political development, involves the prevalence of static and equilibrium-tending models of social change as contrasted with the dearth of genuinely dynamic social theories. This condition of general social theory has come to be reflected in theories of administration and organization. As a result, the requirements of social systems in rapid transformation for dynamic (non-equilibrium) theories of political and administrative change have barely been met simply because few workable theories of non-equilibrium change were available for either predictive or prescriptive purposes.

"Hard" vs. "Soft" Social Science Theory

The success in the physical sciences of what has been called the hypothetico-deductive method has led to many attempts to extend the use of that method to studies of the human world. Attempts to apply this procedure to the social sciences quickly produced some sharp dilemmas. Many of the traditional concerns of political science proved quite untractable to treatment by the hypothetico-deductive method, and it was this issue which divided social scientists in "hards" and "softs." The issue, as Rapoport has pointed out most cogently,

is not whether social science, in particular the study of politics, can be made fact-oriented and so "scientific" or whether it is destined to remain on the conceptual level and close to the humanities. Obviously political science can be made "hard" by properly selecting the objects of study; but this is done at a price—namely, a disengagement from the traditional pattern of thought which has given rise to political theory. This price is deemed too high by many.[44]

The approach Rapoport considers to hold the best promise to bridge the hard-soft gap is the model approach. Both traditionalists and positivists use models, though they mean quite different things by the term. For the former, models are usually analogical and metaphorical, such as the "balance of power" of international relations theory. For the latter a model is a rigorous description of observed events. Thus the positivist expects "productiveness," whereas the traditionalist seeks for "suggestiveness" in his models. Two types of models, the "sytem-theoretical" and the "game-theoretical," might meet this bridge-building need:

The purpose of such models is not primarily prediction (which is the positivist's concern); much less control (which is the pragmatist's concern); rather it is "understanding," which is the concern of traditionally oriented theory in the social sciences. There is a proviso, however—namely, that criteria of understanding are to be rigorous, not merely intuitive.[45]

Both of these models, as Rapoport demonstrates in some detail, have great heuristic value, that is to say, they tell us "where to look," and thus further the search for relevant data. Both types of models can be perfectly rigorous—satisfying the canons of the hard theorists—while also generating understanding and insight and thereby meeting the demands of the soft theorists.

It has seemed important to develop in some detail Rapoport's suggestions for bridging the gap between hard and soft social science, because this kind of estrangement exists in the field of administration and organization theory. The analysis which follows of the work of a number of theorists will reveal that most would tend to cluster toward the "soft" end of the spectrum. Nevertheless, determined efforts have been made to introduce the tools and methods of the "hard" social sciences into the

44. *Op. cit.*, p. 12.
45. *Ibid.*, p. 17. For a similar case of "understanding" with the aid of rigorously developed criteria see the essay by Schutz cited in n. 20 above.

literature. The results have been predictable: much friction and talking at cross purposes, little light and meaningful dialogue. Perhaps some knowledge about the ways in which the gap can be bridged will stimulate efforts along these lines.

Static and Dynamic Elements in Social Science Theory

The last issue to be addressed concerns the essentially static character of much of social science theory. It has seemed best to deal with this by attempting a simple classification of these theories with respect to the presence or absence in them of static and dynamic elements. I have dealt in another place with some of the major theories of social change and need not repeat these arguments here.[46] The typology which follows relies heavily on that earlier analysis, though some of my judgments concerning the presence or absence of dynamic elements in certain theories have undergone some change. In turn, the analysis of organization theories below will reveal a type of distribution among the three categories of organizational change closely resembling that of the general theories.

Social science models fall into three broad categories. (1) Steady state models or static models can account for features of a system or subsystem at a given point in time but cannot accommodate change in any form. (2) Equilibrium models can accommodate "relatively small changes," but these small changes "tend to be counteracted by the effects of their repercussion on other parts of the system in such a way that the original state tends to be restored."[47] A familiar example of an equilibrium model of politics is the group process model of David Truman.[48] (3) Nonequilibrium models are fashioned in such a way that changes going beyond those of equilibrium-tending range are considered as a legitimate part of the system. In such models change is not irrelevant or dysfunctional, as it is in the other two, and processes

46. "Political Development: Approaches to Theory and Strategy," in John D. Montgomery and William J. Siffin, eds., *Approaches to Development: Politics, Administration and Change* (New York, 1966), pp. 15–47.
47. Talcott Parsons and Neil E. Smelser, *Economy and Society* (Glencoe, Ill., 1956), p. 247.
48. *The Governmental Process: Political Interests and Public Opinion* (New York, 1951).

which lead to system transformation are part of the model. It is a testimony to the dominant position of static and equilibrium theories in the social sciences that no term has yet been developed for a category of models which is neither a steady state nor an equilibrium type.

In his study of social time, Moore observes that the dominance of static models in the social sciences has caused theorists to slight the temporal aspect of social life. He points out that the social sciences like "all analytical sciences tend to perfect descriptions of elements and observations of combinations before they develop the capacity to observe orderly transformations in the course of time."[49] In the early development of social science models two major types were common: the mechanistic and the organic. The paradigm of the mechanical model was the clock, which

implied the notion that the parts were never significantly modified by each other, nor by their own past, and that each part once placed in its appropriate position . . . would remain in place and would continue to fulfill its completely and uniquely determined function. . . . The notions of irreversible change, of growth, of evolution, of novelty, and of purpose all had no place in it.[50]

The organic model, on the other hand, did provide for interdependence of parts, both with respect to structure and function, but it, too, "excluded all possibilities of major internal reorganization, and of any evolution. . . ."[51] As later social science theories abandoned such essentially static notions in favor of equilibrium models, among organization theorists some of the earliest models were of the steady state type, whereas later writers adopted chiefly equilibrium models. These, as we will see, are the dominant type of theory today.

There are presently in use a wide variety of equilibrium social science models. Of these, models using structural-functional analysis are the most prominent; others which will be discussed briefly are game theory, ideal-type models, and simple models of input-output theory.

49. *Op. cit.*, p. v.   50. Deutsch, *op. cit.*, p. 27.
51. *Ibid.*, p. 33.

Structural-functional models with their stress on system, on equilibrium, on common values, and on boundary maintenance neglect almost completely—and necessarily so—the problem of change.[52] Various friendly critics of the model have attempted to defend it against the charge of being a steady state construct. In one way or another they try to build in "contradictory requirements," "processes for the institutionalization of change," and other devices which will then render the structural-functional model a dynamic one. Less friendly critics suggest bluntly that the demands of system and subsystem harmony, and of a coherent single value pattern, require such a complete absence of strain that no useful social analysis is possible by relying on such a rigidly equilibrium-tending model. However, not even the most severe critics suggest that structural-functional analysis is *completely* static, but rather that it can only accommodate a very restricted range of changes. It is here that the most profound difficulties begin to arise, for an equilibrium model is bound to be of only limited relevance for a society undergoing rapid transformation.

The same kind of criticism can also be levied against other models in this category. Ideal-type analysis, though most suggestive in some ways,[53] nevertheless cannot be used to show how a particular social pattern came into being, how it was destroyed, or how much change it would have been able to stand in that period of time. Though several ideal-types could be used to form a developmental pattern, it remains doubtful whether one could specify how or why change took place in moving from one stage to another.

On examination, game theory, which has caused considerable excitement as a conceptual tool, turns out to be an almost static theory. In its classical form there can be no changes in the rules of the game, in the capabilities of the participants, etc. Though some efforts have been made to add dynamic elements to the game models,[54] the changes permitted can by the very nature of

---

52. See Diamant, "Political Development," pp. 29–33, for a more extended discussion of structural-functionalism.

53. I have attempted to make a strong case for the utility of ideal-type analysis in "The Bureaucratic Model," pp. 62–65, 86–87.

54. See Deutsch, *op. cit.*, pp. 58–59.

the game be only equilibrium-tending: they cannot lead to the creation of another game.

Another form of the equilibrium model which has caught the attention of some political scientists is the input-output model, the general outline of which was loosely adopted from economic theory. David Easton developed such an input-output model several years ago, and in the form in which it was then presented, it certainly resembled an equilibrium model. "Demands" and "supports" were inputs into the system and "decisions or policies," the outputs; part of the outputs were put back into the systems as inputs.[55] More recently when Easton published his fully developed general theory of the political system, he seemed to have transcended the earlier simplistic input-output model, and the result must now be placed in the non-equilibrium- rather than the equilibrium-model category, if only on the basis of the more sophisticated feedback system he has developed.[56] A similar shift from equilibrium to non-equilibrium theory has occurred in the work of Gabriel Almond. His introductory chapter in *The Politics of Developing Areas* was indistinguishable from the early input-output model of Easton, but an examination of his more recent theory of political development shows a much greater sensitivity to the need for non-equilibrium change in models of rapid political transformation.[57]

This shift from equilibrium to non-equilibrium models of the political system is a strong indication of the increasing dissatisfaction with such theories of change (or with the general lack of change models in social theory). This is not to suggest that there did not exist, as far back as the beginning of the previous century, a variety of process and conflict theories of social, and especially historical, change that were able to avoid most of the shortcom-

55. "An Approach to the Analysis of Political Systems," *World Politics*, IX (1957), 383–400.
56. *Systems Analysis*, pp. 21–33, 363–381.
57. "A Functional Approach to Comparative Politics," in Gabriel A. Almond and James Coleman, eds., *The Politics of Developing Areas* (Princeton, 1960), pp. 3–64. Almond's more recent statements can be found in "A Developmental Approach to Political Systems," *World Politics*, XVII (1965), 183–214, and in greater detail in Gabriel A. Almond and G. Bingham Powell, Jr., *Comparative Politics: A Developmental Approach* (Boston, 1966). In the latter work see especially pp. 25–27, 34–41, 299–332.

ings of equilibrium theory. Unfortunately, most of these theories, though they attempted to account for conscious processes of change and transformation, dealt with these phenomena on the macro-level of society or of human experience as a whole. Thus it was difficult, if not impossible, to derive from them specific propositions and concepts about change in the various subsystems of the social system.[58] More directly relevant to our present concerns is the one recent social science model that has shown the greatest promise in being able to deal with non-continuous changes and with processes of system transformation which go beyond restoration of a previous balance; this is the cybernetics model.

The essential elements of the cybernetics model are the feedback mechanism and the ability of the system to respond to what the feedback carries back into it. Deutsch defines feedback as "a communications network that produces action in response to an input of information, and which includes the results of its own action in the new information by which it modifies its subsequent behavior."[59] Easton's feedback loops fulfil very much the same function.[60] But feedback alone would only carry us a little way beyond equilibrium. In the Deutsch model two other processes are added, learning and consciousness. The former is defined as feedback of data for changing the network, i.e., goal change; the latter constitutes the process of classifying, storing, and the subsequent bringing out of storage and the recombining of messages. For Easton the complete feedback circuit is equally complex, and performs equally effectively the tasks of enabling the system to monitor the environment as well as itself to produce, as completely as possible, the information necessary to respond to a wide variety of challenges:

It is the fact that there can be such a continuous flow of effects and information between system and environment, we shall see, that ultimately accounts for the capacity of a political system to persist in a world *even of violently fluctuating changes*. Without feedback and the capacity to respond to it, no system could survive for long, except by accident.[61]

58. Deutsch, *op. cit.*, pp. 35–38.   59. *Ibid.*, p. 88.
60. *Systems Analysis*. See especially the diagrams on pp. 30, 32, 374, 378, 381.
61. *Ibid.*, p. 32. Emphasis added.

St. Mary's College Library
Winona, Minnesota

The advantages of the cybernetics model are many. Kaplan suggests that: ". . . models of this kind are far more effective than philosophical dialectic in freeing behavioral science from the stultifications of both mechanistic materialism and mentalistic idealism."[62] There is also the special relevance of feedback models for the analysis of social systems undergoing rapid social, political, and economic change; it would surely be shortsighted to expect any useful sort of "fit" for such a society from an equilibrium model. Finally, feedback models, unlike previous dialectical conflict and evolutionary process models, enable us to deal with very small subsystems of the social system and to develop specific (even if not always quantifiable) data and propositions about structural and functional changes in them.

There are a number of disadvantages, as well. Cybernetics models are essentially communications models: they can tell us quite a bit about the flow of messages but practically nothing about their content. Obviously, the content of messages processed by a political system is as important—if not more important —than the mere pattern of communication flow. Then there is also the fact that the cybernetics model is, in Rapoport's terms, a system-theoretical model and like these models might well be quite suggestive about new data and where to search for them, but will not meet the demand of the "hard" theorists for verifiability and predictability. It is "only" a heuristic model; but if it does this job well, its advantages will have outweighed its shortcomings.

It has been suggested that organization theory by its very nature can be only equilibrium theory: It is preoccupied with the needs of a "going concern" and simply cannot tolerate violently fluctuating changes. If this is indeed the case, then cybernetics models with all their dynamic qualities, their flexibility, and openness will fit only with difficulty into the literature on organization and administration. However, only a full-scale inquiry into the literature will reveal the presence or absence in it of concepts of change and of a temporal dimension, and thus the possibility of integrating the cybernetic model into it.

62. *Op. cit.*, p. 292.

Time in Models and Theories of Organization and Administration[63]

A review of the organization and administration literature such as the one undertaken for this study leaves one with a bewildering sense of diversity. Others must have had similar experiences, for there have been a number of attempts to sort out and classify that literature. In some instances models and theories were historically arranged, whereas in others they were grouped into decision-making, bureaucracy, and system model categories.[64] None of these fits the needs of the present assignment, however, and the classificatory scheme shown in the table "Organization Change and the Social System" was devised in order to locate these theories and models in relation to criteria of change and temporality.

Three points need to be made about the scheme which is laid out in the following chart. The first is an admission of partial failure. Though it was possible to classify the models and theories according to broad criteria of change and dynamics, it proved impossible to find equally discrete categories of timing or temporality. Such findings as were possible are explored more fully later in this section. Second, the distinction between the more general notion of change and the more restricted concept of timing developed in the first two sections has been carried forward into this part of the investigation. It seemed useful again to distinguish between the nature of change in the social system and in organi-

---

63. It seemed that no useful purposes would be served by documenting fully the literature being analyzed in this section. It is familiar to scholars and practitioners alike. A most excellent and exhaustive bibliography, at least to circa 1962, can be found in Bertram Gross, *The Managing of Organizations: The Administrative Struggle* (New York, 1964), II, 893–948. See also Dwight Waldo, "Theory of Organization: Status and Problems," in *The Study of Organizational Behavior: Status, Problems and Trends,* Papers in Comparative Public Administration, Special Series, No. 8, Comparative Administration Group (1966), pp. 1–28, for references as well as a temperate and judicious review. At the end of this present chapter (pp. 132–134), there appears a listing of the principal works consulted in arriving at the classification of writers which appear in the chart on p. 114.

64. See Waldo, *op. cit.*; Gross, *op. cit.*, I, 91–243; and James G. March and Herbert A. Simon, *Organizations* (New York, 1958), chaps. ii–iii.

zations on one hand, and questions of timing—synchronization, sequence, and rate—on the other. Finally, taking an essentially ecological view of the nature of organization and administration, it seemed useful to determine whether the various theorists and their constructs would cluster in a particular way if their conception of the nature of the social system was related to their conception of organizational changes; the results of following up this lead will be discussed later.

The analysis of the chart which follows will be in three parts. In the first part the typology of social systems used in the chart will be explained, and the findings derived from the clustering of

Organizational Change and the Social System: Major Alternative Conceptions in Theories of Administration and Organization

| | | NATURE OF ORGANIZATIONAL CHANGE | | |
		STEADY STATE	EQUILIBRIUM	NON-EQUILIBRIUM
NATURE OF SOCIAL SYSTEM	ORGANIC	Follett	Blau & Scott Eisenstadt Etzioni Gouldner Haire Merton Parsons Riggs Selznick Weber	Argyris Deutsch Easton Gore Gross
	MECHANISTIC	Fayol Gulick Mooney Taylor Urwick	Barnard Mayo March Presthus Roethlisberger Simon	Crozier

See pp. 132–134 for an appendix listing principal works consulted in constructing this chart.

theories and models will be interpreted. The second part will be devoted to defining the categories of organizational change and the resulting distribution of theories over the various categories. Finally, the implications for timing of the various models will be explored; it is here that the partial failure of the present effort is revealed most clearly—the absence of neat categories and easily classifiable findings concerning timing and temporality.

Categories of the Social System

The categories of social systems have been taken from the current literature of sociological theory. They resemble, among others, those of Martindale, who divides contemporary social theory into "holistic" and "atomistic" social system types.[65] One might argue that the category labeled "mechanistic" does not use the term in the narrow technical sense of a deterministic, classical mechanistic system, and that "individualistic" or indeed "atomistic" would have been more appropriate. The difficulty encountered in this enterprise was that theorists who were avowedly "organic" in their conception of society tended to state their position clearly, whereas those who were not often did not clarify their stand on this broader question. Thus, it seemed safer to say that their conception of society in a very broad sense is a mechanistic one, and the term now covers both the more radical individualistic theorists, like Taylor and Urwick, and those who conceive of a social sytem, but not in organic terms, like Presthus.

Three other points concerning the social system categorization require some comments. First, as in several other respects the towering influence of Talcott Parsons on social science theorists can be quickly perceived; one can almost create a division of Parsonians vs. "the rest." Because it seemed that Parsons' notion of the social system is an essentially organic one, all the Parsonians were classified accordingly. Pre-Parsonians as well as current non-Parsonian theorists divided themselves among the organic and mechanistic category without revealing any particular pattern.

65. Don Martindale, "Introduction," in Zollschan and Hirsch, *op. cit.*, p. xxxvii.

Second, it appeared that a number of writers whose conception of the social system was mechanistic, nevertheless held an essentially organic view of the nature of organizations; this is surely true of Barnard who defined organization in interactionist terms, as well as of Mayo and Presthus. Though Fayol was classified as mechanistic—and one would assume that most of the contributors to the *Papers on the Science of Administration,* with the one exception noted on the chart, would hold mechanistic and steady state views about the nature of organization—a close examination of some of his writings revealed an almost Barnardian notion of organizational character.[66]

Finally, an examination of the clustering of theorists supports, at least in part, our "ecological hunch" about administration and its environment. One would assume that it would not be easy to combine an organic view of society with a steady state or static view of organizations on one (upper-left) point of the grid or a mechanistic conception of society with a non-equilibrium or dynamic view of the organization on the opposite (lower-right) point. These two cells are not empty, though they contain only one name each and the decision on one of them—Crozier—is far from unambiguous. This nicely balanced pattern might, of course, simply reflect two shortcomings: one, that the dimensions on the two sides of the grid are not really two distinct variables, and two, that the error simply is the result of a highly selective coverage of the literature. As far as the first is concerned, I would suggest that I have followed what seemed to me a reasonably clear distinction between societies and organizations which is fully documented in the literature.[67] It would be difficult not to plead guilty to the second shortcoming, at least in a qualified sort of way. I will gladly accept correction if my effort leads others to further research on the basis of my criteria.

66. Such formulations as "unity, continuity, flexibility, precision . . . are the broad features of a good plan of action" or "time is required for an employee to get used to new work" came as a surprise. These quotations are from Henri Fayol, *General and Industrial Management* (London, 1949), pp. 45 and 38–39, respectively.

67. See especially Waldo, *op. cit., passim,* and the literature cited by him in nn. 1–8.

Categories of Organizational Change

The categories of organizational change follow those established earlier for the typology of social systems. Again, we will note the dominance of equilibrium models. There is also a rising interest in non-equilibrium theories among specialists in administration and organization though not as great as it was found to be among general social science theorists.

Steady state models. The first category is not properly a category of organizational change at all. In fact the writers so designated are not concerned with organizational change but simply want to assure, in one form or another, that the stated tasks or goals of the organization are carried out efficiently. March and Simon divide the writers in this group into two categories: the Taylorites who focus on the basic physical activities involved in production (time and motion studies, etc.) and the Gulick-Urwick group who are chiefly concerned with "grand organizational problems of departmental division and work coordination."[68] March and Simon also include Weber in the Gulick-Urwick organizational design category.

In our steady state group, Urwick and Mooney exemplify best the "classical" organization theorists and their total preoccupation with marshaling or, as we will suggest later, mobilizing material and manpower for the status quo goals of the organization. Taylor has to be included in this group, though (as March and Simon point out) his preoccupation and that of his disciples runs along different lines. But in his case, too, the goals and the nature of the organization are given and unchanging, and concern is with maximizing efficiency in attaining these goals.

Two interesting "deviants" in this group are Mary Parker Follett and, surprisingly, Luther Gulick. Most significant in Follett's work are her organic conception of society and her thoroughly communitarian sentiments—the latter term is used advisedly. Though these sentiments are perhaps more clearly discernible in

68. March and Simon, *op. cit.*, pp. 12–22.

her non-technical writings, her excitement about the possibility of genuine social relations in an industrial society is ever present and reminds one of John Dewey. Like the latter she was misunderstood and has generally been forgotten by social scientists and philosophers alike. For her, society as well as organizations are "whole," life is continuous, and it is for us to see the connection between one moment and another. She aims for what she calls a total relatedness where parts are not added to one another but "where each part has been permeated by every other part." Though she is critical of control in the Urwick-Mooney sense of the term, her preoccupation with what she calls co-ordination leads me to suspect that she, too, does not really have much concern with goals and goal change, and thus ultimately with organizational change.

A thorough re-examination of Luther Gulick's contribution to the *Papers on the Science of Administration,* as well as of some of his later writings in the light of the current perspective of change and timing, produced perhaps the most surprising results altogether. Though the popularizer of POSDCORB has been retained in the steady state classification, if only because of the centrality to his writings of POSDCORB, there are passages which would lead one to categorize his basic orientation in our present scheme as dynamic (non-equilibrium) and organic. He demands "more elaborate provisions for those agencies of management which concern themselves with the processes of adaptation"; he warns those preoccupied with organizational mechanics that they must "regard their basic problem of organization as dynamic"; and he concludes that "a principle of organization appropriate at one stage may not be appropriate at all during a succeeding state." If these views come as a surprise to those who identify Gulick with POSDCORB, they might nevertheless quickly recover and suggest that Gulick ought to have practiced what he preached but that, on the whole, he failed to do so. I tend to agree with these strictures.

Equilibrium models. The second category, equilibrium models, is one in which change is assumed to take place in such a way that the system (or organization) which was in balance before change was initiated will return to its equilibrium position at the end of the change process. But on the whole, change is considered to be dysfunctional and has, properly speaking, no place in such a model.

Two features of the equilibrium model deserve special attention. The first of these concerns the nature of goals and purposes. For the steady state theorists, as was suggested earlier, the goals and purposes of the organization were given, or, as Urwick put it, they were of secondary importance, for there were principles governing human organization which could be "studied as technical questions, irrespective of the purpose of the enterprise . . . or any constitutional, political or social theory underlying its creation." Equilibrium theorists, on the other hand, recognized that goals and purposes could be of an infinite variety and that they could become sources of disagreement and conflict which could threaten the system. However, though they included a statement of goals and purposes as part of their equilibrium-type models, they avoided the problem of *change* in goals and purposes. Thus Blau and Scott recognize the possibility of conflict among the multiple purposes and goals in an organization as leading to change in the organization, but they by-pass the question of goal change itself.

The second of these, closely related to that of goals, is the maximizing vs. satisficing issue. The concern of steady state theorists was with efficiency, that is to say, with the most rational arrangement conducive to maximization of goal attainment. Again, the failure of steady state theory to prove relevant to both "real-life" problems of organizations as well as to the demands of the increasingly sophisticated academic analysts led to an abandoning of steady state as well as maximizing assumptions and, instead, to an acceptance of more modest attainments. Herbert Simon in elegant mathematical form, and Charles Lindblom in his homely phrase "muddling through" both have argued the case for satisficing. Equilibrium surely implies something less than maximum, for a balance can be maintained only if there is no insistence on maximal demands, goals, etc. Could it be that the coincidental shifts from steady state to equilibrium and from maximizing to satisficing models are temporal as well as logical sequences?

Speaking historically, Weber's bureaucratic model set the stage for the development of equilibrium theory. Even though he chose to construct an ideal-type bureaucratic model (essentially a steady state system), Weber was not insensitive to problems of change and conflict—dysfunctional as they might seem to be for that most powerful instrument of complex organizations—bureaucracy. However, the notion of dysfunctional conflict was pursued vigorously and extensively chiefly by the neo-Weberians like Merton, Gouldner, and Selznick. To them the dysfunctional consequences of bureaucracy—dysfunction in structure, operation, and behavior (personality)—were so severe that they almost caused the destruction of the bureaucratic system. It would seem that as a result they should have accepted, explicitly or implicitly, a non-equilibrium change model. I would suggest that none of these three writers, nor any others in the Weber-Parsons tradition, ever took the step that would have carried him beyond the equilibrium model. According to them, the bureaucratic model becomes distorted, but it does not really change into some other form, does not really profoundly alter its goals. Gouldner might recognize the trap of the "metaphysical pathos of the iron law of bureaucracy," but he surely gives no indication that he has been able to avoid it.

The source of the organic concept of society of most modern equilibrium theorists is the social system analysis of Talcott Parsons; and it has been the essentially equilibrating nature of structural-functional analysis which, as was suggested in the preceding section, has contributed to the popularity of equilibrium models in the first place. By invariably reaching back to Weber's bureaucratic model and by relying steadfastly on the stability of the four aspects of the social system, Parsons always manages to produce a form of equilibrium analysis even when he is engaged in constructing paradigms of an evolutionary process.[69]

69. "Evolutionary Universals in Society," *Am. Soc. Rev.*, XXIX (1964), 339–357.

At least two writers in this organic-equilibrium group have dealt at some length with administration in other than advanced Western settings: S. N. Eisenstadt and Fred W. Riggs. The former is concerned chiefly with what he called historic bureaucratic societies, whereas the latter has devoted considerable attention to bureaucracies in so-called transitional societies. Though Eisenstadt has attempted to argue the case for a dynamic element in structural-functional analysis, his most extensive work, *The Political System of Empires,* is a detailed analysis of a bureaucratic system in a condition of equilibrium—a balance between traditional and non-traditional forces and elements. In the same way Riggs's prismatic model represents a political and bureaucratic system's having achieved a similar balance. Admittedly, both Eisenstadt and Riggs recognize the possibility of disruption of this balance and of change to another system, but their preoccupation seems to be with balance rather than with change.

The remaining writer in this group, Haire, by constructing what he called a biological model might well be considered falsely identified in the equilibrium category. But on closer examination it appears, first, that the biological growth laws which he uses to measure certain forms of organizational growth are at best very ill-fitting analogues of organizational growth, and, second, that Haire's first concern is not growth but equilibrium.

Two facts stand out when examining the group of writers in the equilibrium-mechanistic cell. First, these writers are identified by their preoccupation with what Gross calls "people-in-organization"; this certainly holds true for Barnard, the human relations school (Mayo and Roethlisberger), and Presthus. Second, in Simon we have the most articulate proponent of the satisficing argument.

Simon's own formulation and what he calls the "Simon-Barnard equilibrium model" both conceive of the organization as a system "which receives contributions in the form of money and effort, and offers inducement in return for these contributions." In this, as in any other equilibrium model, conflict is of course possible. In the Simon-Barnard (or Simon-Barnard-March) model, the conflict arises when the inducement-contributions balance gets out of kilter; even so, the authors remain preoccupied with organizational equilibrium rather than with change.

The concern with people-in-organization is found most pronouncedly in the now classical studies of Mayo and Roethlisberger (with Dickson) and more recently in Presthus.

Like the neo-Weberians who concentrate on the dysfunctional consequences of bureaucracy, the so-called human relations school focuses on dysfunctions, but less in organizational terms than in human terms—though Merton's treatment of the relationship between bureaucracy and personality should not be overlooked. We are not concerned here with the supposedly undemocratic and manipulative implications of the Hawthorne studies. On the question of organizational changes, these writers are clearly committed to the notion of equilibrium—of the proper balance to permit goal achievement, as well as balance between the organization and the environment.

There seems to be, in Presthus, little concern with change beyond maintenance of equilibrium (perhaps no more than steady state, in effect). Of his three personality types only one, the "upward-mobile," is attuned to the organization at all, and he accepts its imperatives willingly. The "indifferent" ultimately rejects the organization altogether, whereas the "ambivalent" neither accepts nor rejects it. Obviously none of these three types can possibly be (directly) a source of organizational change.

Non-equilibrium models. This brings us to the last category of organizational change, non-equilibrium. Under it are subsumed all forms of change other than those identified in the previous two groups, including the sort of change in cybernetics models, moving equilibria, etc. It should be noted that if the names of Deutsch and Easton are eliminated from this cell as not being concerned specifically with either administration or organization, then the number in this category is small indeed; one need only add that the inclusion of Gross in this set of cells probably raises more questions than can be answered at this time.

I have included Deutsch and Easton, whose general system work was analyzed earlier, because of the relevance of cybernetics models for organization theory. Unlike the global evolutionary and process theories which operate only at the level of whole societies, communications models lend themselves to the handling of discontinuous change at the level of subsystems of various sizes. It is unfortunate that so little use has been made of them in the organization-administration literature so far.

Because there is little that can be said in a systematic manner about the four writers in this category, they will simply be discussed seriatim, taking the three in the non-equilibrium-organic group first.

Argyris, whose views concerning the nature of society and organizations are principally organic, nevertheless, sees organizational development not as a process of balance but of conflict. Existing organizations committed to an essentially rational-maximizing strategy of getting the job done, non-emotional rational individual behavior, and direction by superiors, will decay unless the principles of Rogerian-Maslowian psychology are applied to patterns of organizational behavior. The aim is authentic relationships which can only be achieved if non-evaluative, descriptive feedback, openness, experimentation, and risk taking are increased in the system. It could be argued that Argyris's description of existing organizations is essentially of the equilibrium type, but what is of most interest to us—and certainly to Argyris himself—is the problem of organizational change. One might add that once the "ideal" organization has been attained, equilibrium at this higher level will be established. Even on this interpretation of Argyris's work he would still have to be classified as non-equilibrium, which we have defined here as including models of moving equilibrium.

In Gore's model the conception of the organization as a rational system of action will coexist with the conception of the organization as a "collective, heuristic strategy." Although the "rational process" of the classical model assumes stability of goals, Gore's "heuristic process" focuses on value change leading to eventual consensus, essentially a form of a moving equilibrium. The primary purpose of the decision-making process, with its rational and heuristic components, is to bring about structural change necessitated by shifts in goals and power; only secondarily is it concerned with maintenance of equilibrium.

It is doubtful whether Gross's *The Managing of Organizations* can be accommodated in any single category. Gross's enthusiasm for organizations and especially his unbounded confidence in the future as an organizational future suggest that he is pretty much satisfied with organizations as they are, that they will continue to operate in their present fashion, except that there will be more of them and they will cover a wider range of our daily lives. This has all the earmarks of an equilibrium model: that is to say, whatever changes will take place will not really upset existing balances, will not alter current goals, and will not result in a state recognizably different from the present. To be sure, improvements will have to be made, goals will have to be better clarified; but the world of organizations is already well on the way to becoming the dominant mode of life. Though it is a systems model more nearly on the order of Deutsch and Easton, it does not have the conceptual sharpness of these two constructs. But Gross's profound concern for organizational purposes, the manner in which purposes are broadly defined, and their constantly stressed multiplicity leads him to change and conflict as the motivating forces in organization: "The unifying purposes of any organization are constantly changing in response to new situations." Change can come about for many reasons, including "divergences between interest satisfactions for members and for nonmembers, between quantity and quality of output, between survival and growth, between mobilization logic and growth logic, between small groups and larger group codes, between technical and administrative rationality . . . between the short-run and the long-run aspects." It is too early to say whether the Gross model can be made operational for research or practice, but it has a dynamic which has not been muted even by its Brobdingnagian proportions. One cannot but give it the benefit of the doubt on the question of non-equilibrium dynamics.

It was suggested above that one would expect the non-equilibrium-mechanistic cell to be empty: a mechanistic view of society could not very well go hand in hand with a dynamic view of organization. The identification of Crozier as fitting this category is probably of doubtful validity. The judgment concerning his mechanistic view of the social system is based chiefly on his rather individualistic interpretation of French society; his brief reference to the United States and the USSR did nothing to dispel this impression. The classification as a non-equilibrium theorist rests on two grounds: (1) he identifies the bureaucratic system as a feedback "error-information-correction" process; and (2) in his dysfunctional model of bureaucracy, change comes about only when enforced from the top down and in crisis situations—essentially a non-continuous, non-equilibrium mode of change.

Implications for Time and Timing

It would have been a most dramatic conclusion of this categorization of theories of organization and administration to be able to identify precise notions of time and timing with each of the six categories in the matrix, or at least with each of the categories of organizational change. But the evidence, at least as far as I was able to interpret it, simply could not be mustered. Nevertheless, a number of observations suggested themselves, as well as some categories of time which, I would hope, go beyond abstractions such as those specified by Gurvitch. Let me repeat: my concern here is with what Moore calls timing and its three aspects: synchronization, sequence, and rate.

First, certain differences in perspectives suggest themselves for each of the three categories of organizational change. Steady state models which focus on the maintenance of the status quo will have a rather restricted time horizon and, because of their almost exclusive concern with the efficient working of a complex mechanism, will tend to emphasize cyclical time. It should be added that because all complex organizations are concerned with synchronization, sequence, and rate it will be impossible to specify a difference in emphasis on these three aspects of timing among the three kinds of organizational change. Later on, in the discussion of time and development in the following section, some suggestions will be made concerning certain preoccupations of developing systems with specific aspects of timing.

In both equilibrium and non-equilibrium models, increased attention is paid to longer time perspectives and, thus, there will be a greater emphasis on linear time. In the equilibrium model there will, by its very nature, be some form of balance between cyclical and linear time. Especially those theorists who stress goals will obviously pay greater attention to linear than to cyclical time. The non-equilibrium model with its emphasis on rapid and far-reaching change and on discontinuity will surely be least concerned with cyclical time. Models of this kind will perhaps tend to play down the synchronization and sequence aspects of timing, and stress rate, since their principal concern is, after all, with rapid change and thus with the rates of events over time. It is important that changes are brought about quickly, and, if necessary, at the price of sacrificing finely meshed synchronization and the sequential ordering of events. Metaphors such as "storming," "great leap forward," etc. dramatize this preoccupation with rates of change.

Second, the fundamental notions of cyclical and linear time, as suggested above, are implicit in much of the literature. As was suggested in the opening section, not even Eliade, who developed these categories, assumed that modern man would operate only on linear time; cyclical time would survive, though not in the sacral form in which it was significant for archaic man. One way in which the cyclical-linear categories suggested a distinctive time perspective has already been discussed. As will be seen from the subsequent discussion it will enter our considerations at many different points.

Third, there might well be a significant difference in time perspective between maximizing and satisficing models of organization. In the first place, the maximizer will obviously press for full utilization of time in order to achieve maximum efficiency. To the satisficer a variety of goals including individual demands or group demands will be significant, and he will most likely try to bargain time for demands and satisfactions. Next, one needs to consider the following paradox. Although the satisficer will have a shorter time horizon than the maximizer, he does not assume that long-range ordering of preferences is possible (planning); he will more likely think in linear terms which are more flexible than the fixed cycles of astronomical time which are the tools of the rational maximizer. Perhaps linear and cyclical time in this context are not synonymous with long-range and short-range outlooks, respectively. Finally, one might want to suggest that the satisficer, focusing on "bounded uncertainty," will more likely find congenial the phenomenological time conception of a Shackle and Husserl than would a maximizer.

Fourth, the linear-cyclical categories seem most useful and suggestive for giving time perspective to certain aspects of administration. Selznick's distinction between critical and routine decisions; the much maligned, but still useful, policy-administration distinction (or perhaps creativity-routine or development administration-routine administration); the differences in time perspective between those near the top or the bottom of the hierarchy (another form of distinguishing between creative and routine work); all these suggest different positions on the linear-cyclical spectrum. Critical decisions, policy formation, top of the hierarchy, all suggest cyclical or short-range concerns. These are not, repeat *not,* polar opposites but mixed types located along a spectrum. Though admittedly a simple one-dimensional model, it, nevertheless, suggests a new dimension of viewing the structure and functioning of administration. One might also add that as an organization shifts in its tasks from development and creativity to routine administration, the time perspective of the entire organization, including those in policy positions, will shift markedly from linear to cyclical forms.

Fifth, a most interesting aspect of time in organizations is the division between time devoted to organizational responsibilities (public) and that devoted to personal and family concerns (private). It will be recalled that for Weber the distinction between public office and private life was one of the hallmarks of legal-rational bureaucracy. But much of the "lore" and science of management and leadership seems to indicate that both public and business executives find their entire lives taken up, often quite voluntarily, by their job. If one adds to this the increasing emphasis on the communitarian nature of the business corporation, at least in the United States, one can call the time demands of executive responsibility totalitarian—the executive's entire time has become public time. There is also general agreement in the literature that as one descends the hierarchy, as one goes from critical to routine decisions, the time demands of the job become less severe. The routine job is a nine-to-five affair, but the executive takes home a full brief case. This would indicate that the demands of cyclical time in routine jobs are well defined "in time," whereas the demands of linear time (planning, creativity) are unlimited. An attempt was made to determine whether Weber's distinction between the claims of expertise and incumbency of office on the part of administrators would yield significant differences in time perspective; none could be found.

Sixth, time emerges as one of the principal tools of the organizational mobilizer in almost all models of organization and administration. Many current writers carefully try to distinguish their own approaches from those of the classical organization theorists and the human relations school. They tend to accuse their precursors of either an open (Taylor, Urwick, Weber) or of a more refined and concealed but, nevertheless, deep-rooted anti-democratic bias (human relations school). However, an examination of some of these same writers revealed the following situation. In at least two prominent cases time and timing were discussed chiefly under headings of control. The implication seems to be that "time" is simply an element of command, a concern of those in control of the organization, a tool which enables them to direct the organization along lines determined by them.[70] In fact, it is difficult to avoid the impression—"impression" here being not something vague and fleeting, but that which presses upon one's consciousness—that the theory of administration and organization is a theory of command and control in which other considerations, such as democratic decision-making

70. Two specific examples would be Gross, *op. cit.*, I, 348, 360–362, and II, 791; and Peter M. Blau and W. Richard Scott, *Formal Organizations: A Comparative Approach* (San Francisco, 1962), pp. 169–170.

or individual self-activation (Argyris) are always means to other ends. One has to agree that the non-equilibrium theorists are considerably more sophisticated than the other categories of theorists, but they share with the others a preoccupation with command and control. One is tempted to add that their being more sophisticated only enables them to create more effective (because apparently non-coercive?) control systems.

Conclusion: Time, Administration, and Development

This paper has dealt at some length with aspects of timing and change in models and theories of administration and organization. This was done not because of a primary interest in the narrower, more technical issues of social science methodology and philosophy. Rather this resulted from a concern with the role and function of administration in development and for the availability of effective tools and concepts for dealing with phenomena of rapid social and political transformation. The search for dynamic instruments, the preoccupation with change and timing, sprang from this commitment to problems of modernization and development. Thus, we must ask now: is it likely that these models and theories, given the presence or absence in them of dynamic qualities and of timing, will help us analyze, understand, and perhaps even predict the course of development and modernization? The answer to this question is in four parts.

First, it has been the position of this essay that static models and theories will be of little help in analyzing systems in rapid transformation. At the outset of the present study it seemed that models and theories of administration and organization suffered from a twofold debility when viewed from the perspective of development and modernization. Most models were static, that is to say, they could be used only to deal with conditions, states, and data at a given point in time. They could not explain how a given state came into being, how it would change, and what would be the conditions of change. At best, one could argue that models constructed at different points in time would yield a series of "still" pictures, but certainly no more than that.

A second failing seemed to be that even those models and theories which were not fully static tended toward equilibrium conceptions; they can accommodate some amount of change and conflict but generally view conflict as dysfunctional and cannot really cope efficiently with violently fluctuating and discontinuous (revolutionary) change. I have already reported on the general condition of social theories of change from the perspective of development.[71] The current analysis of organizational change reveals a similar situation. To the question of whether the picture in the organization and administration literature is more promising than in general social theory, the answer must be a firm "yes *and* no." It is less bright because those social theories that seemed to handle change most effectively—various evolutionary and conflict process types—simply operated at too macroscopic a level to be of much direct use in the analysis of organizational change. But the picture also is brighter because considerable progress has been made (as was documented earlier) in the development and application of non-equilibrium models, chiefly of the cybernetic variety.

Second, the division in the literature between rational-maximizing and satisficing models of organization is particularly germane to problems of development and modernization. There is no doubt that models which are uncompromisingly rationalist and maximizing in character will have little or no relevance for the situation in which developing societies find themselves today. This is so for a number of reasons. Uncompromising demands for rational organization cannot possibly be met for lack of skilled manpower. Furthermore, the maximizer's preoccupation with the clock will founder on the rocks of cultural norms still attuned to patterns of cyclical time—not the cyclical time of the astronomical devices but the cyclical time of the sacred myth and seasonal rhythm. Because of that, they will have difficulty projecting plans into a distant future: the linear time of long-range planning will be beyond their grasp. On the other hand, they might be able to

71. See above n. 46.

respond more effectively to suggestions of "muddling through," and to the satisficers' position that individuals as well as governments are incapable of total rationality and long-range forecasting.

Third, we must guard against misinterpreting as relevant to development situations certain time phenomena of post-industrial societies. One must carefully qualify any discussion of cyclical time in contemporary societies, for the cycles of astronomical time are physically, philosophically, and psychologically a world apart from the cyclical time of archaic man. In the same way, it might be misleading if we were to say that post-industrial man has returned to the condition of primitive man because "time" does not seem to exist for either of them: for one, because it never "existed," for the other because it has been "abolished." It has also been suggested that the concern for the values of participants in organization which began with the Hawthorne experiments, and has continued into the present day in such theorists as Gross and Argyris, is no more suitable for "transfer" to developing societies with their diffuse and particularistic values than the legal-rational model of Weber and Urwick. Looking at the historical development of Western social systems, Moore observes that "as new forms of production, exchange, and mobility become very general, some partial restoration of the prior, richer fabric of social relations becomes evident. . . . But the conclusion claims too much. . . . The informal organizations and 'human relations' policies found in complex bureaucracies are not the same as the pre-industrial work organization. And so on. The wheel turns but it also moves across a changing terrain."[72] The neo-mercantilism and the neo-feudalism of the post-industrial society would seem to be no more easily exportable than the finance capitalism and Taylorism of fifty years ago.

Finally, I want to conclude this discussion with a paradox. (It might well be that the contradiction I claim to see results chiefly from a certain use of words—but then it is always possible to call on the Red Queen in defense of such practices.) A great many

72. Wilbert E. Moore, "Predicting Discontinuities in Social Change," *Am. Soc. Rev.*, XXIX (1964), 331–338.

students of the politics of new states have identified the primary need of these states to be acquiring the capacity to marshal men and resources for the development tasks by any means at their disposal. The term "mobilization system" has come into wide use for such a political system. It is possible to use this term in very much the same way to characterize, as I have done toward the end of the preceding section, much of the theory of administration and organization. In both cases we obviously have identified a process of marshalling resources by an elite. If it is correct to say that the political systems of new states tend to be mobilization systems, and if much of current organization theory can also be characterized as mobilizational, why is it we hear continuous complaints that "Western" organization, "Western" administrative structures and processes are simply not relevant for these new states? Why is a mobilizational administrative system not appropriate for a mobilizational political system?

It is impossible to dismiss these questions with the all too familiar platitudes about culture clash, principally because some of the same questions could be raised about the relevance of these instruments even under conditions of (relative) cultural homogeneity. Is it because mobilization is not enough? Is it because technical expertise, planning, synchronization, etc. still leave unanswered questions that trouble both pre-industrial and post-industrial man? Has time, after all, remained as untractable as it was for the author of Ecclesiastes?

Appendix. Principal Works Consulted for Classification of Authors in the Chart *Organizational Change and the Social System*

Argyris, Chris. *Interpersonal Competence and Organizational Effectiveness.* Homewood, Ill., 1962.
———. *Personality and Organization.* New York, 1957.
Barnard, Chester I. *The Functions of the Executive.* Cambridge, Mass., 1938.
Blau, Peter M., and W. Richard Scott. *Formal Organizations: A Comparative Approach.* San Francisco, 1962.
Crozier, Michel. *The Bureaucratic Phenomenon.* Chicago, 1964.

Deutsch, Karl W. *The Nerves of Government: Models of Political Communication and Control.* New York, 1963.

Easton, David. *A Systems Analysis of Political Life.* New York, 1965.

――――. *A Framework for Political Analysis.* Englewood Cliffs, N.J., 1965.

――――. "An Approach to the Analysis of Political Systems," *World Politics,* IX (1957), 383–400.

Eisenstadt, S. N. *Essays on Comparative Institutions.* New York, 1965.

――――. *The Political System of Empires.* New York, 1963.

Etzioni, Amitai. *Modern Organizations.* Englewood Cliffs, N.J., 1964.

――――. *A Comparative Analysis of Complex Organizations: On Power, Involvement and Their Correlates.* New York, 1961.

Fayol, Henri. *General and Industrial Management.* London, 1949.

――――. "The Administrative Theory in the State," in Gulick, Urwick, and Mooney, see below.

Follett, Mary P. *The New State: Group Organization the Solution of Popular Government.* New York, 1918.

――――. *Dynamic Administration: The Collected Papers of Mary Parker Follett,* ed. Henry C. Metcalf and L. Urwick. New York, 1940.

Gore, William J. *Administrative Decision-Making: A Heuristic Model.* New York, 1964.

Gross, Bertram M. *The Managing of Organizations: The Administrative Struggle.* New York, 1964.

Gouldner, Alvin W. *Patterns of Industrial Bureaucracy.* Glencoe, Ill., 1954.

Gulick, Luther H., L. Urwick, and James D. Mooney. *Papers on the Science of Administration.* New York, 1937.

Haire, Mason. "Biological Models and Empirical Histories of the Growth of Organizations," in *Modern Organization Theory,* ed. Mason Haire. New York, 1959.

――――. *Psychology in Management.* 2nd ed. New York, 1964.

March, James G., and Herbert A. Simon. *Organizations.* New York, 1958.

Mayo, Elton. *The Human Problems of an Industrial Civilization.* New York, 1962.

Merton, Robert K. *Social Theory and Social Structure.* Rev. and enl. ed. Glencoe, Ill., 1959.

Mooney, James D., and Alan C. Reiley. *Onward Industry! The Principles of Organization and Their Significance to Modern Industry.* New York, 1931.

Parsons, Talcott. *The Social System.* Glencoe, Ill., 1951.

――――. *The Structure of Social Action: A Study in Social Theory with Special Reference to a Group of Recent European Writers.* 2nd ed. Glencoe, Ill., various dates, 1948–66.

———. "Evolutionary Universals in Society," *Am. Soc. Rev.*, XXIX (1964), 339–357.

Parsons, Talcott, and Edward A. Shils. *Toward a General Theory of Action.* Cambridge, Mass., 1951.

Presthus, Robert V. *The Organizational Society: An Analysis and a Theory.* New York, 1962.

Riggs, Fred W. *Administration in Developing Countries.* Boston, 1964.

———. *The Ecology of Public Administration.* New York, 1961.

Riggs, Fred W., and Edward W. Weidner. *Models and Priorities in the Comparative Study of Public Administration.* Comparative Administration Group, American Society for Public Administration. Chicago, 1963.

Roethlisberger, Fritz J. *Management and Morale.* Cambridge, Mass., 1941.

———. *Management and the Worker: An Account of a Research Program Conducted by the Western Electric Company, Hawthorne Works, Chicago.* Cambridge, Mass., 1943.

Selznick, Philip. *Leadership in Administration: A Sociological Interpretation.* Evanston, Ill., 1957.

———. *TVA and the Grass Roots: A Study in the Sociology of Formal Organization.* Berkeley, Calif., 1949.

Simon, Herbert A. *Administrative Behavior: A Study of Decision-Making Processes in Administrative Organizations.* New York, 1957.

———. *Models of Man, Social and Rational: Mathematical Essays on Rational Human Behavior in a Social Setting.* New York, 1957.

———. *The New Science of Management Decision.* New York, 1960.

Taylor, Frederick W. *Scientific Management: Comprising Shop Management, the Principles of Scientific Management, and Testimony before the Special House Committee.* New York, 1947.

Urwick, Lyndall F. *The Elements of Administration.* New York, 1944.

———. *The Pattern of Management.* Minneapolis, 1956.

Weber, Max. *Wirtschaft und Gesellschaft.* Part III of *Grundriss der Sozialoekonomik,* ed. S. Altmann *et al.* Tübingen, 1922.

———. *Gesammelte politische Schriften,* ed. Johannes Winkelmann. 2nd ed. Tübingen, 1958.

———. *The Methodology of the Social Sciences.* Trans. and ed. Edward A. Shils and Henry A. Finch. Glencoe, Ill., 1949.

Chapter 5

New Time in Old Clocks: Productivity, Development, and Comparative Public Administration*

Warren F. Ilchman

Time will consume all things including itself.
Hindu proverb

He that riseth late, must trot all day.
Ben Franklin

If you knew Time as well as I do, you wouldn't talk about wasting *it*. It's *him*. Now if you only kept on good terms with him, he'd do almost anything you liked with the clock.
Lewis Carroll

Theorists and practitioners of public administration, perhaps above all in the United States, have always been aware of the temporal dimension, whatever their difficulties in defining it or making it explicit. They have been concerned with the careful use of objective time as a resource for advancing rationality. They have explored the subjective impact of "time serving" on fatigue and morale and hence its effect on productivity. The very concept of productivity is measured partly in temporal terms. Temporal ordering has been central to the studies of decision-making and communications. Development of organization theory has been stimulated by the attempt to understand and control

* The author wishes to acknowledge the Rockefeller Foundation for making possible a field trip to South Asia and the Middle East and later "time" to think about problems of development, his colleagues in the Berkeley Seminar for many of the ideas that appear herein, and to Mr. Allan Samson, Miss Mary Oppenheimer, Mrs. Mary M. Skinner, and Mrs. Joyce M. Munns for their research assistance.

"change." More recently, students of comparative administration have adopted the ideas of historical stages and "synchronized" systems in time. Technical assistance practitioners refer to the export of administrative practices as "premature" or "ripe," relying essentially on temporal ideas. The very words "development" and "modernization" refer to processes through time, positing a linear course. And an objective of research in public administration (as in the natural and social sciences generally) is prediction —the use of the future and probabilities in time. Indeed, public administration—its assumptions, methods, objectives, and values —can be described as obsessed with "time."

This essay is both external to this characteristic obsession with time and part of it. The intention of what follows is to understand, in a preliminary fashion, the concern with time as part of the intellectual, industrial, and urban development of western Europe and especially to examine the administrative systems of non-Western nations in terms of their hospitality to Western time-oriented institutions and values. In the present intellectual subdivisions of public administration, this essay belongs to the untidy area labeled "development administration." Simply, the words "development" and "administration" mean both the self-conscious inducing and ordering of change by the agents of the state and the acquiring of a capacity by the government to induce and order change. Development administration, for my purposes, is concerned with increasing the capacity of the state to produce goods and services to meet and induce changing and expanding demands. The central analytic focus of the field of development administration is the comparative efficiency of administrative systems. These concerns—"change," "increasing capacity," "expanding demands," and "comparative efficiency"—are informed by a high value placed on time as a resource and center upon public institutions for the management of the use of time.

A New Temporal Metaphor: From Cyclical Time to Progressive Time

To understand the essence of this "industrial" conception of time it is important to examine it in terms of its social power as a

metaphor. By social power, I mean the codification or simplifica-
tion of reality in such a way that action is impelled on the part of
relevant persons. A host of diverse phenomena can be reduced by
means of a metaphor to a system which can be understood in that
it attaches values or significance to aspects of empirical reality,
yields predictions about the continuity and change in this reality,
and guides choices.[1] Thus, according to my argument, a particular view of time, arising in the sixteenth and seventeenth centuries in western Europe, provided a symbolic system for the ordering of human affairs. This view of time became a component of
ideology, even the most important component, for the state and
its members.

At the risk of vulgar idealism and making independent a variable which, at most, may be intervening, I would argue that the
most important element of the ideology appearing in western
Europe during this period was a belief in progressive time. This
view, while losing its impact on science and the arts in the late
nineteenth and twentieth centuries, remained dominant in politics, economic life, and social structure.[2] "Progressive time," as a
metaphor, conceived of time as pushing *forward* toward expanding productivity, *through* human co-ordination and the exploitation of advancing technology, *for* a better collective life. Time is
thought to be linear, an arrow pointing "upward." In this symbolic system, past states are thought to be lower, future states,
higher; human choices in the present are ordered to achieve a
more desirable future state. The future, held in control by present
choices, yields a criterion for policies, public and private. From
the point of view of the state, progressive time yields the politics
of expectation, the politics of collective improvement in time, the
politics of instrumentalism, in which the present becomes devalued for the sake of the future.

The metaphor of progressive time transforms the traditional
view of temporal ordering as cyclical and subservient to the

1. Clifford Geertz, "Ideology as a Cultural System," in David E. Apter, ed.,
Ideology and Discontent (New York, 1964), pp. 44–76.
2. See, for example, Ernst Cassirer, *Substance and Function and Einstein's
Theory of Relativity* (Chicago, 1923), pp. 417–420, 449–456; H. Stuart Hughes,
*Consciousness and Society: The Orientation of European Social Thought,
1890–1930* (New York, 1958), *passim.*

traditional conception of space. No longer is time thought to be a circle, a continuous repetition of birth, maturity, and decay, a threat to the highly valued public sacred space. Indeed, progressive time reinterprets the time relevant to human discipline as productivity time. Here everyday temporal discipline becomes "timing," which has as its components synchronization, sequence, and rate. According to Wilbert E. Moore, *synchronization* requires "the simultaneous actions by a number of persons, or at least their presence at a particular time." He defines *sequence* as the requirement that actions follow one another in a prescribed order, and conceptualizes *rate* as the critical frequency of events during a period of time.[3] The assumption is that through proper timing the promise of progressive time will be fulfilled. Indeed technology becomes, among other things, applied time control, and productivity becomes the measurement and organizing principle for public and private goals and means. Space, which was once a more powerful organizing metaphor than time, becomes in this system subordinate to progressive and productivity time. Space as "distance" is thought to be an impediment to productivity and thus as requiring temporal organization through centralization and improved communications.

The argument of this essay, then, is that the dominance in industrial society of this time consciousness represents a transformation of the impelling metaphor *from* a view of time as basically cyclical and subservient to spatial concepts *to* a view of progressive time and timing in which spatial concepts are subordinated. A state dominated by spatial concepts is oriented toward law and order and qualitative judgments. Space is its own product. A state dominated by linear time is oriented toward productivity and quantitative judgments. Time is a measurement of another object.

The argument has considerable explanatory value. It partly explains many of the dominant institutions and values of contemporary industrialized states. It partly explains the conflict in technical assistance between agents of industrialized and non-industrialized regimes. And it partly explains some of the basic internal

3. *Man, Time, and Society* (New York, 1963), p. 8.

problems of those nations undertaking industrialization. For instance, it illuminates the intra-bureaucratic conflict between those civil servants concerned with law and order and those concerned with productivity, and the conflict between governors, especially administrators, and the governed as deriving from different time conceptions. But to assert an argument's utility is not to demonstrate it. That task follows.

Archaic and Traditional Time

Progressive time and the importance of timing are rather recent as impelling and organizing metaphors. Sebastian de Grazia speaks of this image of progressive time as follows: "One can speak of images of time. . . . The one that fits the modern conception is linear. Time does not repeat itself, it ticks off in a straight line, goes from t to t in a continuum, runs in an even flow or in a stream with graduated steel banks, moves like the assembly lines or the ticker tape."[4] If a general period could be assigned to the rise and dominance of linear time in the West, it would be the sixteenth through the nineteenth centuries. A view of time as cyclical and subservient to space can be said to have prevailed until that period, and there are traces of the older view in modern thought as well.[5] The conception of time as a circle or a placid pool appears to be almost universal among archaic, primitive, and traditional cultures. Practices or institutions deriving, in part, from this conception are remarkably comparable across cultures. Mircea Eliade has found in his studies of traditional cultures a persistent theme in the abolition of profane time, the time of the linear concept, through the medium of myths of exemplary models. Myth itself serves to reactualize exemplary events—the Creation, the Founding of the State, the Giving of the Law, the Act of Sacrifice, and so forth. Myth summons a "timeless time" to serve as a guide for discipline.[6] The Mesapotamian empires, the Egyp-

4. *Of Time, Work, and Leisure* (Garden City, N.Y., 1964), p. 303.
5. See, for example, the plays of T. S. Eliot and Samuel Beckett.
6. See *Cosmos and History: The Myth of the Eternal Return* (New York, 1954), pp. 51 ff.

tian dynasties, and the empires of the Persians conceived of time only in static spatial terms. Time in terms of human events represented decline or the combination of forces, divine and demonic, bringing at once creation and destruction. Time was qualitative and concrete, even personalized. It shared none of the characteristics of modern time—quantitativeness, abstractness, and universalism. According to Henri Frankfort and his colleagues, there was in archaic societies a poorly developed sense of human succession and sequence with which one could develop a universal causality. Of the three metaphysical dimensions, space seems to have provided the impelling metaphor; the control of space was used analogously for the control and understanding of time.[7]

Similar conceptions of the time of human experience appear in all the Great Traditions, although considerable variation exists in their assumptions of, and attitudes toward, cosmic time. Hinduism and Buddhism treated profane time as illusion, as the endless cause of rebirth. As one commentator puts it, "time is an all-embracing, all-annihilating principle, in the onflow of which everything that comes into existence again vanishes after the expiration of time."[8] Indeed, insofar as the concept of sin existed in the two Indic traditions, it was the belief that nothing existed out of time. *Moksha* or *nirvana* consisted of overcoming one's history. Both religions sought an escape from time to an engulfing space.[9] In other usages of time, it was seen as the principle of creation and destruction, over which in divine detachment, Shiva danced.[10] From a human perspective, the "history" of the world vanished into temporal infinity. A single day in the life of Lord

7. *Before Philosophy: The Intellectual Adventure of Ancient Man* (London, 1949), pp. 11–38. See also Jean Cazenueve, "La perception des etendues dans les societes archaiques," *Cahiers Internationaux de Sociologie,* XXXVII (1964), 107–112.

8. Heinrich Zimmer, in Joseph Campbell, ed., *Myths and Symbols in Indian Art and Civilization* (New York, 1946), p. 211.

9. Mircea Eliade, "Time and Eternity in Indian Thought," in Joseph Campbell, ed., *Man and Time: Papers from the Eranos Yearbook* (New York, 1957), pp. 173–200. See also S. Das Gupta, *A History of Indian Philosophy,* 5 vols. (Cambridge, 1922–55); Ananda K. Coomaraswamy, *Hinduism and Buddhism* (New York, 1943); F. S. C. Northrop, *The Meeting of East and West* (New York, 1946), pp. 366–401; Hajime Nakamura, "Time in Indian and Japanese Thought," in J. T. Fraser, ed., *The Voices of Time* (New York, 1966), pp. 77–91.

10. Zimmer, *op. cit.,* pp. 3–22, 151–174.

Brahma was twelve thousand years, a *Mahayuga,* divided into four *yugas* of increasing moral degeneration, until the next day began for Brahma in perfection. The life of Brahma was calculated at the humanly incomprehensible three hundred and eleven thousand billion years. The festivals and religious acts of Hindus and Buddhists alike reactualize the time-destroying myths.[11] For human timing and its discipline, Hinduism and Buddhism were both inhospitable. The discipline and control of action in yoga were seen as aids to the abolition of time. Human effort was ultimately thought futile and arrogant, as seen in the legend of Indra. When action in the world was not rejected, the fruits of action were not to be enjoyed.[12]

The Great Traditions of China, excluding its variant of Buddhism, viewed time in cyclical terms, but took different stances toward it. Where Hinduism sought to abolish time, the Taoist for instance sought to abolish change, and treated time as something to be preserved endlessly. The Book of Changes, for example, sought to show persistence despite change. The normative guides advocated the human attainment of a standard of pre-established harmony to avoid an otherwise inevitable degeneration. The hope was to achieve pure duration, endless and identical survival, an unlimited repetition of sameness. As in other traditions, time was spoken of in spatial terms and its anti-change characteristics were exemplified through the imagery of the placid pool. Finally, in relation to acts, the Taoist ethic strongly advocated passivity or immobility. Human choices were to approximate the revered pre-established harmony.[13]

Greek and Roman thought, with a few exceptions, treated time as cyclical. Time was subject to perpetual return and influenced by astronomical movements which determined its course. But Greek thought differed from the Great Traditions of Asia. These differences were made especially clear by Ernst Cassirer:

11. Eliade, "Time and Eternity," pp. 173–200.
12. Eliade, "Cosmical Homology and Yoga," *Jour. Ind. Soc. Oriental Art,* V (1937), 188–203.
13. Hellmut Wilhelm, "The Concept of Time in the Book of Changes," in Campbell, *op. cit.,* pp. 212–232. See also Joseph Needham, "Time and Knowledge in China and the West," in Fraser, *op. cit.,* pp. 92–135.

Thus, while Indian thinking is oriented essentially toward the transience of the temporal world and Chinese thinking toward its permanence; while Indian thinking one-sidedly stresses the factor of change and Chinese thinking that of permanence—Greek thought establishes a pure inner balance between the two factors. The ideas of variability and substantiality fuse into one and from this fusion arises a new feeling, which might be called the purely speculative feeling of time and presence.[14]

This "speculative feeling," of course, marked a late development of Greek thought on time. In early Greek mythology, Chronos was thought of as a being who continuously begot children which he himself devoured. In later Greek thought, the circle of time, although not something from which to escape as in Hinduism, became a statement of perfection and the image of the determining law of the universe. Human history, as presently conceived, was for the Greeks an endless chain of creation, growth, decay and destruction, and re-creation. Because no point in time could be conceived of as unique, there could be no conception of linear development. Indeed, as Aristotle pointed out with his illustration of the Trojan war, the "after" of the present might be a "before."[15] For Plato not only was time cyclical, but the objective of the humanly impossible *Republic* was the arresting of change—that is, the governmental control of change in the public space and the education of its inhabitants to that end. And, as in other traditions, time is conceived of exclusively in spatial terms. As Plato argues, "The time which is the determination and measured by the celestial sphere is the mobile image of the immobile eternity which it imitates by moving in a circle."[16] Change and movement are inferior to permanence and perpetuity and cannot be understood without the latter. The implications of this view for action and/or knowledge are obvious.

Though out of chronology, a brief note should be added about

14. *The Philosophy of Symbolic Forms,* trans. Ralph Manheim (New Haven, 1955), II, 136.
15. *Problems,* trans. W. S. Hett (Cambridge, 1936–37), I, 367.
16. *Timaeus,* 37c–38a. See also J. Alexander Gunn, *The Problem of Time: An Historic and Critical Study* (London, 1929); Cornelius Benjamin, "Idea of Time in the History of Philosophy," in Fraser, *op. cit.,* pp. 3–30.

Islam. Here substantial differences exist, as Islam was marked by a future-oriented prophetic tradition. Time becomes the revelation of God's order which encompasses the acts we perform as responsible beings. But there is no conception of continuous duration in Islam, only instants. Especially common is the thought that human time is the pause between two divine interventions, creation and judgment, when responsible men expiate for their past.[17] In Islamic countries, the development of time reckoning was of low order, as evidenced in the inadequate calendar and unsophisticated development of tenses in Arabic.[18] Theologically, Islam was premised on the hope for the divine interruption by Timeless Being and the abolition of human time in paradise. The Ismaili variant of Islam embraced a frankly cyclical conception of time.[19] And the chief historiographer of Islam, Ibn Khaldun, clearly saw mundane time as cyclical. In the *Mugaddimah* Ibn Khaldun wrote: ". . . the life [span] of a dynasty corresponds to the life [span] of an individual; it grows up and passes into an age of stagnation and thence into retrogression."[20]

Finally, this brief and inadequate survey of the time attitudes of the Great Traditions must consider the Christian conception of time. As in Islam, Christianity's "superhuman" temporal ideas were not cyclical. Both were linear, positing a point in time for creation and direction in time toward the fulfilment of God's promise. The Christian God acted in history and was the fulfilment of human history. Time unfolds from past to future. In time the Christian found meaning; life itself was immersed in time. The Greek conception of circularity was early branded as heresy. Golgotha would not recur.[21] But to say this is not to suggest that modern time conceptions are the same as those held by Christians. In Christian thought, there were two times—one sacred

17. Louis Massignon, "Time in Islamic Thought," in Campbell, *op. cit.*, pp. 108–114.
18. *Ibid.*, p. 110.
19. Henry Corbin, "Cyclical Time in Mazdaism and Ismailism," in Campbell, *op. cit.*, pp. 144–172.
20. *The Mugaddimah*, trans. Franz Rosenthal (New York, 1958), I, 346.
21. Henri-Charles Puech, "Gnosis and Time," in Campbell, *op. cit.*, pp. 38–84, esp. 50. See also Herbert Butterfield, *History of Man's Attitudes Toward the Past: Their Role in Civilization* (London, 1961); J. L. Russell, "Time in Christian Thought," in Fraser, *op. cit.*, pp. 59–76.

and the other profane. The latter was marked by circularity: e.g., Rome's rise and fall, human governments given to creation and degeneration. Second, the objective of history or man's temporal life was the destruction of time. In its mystical variant, men like Master Eckhart thought that human time was an obstacle to oneness with God.[22] And the Eucharist and Church calendar partook of the timeless myth of eternal return—not to the beginning but to the act of Christ and to the promise of history. Confession, in addition, was an act to eliminate the past. Indeed, as J. B. Bury points out, the persistence of the concept of Providence made "progress" impossible.[23] Much of this can be found in one of the foremost theoreticians of time, St. Augustine, who devoted only one book in *De Civitate Dei* to human events and insisted that human actions, other than restoration with God, were futile. The reward for action was everlasting life in timeless space. It was other-worldly "progress."[24] St. Augustine consoled the early Christians:

As therefore we are saved, so are we made happy by hope. And as we do not as yet possess a present, but look for a future salvation, so it is with our happiness, and this with patience; for we are encompassed with evils, which we ought patiently to endure . . . for what does it matter under whose government a dying man lives.[25]

In each of these traditions, human time was thought, in some sense, to be cyclical. In two of them divine time, which intervened in human time, was thought to be linear, but in all of them a timeless space was valued. Time was either conceived of in spatial terms, or at the end of time there was reunion in space. At the risk of exaggeration, I should like to argue that this had an effect on governments and administration. Three variations on the highly valued space and devalued time metaphor existed. In these traditions, government served a change-controlling func-

---

22. Eliade, "Time and Eternity," pp. 198–199.
23. *The Idea of Progress* (New York, 1955), pp. 20–21.
24. Gilles Quispel, "Time and History in Patristic Christianity," in Campbell, *op. cit.*, pp. 85–107; Hannah Arendt, *Between Past and Future* (Cleveland, 1963), pp. 65–68; Oscar Cullman, *Christ and Time* (London, 1951), *passim*; Theodor Mommsen, "St. Augustine and the Christian Idea of Progress," *Journal of the History of Ideas*, XII (1951), 346–374.
25. *De Civitate Dei*, XII, 13.

tion. Space was essentially the chief organizing image. For Hindu and Chinese thought, government represented an earthly approximation of the arrangement of the cosmos. In Hindu thought, the capital was the exemplary center which was a macrocosm of the supernatural order, "an image of . . . the universe on a smaller scale." Governments existed to approximate heaven's harmony or dictates and to resist the otherwise inevitable decay.[26] In Greek thought, governance was equated with the maintenance of the public space in which one might seek moral perfection or immortalizing recognition for superior acts. Hannah Arendt amplifies this point:

> To strive for immortality can mean, as it certainly did in early Greece, the immortalization of one's self through famous deeds and the acquisition of immortal fame; it can also mean the addition to the human artifice of something more permanent than we ourselves; and it can mean, as it did with the philosophers, the spending of one's life with things immortal. In any event the word designated an activity and not a belief, and what the activity required was an imperishable space guaranteeing that "immortalizing" would not be in vain.[27]

Finally, for the later Christians and Muslims, the state was ordained by God to provide a life-space in which man, assisted by religious authorities, could work out his personal salvation.

The foregoing should not be interpreted as arguing that the Great Traditions were totally oblivious to human time. For religious and great hydrological purposes, impressive and often accurate calendars and other methods of time reckoning were developed—though these, owing to the methods of production and character of religious worship, did not embody the divisions of time which characterize the present timing periods.[28] Nor was the possession of these time-reckoning devices or knowledge of them widely diffused. Also it should be added that the Great Tradi-

26. R. Heine-Geldern, "Conceptions of State and Kingship in Southeast Asia," *Far East. Quart.*, II (1942), 15–30.
27. *Op. cit.*, p. 71.
28. Karl Wittfogel, *Oriental Despotism* (New Haven, 1957), pp. 29–30. See also F. Lionnais, *The Orion Book of Time* (New York, 1959); G. H. Baille, *Clocks and Watches* (London, 1951); J. Cowan Harrison, *Time and Its Measurement from the Stone to the Nuclear Age* (New York, 1958); B. Richmond, *Time Measurement and the Calendar* (Leiden, 1956); Willis T. Milham, *Time and Timekeepers* (New York, 1929).

tions had dissenting opinions on time's circularity and the impossibility of progress, such as those of Han Fei-Tzu and the legalists in China and the heretical Dahariyun of Islam.[29] But these, of course, were minority opinions. Likewise, although significant points in time were selected for reckoning years, such as the birth or reign of Alexander, Chandra Gupta, Seleucus, the various Chinese and Egyptian dynasties, or Diocletian, these points were not deemed as partaking of a progressively linear course. Indeed, these points marked the "greater beginning," from which all subsequent events were less glorious. Thus, in summary, "premodern" time conceptions suggest that space was the more dominant organizing metaphor, that the time of human events (as opposed to divine intervention into history) was devalued, and that human action, unless aimed at comporting with the changeless (which defined the function of education), was thought to be futile.

The Rise of Progressive Time

The sixteenth and seventeenth centuries marked a watershed in time conceptions. With growing force, the conception of linear or progressive time and the institutions of timing marked western European development.

That western Europe was its venue is not surprising. The contribution to modern time conceptions was heavily influenced by the Christian tradition. Let me briefly explain. Implicit in the Christian view of time as linear from Creation, the Fall and the Parousia, to the Second Coming, was a movement toward a highly valued end. What came *later* gave significance to earlier acts and events. A second contribution of Christian thought was the *universality* of the process for all mankind. All the wicked would be damned, the righteous rewarded; the judgment and the movement toward judgment encompassed everyone—a stream in

29. John T. Marcus, "Time and the Sense of History: East and West," *Comp. Stud. in Soc. and History*, III (1960), 123–139; Louis Massignon, *op. cit.*, p. 108. See also P. A. Sorokin and R. K. Merton, "Social Time: A Methodological Analysis," *Am. Jour. Soc.*, XLIII (1939), 615–629.

which all human beings, living and dead, were moving. A third contribution, though not unique to Christianity, is the sacredness of self. When robbed of its transcendental character, it could encourage the acceptance of this-worldly gratification, of hedonism.

There are other contributions as well. St. Augustine's distinction between the time of things and the time of pure experience, the ultimate subjectivizing of time, could permit, through later elaboration, the mental image of man's temporal progress as well as the internalization of the imperatives of timing. From the monastic tradition of Christianity, work (or productive action in time) had a dignity and redemptive quality, although its monastic justification was preparation for the extinction of time in salvation.[30] This theme can later be found as central in the Protestant Reformation. For Luther, Calvin, and Wesley, work was the moral or right thing for human existence. The Puritan conception of the "elect," with its inducement for rational reordering of life, was later conducive to timing. This can be easily seen in the exhortations for human temporal discipline in the Puritan divines, such as Richard Baxter.[31] And finally, the commitment to timing and productivity arising from the Protestant variant of Christianity can be found in the elimination from the calendar of over one hundred saints' days, thus reducing the non-economic impediments to expanding productivity.[32]

The Renaissance revived an interest in mundane life and asserted that knowledge should serve human ends; and it is in understanding certain forces in the mid-sixteenth century and in subsequent centuries in the fields of science, social thought, industrialization and technology, and nationalism that the rise of linear time and the institutions of timing can be fully understood. Needless to say, the development of modern, industrial, urban-

---

30. De Grazia, *op. cit.*, pp. 36–40.
31. Max Weber, *The Protestant Ethic and the Spirit of Capitalism* (New York, 1958), pp. 106, 155, 181. For the contribution of Christianity and especially its chiliastic sects, see Norman Cohn, *The Pursuit of the Millenium* (Fairlawn, N.J., 1957); E. Tuveson, *Millenium and Utopia: A Study in the Background of the Idea of Progress* (Berkeley and Los Angeles, 1949); Morris Ginsberg, *The Idea of Progress: A Re-evaluation* (Boston, 1953).
32. De Grazia, *op. cit.*, p. 291.

ized, and nationalized societies is too well known to be dwelt upon here. But certain features, taken out of their contexts—and
passing lightly over their inherent complexity—should be noted.

In the realm of social thought, which is certainly subordinate to
the impact of science, several important intellectual agreements
had to be struck. The first agreement was one concerning the
sequence of history. Contrary to the assumption of the Renaissance, which assumed the superiority of ancient learning, the
formulators of the doctrine of progressive time sought to demonstrate that ancient thought was really younger than knowledge
held by those in the present—that is, the past could not know
what is now known, nor could it have built on what since has
been constructed.[33] Although this can be found in many writers of
the period, such as Perrault, Tassoni, and interwoven generally in
the argument between the Ancients and the Moderns, it was most
succinctly put by Francis Bacon:

For the old age of the world is to be accorded the true antiquity; and
this is the attribute of our own times, not that of the earlier age of the
world in which the ancients lived; and which, while in respect to us it
was the elder, yet in respect of the world it was the younger. . . .
From our age . . . much more might fairly be expected than from the
ancient times, inasmuch as it is a more advanced age of the world, and
stored and stocked with experiments and observations.[34]

A second agreement was to view society in non-cyclical terms
—to reverse the typical view of an Ibn Khaldun that an older
society faces the life-cycle probability of death. This was formulated by many, especially eighteenth-century philosophers in
France, who presumed an ever invigorated collectivity moving
from youth to youth.[35] A corollary to this formulation was the
idea that this was not only true for western Europe, but for all of
mankind. One device used in developing this mode of thought
was the concept of stages, seen in Saint Simon, Comte, and the
German sociologists; here the gradual elimination of myth and

33. Bury, *op. cit.*, pp. 78–97; Bruce Mazlish, "The Idea of Progress," *Daedalus*,
XCII (1963), 447–461.
34. Quoted in J. Bronowski and Bruce Mazlish, *The Western Intellectual
Tradition* (New York, 1963), p. 92.
35. Bury, *op. cit.*, pp. 98–126.

the growth of reason, a universal faculty, would cosmopolize the linear accumulation of happiness.[36]

A third agreement was implicit in the first two—the conception of society as a person or as an aggregate, a consensus, a solidarity. This conception assumed that collective advancement resulted in the happiness of each member or, conversely, the pursuit of happiness by individual members advanced the happiness of the collectivity. This device of thinking in aggregate terms spurred during the seventeenth and eighteenth centuries an interest in the collection and use of statistics in order to show changes in mass over time. This conception of society as an aggregate moving through time was also assisted by the assumption of Montesquieu and others that this movement was subject to the same immutable laws of nature as the planets. Society, like the universe, could be interrogated to reveal its secret dynamics and hence permit human intervention for human ends.

This intervention—as another agreement involved in the linear time concept—was seen by Saint Simon, Comte, Fichte, and others as presenting the possibility of social engineering: the devising of an environment capable of creating accumulative human happiness or providing a locus for man's endless moral perfection. And with the assumption of social engineering, especially with Comte, linear time joined hands with the conception of timing. Under all this—which has been abstracted and condensed unmercifully for this essay—lay the concomitant conception of the "proper" knowledge. Beginning, at least, with Bacon and Descartes, but *almost* universal in later periods, the criterion for knowledge became utility—what was conducive to this-worldly happiness. When specified, this knowledge was to relate to shortening and lightening labor, to making material goods more abundant, and to prolonging human life. In this milieu, the characteristic social disciplines of history, economics, and sociology could rise and flourish, for all of them share these assumptions in one way or another.

---

36. See, for example, Bert F. Hoselitz, "Theories of Stages of Economic Growth," in Hoselitz *et al.*, *Theories of Economic Growth* (Glencoe, Ill., 1960), pp. 193–238.

At every point, the development of science in this period was crucial to the concept of linear time. In the first place, nature was redefined as process. Galileo was much more interested in how the heavens worked than how to get to heaven. This de-emphasis on the transcendental significance of nature was made absolutely clear in Descartes, who not only was the first to place time on an abcissa, but more importantly also conceived of a system in which nature could be understood without God.[37] For Kepler and Galileo nature was a secular realm with an independent meaning which even God could not alter. Within this secular realm of immutable laws, a new statement of time was necessary. This was provided by Newton, who distinguished between pure time and sensed time. Newton's "pure" time provided a solid framework for all motion and a means by which to measure all change. Time, in his system, became a universal and abstract quantity.[38]

The second view of time, sensed time, especially in the hands of Locke, allowed for the internalization of time for human history and timing. Imperative for the development of science were new mathematical tools, which when constructed contributed to the developing time conception with their own notions of periodicity, recurrence, and continuous functions. These, in turn, sparked a quantitative propensity in social thought, as seen in the political arithmetic of the mercantilists and the pressure for calendar reform.[39] Furthermore, the developing conception of science was that it was a cumulative body of knowledge, capable of interrogating nature for answers and, with the criterion of utility, having results for human life. This cumulative body of knowledge, though divided into many fields, was also seen to cohere and to be interdependent. Finally, the certainty of progress in the natural world was argued by Darwin when he wrote: "Hence we may look with some confidence to a secure future of equally inappreciable length. And as natural selection works solely by and for the good of each being, all corporeal and mental

37. John U. Nef, *Cultural Foundations of Industrial Civilization* (New York, 1960), pp. 6–35; Herbert Butterfield, *The Origins of Modern Science, 1300–1800* (New York, 1957), pp. 108–128; Hannah Arendt, *op. cit.*, pp. 54–56.
38. Butterfield, *op. cit.*, pp. 164–170; F. C. S. Northrop, *op. cit.*, *passim*.
39. Nef, *op. cit.*, pp. 7–17; 27–37.

environments will tend to progress towards perfection."[40] This idea was imported into social thought generally in the nineteenth century.

But these views operated on the level of high culture. The transformation to linear time and the institutions of timing were assisted by two sets of mediating phenomena—industrialization and nationalism. As to the former, on one level, owing to the close relation between science and technology, common town and city dwellers from the mid-sixteenth century saw an increase in consumer goods, improved modes of transportation and communication, and mechanical improvements in production, to confirm what their "betters" had assumed and discussed in the salon. On a more important level, the industrial process increasingly depended on timing and on an internalizing of its imperatives. Production steadily required a much more accurate means of dividing and measuring time and a sense of obligation for maintaining mechanical, non-human rhythms. The contrast between "agricultural time" and that required by factories discouraged potential workers, and mastering "industrial time" became a major index of labor commitment. The value of timing to human success and the responsibility for using time wisely were the subjects of Methodist sermons, the platitudes of *Poor Richard's Almanac*, and the McGuffey *Readers*.[41] In England, the same exhortations to look at time as a resource arose with such popular writers as Samuel Smiles.[42]

---

40. Quoted in Bury, *op. cit.*, p. 336. For the general relationships of the development of science and the concept of linear time, see E. Zilzel, "The Genesis of the Concept of Scientific Progress," in P. P. Weinger and A. Noland, eds., *Roots of Scientific Thought and Cultural Perspective* (New York, 1957).

41. Benjamin Franklin, *Autobiography* (New York, 1944); *Old Favorites from the McGuffey Readers* (New York, 1936). In *Poor Richard's Almanac*, Franklin asks "Dost thou love life, then do not squander Time, for that's the stuff Life is made of, as Poor Richard says. How much more than is necessary do we spend in sleep, forgetting that the Sleeping Fox catches no Poultry, and that There will be sleeping enough in the grave . . ." (pp. 218–219). A common time theme in the McGuffey *Readers* can be found in the poem "A Moment Too Late," where the child is warned about all the things he will miss if he tarries a bit—"Now you see what a very sad thing / 'Tis to stay a moment too long" (p. 61).

42. Samuel Smiles, *Self-Help* (Chicago, 1881). For example, Smiles writes, "An hour in every day withdrawn from frivolous pursuits would, if profitably employed, enable a person of ordinary capacity to go far towards mastering a science" (p. 157). Smiles's influence is discussed in Asa Briggs, *Victorian People* (New York, 1955), pp. 116–140.

The early factories required longer working days and a regular pact with workers not set by the agricultural season. Sebastian de Grazia claims of the Luddites:

They [the peasants turned workers] acted like bulls hypnotized not by the flashing red cape but by the horror of machinery. All the while the real enemy, the matador, was there behind them, silent, imperturbable, the clock on the wall. Had they destroyed all clocks the industrial world would have remained at most a lively commercial age.[43]

And Lewis Mumford unequivocally asserts the centrality of the clock to industrialization, when he writes, "The modern industrial regime can do without coal, iron, and steam easier than it can do without the clock."[44] It was possible to substitute sources of power and even materials, but nothing could substitute for the co-ordination of a factory, whose workers were socially and culturally conditioned by a reliable objective universal time system. Indeed, a significant index of the spread of timing was the appearance of the cheap pocket clock, appropriately called "watch," in the United States and Switzerland in the 1860's. By 1888, the Waterbury factory alone in the United States was producing 500,000 watches annually.[45] Similary, the Soviet Union in the 1920's, when embarking on massive industrialization, even formed a league for the wearing of watches, to inculcate in a non-industrial population the importance of and responsibilities for timing.[46] It was in this context of growing complexity and temporal co-ordination, furthermore, that the scientific study of business arose, with its characteristic concern with "time and motion." De Grazia writes, summing up the impact of industrialization: "Over the span of the several centuries, the seventeenth to the nineteenth, a new conception of time developed and spread over the industrial world going hand in hand with the modern idea of work."[47]

43. *Op. cit.*, p. 313.
44. *Technics and Civilization* (New York, 1934), p. 14. See also Georges Friedman, "Leisure and Technological Civilization," *Int. Soc. Sci. Jour.*, XII (1960), 509–521; Allen Clarke, *The Effects of the Factory System* (London, 1898); Daniel Bell, "Notes on Work," *Encounter*, II (1954), 3–15.
45. De Grazia, *op. cit.*, p. 305.
46. Reinhard Bendix, *Work and Authority in Industry* (New York, 1956), pp. 208–209.
47. *Op cit.*, p. 291. See also Adam Abruzzi, *Work Measurement: New Principles and Measurement* (New York, 1952); Georges Friedman, *Industrial Society*

The second popular mediating force was nationalism. Several themes in the philosophical conception of linear time and timing found common political expression. A nation, in the modern sense, ceases to be a "space" and becomes a continuous enterprise in time. It has a past from whence it came (and the various nationalist movements inspired a host of writers of national histories), but it is also a collectivity in time with a forward driving urge. Manifest Destiny, Reichs to live a thousand years, and so forth, emphasized the future orientation. The propensity to aggregate that the philosophers of progress evinced is manifested: the population, in their several functions, contribute to the total ongoingness of the enterprise. Mazzini is a representative advocate of the nationalist concept. His work is rife with time imagery and the need for social co-ordination—for timing. In "On the Unity of Italy," Mazzini wrote:

> No peoples ever die, nor stop short upon their path, before they have achieved the historical aim of their existence. . . . [The nation] must exist in the future. A people destined to achieve great things for the welfare of humanity must one day or other be constituted a nation. . . . The fact of this instinct among people of the national mission to be fulfilled, and the collective idea to be developed, would be enough to prove the necessity of one country, of one form of organization to embody and represent it. That form of organization is unity.[48]

There are many points of connection of these themes and forces to the governance of western Europe. Indeed, far more than the parliamentary and other political artifacts, the artifact of public administration has been most responsive to progressive time and timing. Only a few suggestions can be made here; other essays in this volume will treat some aspects more extensively.

The political thought of the period of the formation of progressive time conceptions revised the function of the state from a preserver of space to an organization to produce, or to assist the citizenry to produce, goods and services in larger amounts to

---

(Glencoe, Ill., 1955); Ralph M. Barnes, *Motion and Time Study* (New York, 1937); John Dos Passos, *The Big Money* (New York, 1936).

48. Hans Kohn, ed., *Nationalism: Its Meaning and History* (Princeton, 1955), pp. 118–121; Joseph Mazzini, *The Duties of Man and Other Essays* (London, n.d.), pp. 1, 19, 52, 55, 70, 171. On nationalism generally, see Hans Kohn, *The Idea of Nationalism: A Study of Its Origins and Background* (New York, 1944), pp. 13–35.

fulfil men's increasing wants. Indeed, the first institutions of the
modern state, the intendants of France, were created to reduce
the impact of space on governments. But the state no longer was
an institution to provide law and order alone. It was a "productive instrument" to advance man's terrestrial felicity. From mer-
cantilist policies to the service state, the course is clear. The role
varied from nation to nation, but a convergence in time marks the
modern state as an enterprise, hopefully profitable, in time. This
fact, seen in policies enacted by parliaments and kings but eventually the province of administrators, is central.

Administrators were called upon to induce change and to control "change's" space-threatening results. Differentiated ministries
and the rapid expansion of the number of civil servants eventually made imperative the need for a science of public management to facilitate the productive efficiency of the state. Public
corporations arose, adopting the temporal co-ordination and opportunities of the private firm. Budgets arose first perhaps as
documents of control, but increasingly became devices for time
control and yardsticks of efficiency. And as characteristic, formally or informally, of all industrial states came the overarching
temporal institutions of planning.

This brief survey of linear time and timing could have been
expanded indefinitely. For every representative institution or
thinker, dozens more could have been added. But the purpose of
the survey was only to delineate the main components of this new
time conception and to view its transforming qualities in another
context—the contemporary non-Western world—to see if "new
time" is relevant to "old clocks." And to that, this essay now turns.

The Diffusion of Progressive Time

The metaphoric phrase "revolution of rising expectations" is
presently in disrepute. Although it was used originally in the
context of the Cold War by hopeful recipients of foreign assistance and their sympathizers in the aid-giving countries to accel-
erate the public and private redistribution of income and skills

from the industrialized to the low-income nations, the phrase should not be abandoned. It captures, even in its exaggeration, the relationship of the ideologies of elites in non-Western areas to the Western ideology of progressive time and the importance of timing. The original implication of the phrase was that there existed a unified demand and commitment of populations in low-income countries to improve their lot. Present disrepute arises from the realization that the phrase was believed by and served to guide the choices of only a narrow-based elite. The "revolution of rising expectations" was an aspiration of the political elites.

The metaphors suggested by the phrase contain many time allusions. The "revolution" to the elites constituted a displacement of an "older" regime, marked by its incapacity to meet the needs of the public, by a "newer" regime girded for improvement. In its usage, the phrase meant not simply a revolution for the few but a revolution involving the nation, in which eventually the curse of backwardness would be lifted. "Rising" implied a continuous linear increase, and the word "expectations" suggested that the patience of hope had been replaced by the assumption that demands would be fulfilled soon.

Since "time" and "space" forbid an extended analysis here of the penetration of Western time into the non-Western areas, we can note that the major factor in this transfer was, of course, the imperialist interlude, especially in the later "civilizing" and "regenerative" programs of colonial powers. Individual colonial civil servants, like F. L. Brayne and Malcolm Darling, imparted a mastery of time through programs of self-help not only to their subjects, but to the native civil servants working under them.[49] Students, both in the new schools and universities in the empires and at the universities in the metropole, imbibed the doctrine of progress and later the time-suffused promises of Marx and observed the transforming qualities of technology in the industrial West. With a "progressive" view of the nation, social customs and economic life met in the intergenerational arena the forces de-

49. See Philip Woodruff, *The Men Who Ruled India* (New York, 1964), II, 207–225, 244–266, 281–299.

fending the old order. The movement of time and its ordering inevitability sustained young intellectuals in their personal searches for identity.[50] Progressive time explained the backwardness of their land and provided a focus for uplift and a weapon to fight the colonial power which held them back. The elites in those areas which escaped colonial tutelage were similarly influenced, directly or indirectly. Even to avoid tutelage required the co-ordination referred to earlier as timing. Thus, as the reality and threat of Western imperialism receded, there was a rise of progressive time thinking and of the politics of expectation.

Certainly there is considerable evidence that in the "newly emerging" nations can be found the organizing and impelling power of the metaphor of progressive time and timing. Alexander Gerschenkron, for instance, has documented in the Soviet case the power of the sense of "backwardness" and the impelling "urgency" for economic development.[51] Mary Matoosian, referring to a wider sample of elites, has demonstrated the use of time —ideas of a golden age and the stream of progress—to explain the need for development in consequence of the sense of "delayed" industrialization.[52] Likewise, Alexander Eckstein, on a more theoretical level, has shown the relevance of temporal comparisons—backwardness, expectation, and urgency, chiefly—to explain the extent of government interventions.[53]

But even more telling evidence can be found in the ideological statements of the non-Western elites. Here the problem of selection is enormous, for virtually every public statement contains vivid time imagery. Phrases such as "the caravan of history," "history in a one-way street," a "modern awakening," "avoiding marking time," "tornadoes of change," sweeping away the "cob-

50. Lucian W. Pye, *Politics, Personality, and Nation Building* (New Haven, 1962); E. R. Hughes, *The Invasion of China by the Western World* (London, 1937); T. E. La Fargue, *China's First Hundred* (Pullman, Wash., 1942); Reinhard Bendix, *Nation-Building and Citizenship* (New York, 1965), chap. vii; Willie Abraham, *The Mind of Africa* (Chicago, 1962).

51. *Economic Backwardness in Cultural Perspective* (New York, 1965), pp. 5–30, 52–71.

52. "Ideologies of Delayed Industrialization: Some Tensions and Ambiguities," *Econ. Dev. and Cult. Change*, VI (1958), 217–228.

53. "Individualism and the Role of the State," *Econ. Dev. and Cult. Change*, VI (1958), 81–87.

webs and grime of the past," "history smiling," "ineluctable, progressive industrialization," "stagnant," "rebirth," "retarded," "normal growth," "arouse people's faith in their destiny," "the road of history," "the elimination of backwardness," "national renewal," "normal development was arrested," and "to escape from the infernal cycle and create progressively and patiently the technical conditions of harmonious development" fill the pages of nationalist tracts and the hours of public exhortations.[54] Like their predecessors in the West—though with variations, of course—these statesmen sound the themes of change and "time forward."

First, the nation is a collectivity with a time that is irreversible, and it shares a general sense of time pushing forward with other nations. For example, Mamadou Dia of Senegal claims, "What must be stressed . . . is that instead of being a static definitive state, the nation is rather an affirmation, a perpetual movement, an unfinished construction."[55] All of the statesmen argue that their countries' comparative backwardness resulted from stunting the normal growth by factors such as colonialism, poverty, and—not inappropriately—"the past." Gamal Abdul Nasser argues, "our spirits were still in the thirteenth century although the symptoms of the nineteenth and twentieth centuries infiltrated in their various aspects. Our minds were trying to catch up with the advancing caravan of history."[56] Habib Bourguiba of Tunisia claims that the Prophet could not imagine that his nation "should be far behind other nations and reduced to its present fate."[57] Nandi Azikiwe of Nigeria insists that "Factors of capitalism and imperialism have stultified the normal growth of Nigeria in the community of nations."[58]

Second, the statesmen of the non-Western world share with the formulators of the conception of progressive time the assumption that action should be valued as a means of exploiting progressive

54. Paul E. Sigmund, Jr., ed., *The Ideologies of Developing Nations* (New York, 1963), *passim.*
55. *The African Nations and World Solidarity*, trans. Mercer Cook (New York, 1961), p. 5.
56. *The Philosophy of the Revolution* (Buffalo, 1959), pp. 50–51.
57. "The Feast of Ramadan," in Sigmund, *op. cit.*, p. 138.
58. *Zik* (Cambridge, 1961), p. 159.

time. Leopold Senghor of Senegal asserts, "the time for philosophizing has passed: the time for action has come. We must gird up our loins and assume all our responsibilities as political militants here and now."[59] Kwame Nkrumah sounds the same sense of urgency implicit in this commitment to action: "What other countries have taken three hundred years to achieve, a once dependent territory must try to accomplish in a generation if it is to survive. Unless it is . . . jet propelled it will lag behind and thus risk everything for which it has fought."[60] Sukarno maintains, ". . . the present is no time for us for too much theorizing. We had better be practical. . . ." Furthermore, this action should be based on technical knowledge and judged on the basis of its productivity.[61] According to Jawaharlal Nehru, "the latest technique has to be followed. To adhere to outworn and out-of-date methods of production—except as a temporary and stopgap measure—is to arrest growth and development."[62] Finally, distinctions among citizens are to be muted for a collective "great leap forward." Thus Sekou Toure of Guinea: "Our desire for progress will be fruitless if individual wills are not identical and do not aim at attaining the same objectives, for internal contradictions will become more and more violent and hold us back, endangering our very independence."[63]

Conflicting Time Perspectives

It is useful to point out, however, that all nationalist leaders have not shared this commitment to progressive time and its political imperatives. Indeed, one of the intergenerational differences among nationalist leaders has concerned the issue of progress. Here the disagreement of Gandhi and Nehru on time is illustrative. For Gandhi, the Golden Age was behind, not forward in time; the objectives of industrialization through advancing

59. *On African Socialism,* trans. Mercer Cook (New York, 1964), p. 67.
60. "Toward a Socialist State," in Sigmund, *op. cit.,* p. 67.
61. "Lecture to the Students of Hasanuddin University, *ibid.,* p. 59.
62. "The Discovery of India," *ibid.,* p. 94.
63. *Ibid.,* pp. 165–166.

technology threatened what was good in India; centralization was abhorrent. In *Hind Swaraj* Gandhi wrote: "In order to restore India to its pristine [*sic*] condition, we have to return to it. In our civilization, there will naturally be progress, retrogression [*sic*], reforms, contradictions; but one effort is required, that is to drive out Western civilization. All else will follow."[64] And on technology, Gandhi wrote, "As long as we cannot make pins without machinery, so long we will do without them. . . . It is necessary to realize that machinery is bad."[65] Nehru, on the other hand, insisted:

Events take place one after the other and the uninterrupted and unending stream of happenings goes on. [A particular event] is but a link in an unending chain. . . . For countries like India a different emphasis is necessary, for we have too much of the past about us and have ignored the present. . . . There is only one-way traffic in time. . . . Destiny marches on and does not wait for our leisure.[66]

Rather than seeing technology as a threat, Nehru insists, "New experiences, new processes, leading to new ideas and new horizons, are necessary. . . . A civilization based on ever-changing and advancing mechanical techniques leads to this."[67] Nehru rejected small-scale and cottage industry as "backward" and became an early convert to centralized economic planning. In this duel between the highly valued timeless space of India, as espoused by Gandhi, and the highly valued notion of a nation pushing forward through time to expanding productivity, as embraced by Nehru, the latter won.

The dichotomy between Gandhi and Nehru is particularly revealing. Both used temporal metaphors to identify what was significant in reality, and to impel certain choices. Both stood at a similar point in time and viewed changes and the human technology required for change with different values. Gandhi's evoking of a Golden Age in the past was inspired by his fear of the dominance of the progressive time of the West and its transforming concept of timing. Nehru, on the other hand, exhorted Indi-

64. *Indian Home Rule* (Madras, 1922), p. 104.
65. *Ibid.*, p. 86.
66. *The Discovery of India* (New York, 1960), pp. 383–393.
67. "The Discovery of India," in Sigmund, *op. cit.*, p. 94.

ans to take his view of time and timing—to think of India as an enterprise in which efficiency and productivity calculations were necessary in order that their enterprise be competitive in an ever ascending competition. Both addressed their views to what, temporally, might be described in terms of progressive time values as a transitional society. In this transition, India may have been more developed than others. But, for the non-Western world on which the major part of this argument rests, it was very typical.

Most of the societies on which time studies have been done have been less differentiated than the nations of our sample.[68] Already it has been shown that the High Culture concepts of time in Chinese, Indian, and Islamic thought were not hospitable to progressive time. Edward T. Hall in *The Silent Language* has given many examples of the cross-cultural conflicts between the traditional view of time and that of the more industrialized West.[69] The cyclical time emphasis in rural areas, reinforced by religious and social factors, makes the acculturation to progressive time and timing one of the great tasks of development. This has also been shown by the bulk of the evidence in Kusum Nair's important *Blossoms in the Dust*. There the attitudes toward work, savings, and investment are contingent on a short-time horizon wedded to a fatalistic long-time horizon. The middle ground of expectation that permits risks in productive techniques and new inputs and advances the opportunity to overcome the low stable equilibrium of production is largely absent.[70]

From the more primitive societies, which now comprise the constituencies of new African nations, the evidence of a time

68. The literature is so vast that only a few especially pertinent works can be cited: B. C. Bundage, *Empire of the Incas* (Norman, Okla., 1963); Paul Einzig, *Primitive Money in Its Ethnological, Historic, and Economic Aspects* (London, 1949); E. E. Evans-Pritchard, *The Nuer* (Oxford, 1949); A. I. Hallowell, "Temporal Orientation in Western Civilization and a Pre-Literate Society," *Amer. Anth.*, XXXIX (1937), 640–676; Dorothy Lee, "Lineal and Non-Lineal Codification of Reality," *Psychosomatic Medicine*, XII (1950), 89–97; Martin P. Nilsson, *Primitive Time Reckoning* (London, 1920); Emmeline M. Plunket, *Ancient Calendars and Constellations* (London, 1903); Julian H. Steward, *Basin-Plateau Aboriginal Socio-Political Groups* (Washington, D.C., 1938); J. Eric Thompson, "Philosophy in Time," in *The Rise and Fall of the Mayan Civilization* (Norman, Okla., 1958), pp. 137–158.
69. New York, 1959, *passim*.
70. New York, 1962, *passim*. Cf. Theodore M. Schultz, *Transforming Traditional Agriculture* (New Haven, 1965).

system antithetical to development is overwhelming. As Melville Herskovitz argues: ". . . a primary requirement in bringing about economic and technological change, or 'development' . . . would be to effect an adjustment on the part of the peoples who have a less demanding time-system to one under which they must become continuously more aware of the passage of time, and revise their habits accordingly."[71] Anthropologists have found languages which cannot easily handle either the conceptions of progressive time or those of timing. Pluralistic systems of time, each part loaded with sacred qualities, make difficult the acquisition of a neutral, universal time in which to undertake the co-ordination implicit in development.[72]

In urban areas, where the seeds of progressive time and timing have been sown, the problem still remains. Labor commitment is rendered difficult by the coexistence of "industrial time" and "rural time," and the frequent alteration of the new worker between them. The non-seasonal constraints of factory work with its impersonal relationships and machine-paced rhythms are difficult for the worker to accept, as is the conception of *selling* one's time and thus making an efficiency calculation about one's effort. Wages geared to a new time-expenditure pattern together with the disappearance of many of the festivals of the year constitute throughout the non-Western world a major barrier to the advantages of Western progressive time and timing.[73] In most classes in urban areas in India and elsewhere, the level of savings and the expenditure on education suggest that the horizon associated with Western time is not present.[74] The shorter time horizon is also shown in investment patterns of entrepreneurs, which are still marked by the time conceptions of merchant life.

71. "Economic Change and Cultural Dynamics," in Ralph Braibanti and Joseph Spengler, eds., *Tradition, Values, and Socio-Economic Development* (Durham, N.C., 1961), p. 128.
72. J. M. Guyau, *La genese de l'idee de temps* (Paris, 1952), p. 6.
73. See, for example, Joseph A. Kahl, "Some Social Concomitants of Industrialization and Urbanization," *Hum. Org.*, XVIII (1959), 53–74; Wilbert E. Moore, "Industrialization and Social Change," in Bert F. Hoselitz and Wilbert E. Moore, eds., *Industrialization and Society* (The Hague, 1963), pp. 299–372.
74. See Jhaverbhai P. Patel, ed., *Planning for a Minimum Income* (New Delhi, 1963); U. Tan Wai, "Interest Rates Outside the Organized Money Markets," *International Monetary Fund Staff Papers* (Nov., 1957).

But it is in government and planned economic development that differences in time perspectives become most relevant to this essay. As I have pointed out, significant elites in the non-Western world have committed themselves and their nations to progressive time and the imperatives of timing—at least abstractly. When these views conflict with everyday political contingencies, the future is often devalued in favor of the present. Other conflicts, owing partly to different time perspectives, exist in the realm of administration. Much of the administration in developing countries, in terms of men and resources, is devoted to maintaining "space," to insuring "law and order" and protection from external enemies. Advocates of development programs, premising their value systems on controlled changes through time, must compete with traditional administrators for scarce resources. This struggle is rather bitter and it often becomes public. Implementers of development programs have claimed virtual sabotage by the "spatial" bureaucrats. Charges of "unproved theory" are made by the "spatial" bureaucrats; the developers insist that the older administrators are backward, "out of the time."

Conflicts also exist between the development administrators and those responsible for fiscal controls. The former charge "delay" as deadening to their exploiting development opportunities, whereas the latter charge irresponsibility in the use of funds. Conflicts even exist among the developers, between those responsible for implementation in the field, and those responsible for long-term projections and for the interweaving of projects for optimal results. The former charge the latter with making unworkable plans, whereas the latter insist that the implementers are not sufficiently bold and forthright. Conflicts also exist among the administrators of various programs of development. These conflicts are over the distribution of scarce resources of the state in terms of plan outlays, access for foreign exchange, and appropriation of foreign economic and technical assistance resources. In the various conflicts, the political process is brought in to settle the issue, though the settlement is never final and insures continuous political activity on the part of all members of the higher bureaucracy.

Elsewhere I have described in greater detail the role conflicts among different categories of administrators and politicians.[75] Here it is necessary only to point out that conflicts stem partly from differing time values and conceptions. In the progressive time commitment and the imperatives of timing, the developers and the nationalist elites get considerable support from the literature of economic development and public administration. This support is strengthened by the claim that the findings in these fields are "scientific" and, perhaps more telling, that their acceptance is prerequisite to large-scale international economic assistance. The economic development literature relates to the Western conception of time. It deals with the cumulative impact of a series of decisions on potentially ever expanding wealth. Although early economists feared the potential for secular decline and stagnation for the economy in the birth rates, the decrease of interest, and the exhaustion of arable lands, most contemporary economists who consider the problem of development in the non-Western world are publicly less glum.[76] No nation has been deemed beyond development. Potential inhibitors, such as population increase and low investment rates, are usually treated as amenable to social policy or technological breakthroughs. The major causal element—whether it is a high savings-investment ratio, entrepreneurship, or the adaptiveness to technological innovation—attests to the importance of these Western time orientations: devaluing the present for the future, the assumption that past techniques are less efficient than the present and future techniques, and the engulfing concern for productivity.

Time, Timing, and Growth

This utilization of time and timing can be demonstrated in a brief examination of the major theories and strategies of eco-

75. Warren F. Ilchman, Alice Stone Ilchman, and Philip K. Hastings, *The New Men of Knowledge and the Developing Nations: Planners and Polity* (Berkeley, 1968).

76. Warren F. Ilchman and Ravindra C. Bhargava, "Balanced Thought and Economic Growth," *Econ. Dev. and Cult. Change*, XIV (1966), 385–399.

nomic growth. In each of the latter, the importance of timing is the central analytic tool. W. W. Rostow, for instance, uses the three timing conceptions: synchronization, sequence, and rate. Sequence is his central concept. Economic growth proceeds by identifiable stages, which follow one upon the other and cannot be skipped. In each state, a synchronization of social, political, and economic forces must be present. Their presence or absence determines whether the successive stages are achieved. His major image of "take-off" implies not only linear growth upward but also is contingent on the concept of rate—capital investment over time. When industries which once gave the push forward to the next stage stagnate in terms of their propelling qualities, others arise. And he estimates the total sequence to be completed in a given number of years.[77]

The more economic and less historical of the theories of economic growth also are expressed essentially in terms of timing. One important strategy, balanced growth, depends on the description of poverty as circular and self-enforcing. The way to break through the vicious circle of poverty to achieve linear growth is to create a *synchronized* group of productive investments in which goods are bought from and by each unit as finished or intermediate products.[78] A second strategy, unbalanced growth, relies on the conception of *sequence*. A series of deliberately unbalancing investments, economic and technological, are made in an economy. In the process, entrepreneurs gain the experience of making decisions for long-term gains, and workers acquire the pace and attention required for modern industry. "Unbalancing" also permits, according to its advocates, the proper sequence of social overhead capital and thus the conserving of the State's scarce resources.[79] A final strategy, W. Arthur Lewis' growth through the utilization of unlimited supplies of labor, relies on the conception of *rate*. Wage rates in the indus-

77. *The Stages of Economic Growth* (Cambridge, 1960), *passim.*
78. P. N. Rosenstein-Rodan, "Problems of Industrialization of Eastern and Southeastern Europe," in A. N. Agarwala and S. P. Singh, eds., *The Economics of Underdevelopment* (New York, 1963), pp. 145–155; Ragnar Nurkse, *Problems of Capital Formation in Underdeveloped Countries* (New York, 1960), chap. i.
79. Albert O. Hirschman, *The Strategy of Economic Development* (New Haven, 1958).

trial and agricultural sectors, prices for farm products, and profit rates are all delicately balanced to show the possibility of attaining high industrial rates of growth despite the under-employment (temporally defined) in the agricultural sector.[80] For all strategies of economic development, there have also been devised temporal quantitative methods, such as linear programming and input-output analyses, which permit the optimizing of the conditions of timing. Strategies of economic development and their tools of analysis, in other words, are conceptions of the use of timing to realize the promise of progressive time—that is, expanding productivity to meet this-worldly material desires.

Time, Timing, and Management

Thus developers, those administrators responsible for programs of economic change, are guided in their substantive economic choices by a body of theory and a set of tools premised on progressive time and utilizing concepts of timing. In the process of implementing these programs, they are further frequently buttressed by the theory and practice of time management developed in American and British public administration. As indicated earlier, the study of public administration arose to handle the question of increasing productivity in the public sector and hence is filled with progressive time imagery and values. This can be easily seen in the abstracted conception of the optimal development decision—"to have the right things in the right quantity in the right place at the right time at the right price." There are three time-related elements in this definition: a notion of consistency, partly defined in temporal terms; a notion of timing, the proper phasing and synchronization; and a notion of efficiency, expressed in a temporally related conception of minimum social opportunity cost given the level of output predetermined by a plan.

Examples of less than optimal development decisions are le-

80. "Economic Development with Unlimited Supplies of Labour," in Agarwala and Singh, *op. cit.*, pp. 400–449; Nurkse, *op. cit.*, chap. ii.

gion and illuminating on the question of managing time: teachers arriving before schools are constructed and schools constructed before teachers are trained; heavy machinery production out of phase with the production of steel; fertilizer arriving after the rainy season; markets developed before adequate transportation and communication; export crops stimulated before port facilities are constructed; a program to encourage agricultural production negated by an import commodity program; training colleges without hostels; new industries without facilities for workers; hospitals without equipment, beds, or doctors; ad infinitum. Instances similar to these can be found in practically every mid-plan review or report of a technical assistance study team.[81] A decision to expand primary education, for instance, at a particular rate and point in time requires a series of earlier decisions, at the proper time and to the proper extent, to develop teacher training and appropriate facilities which, in turn, requires an expansion of secondary education, and so on. It also requires the expansion of the production of building materials, their proper allocation and transportation, and the development of equipment. All of this is geared to a projected demand in terms of birth rates and must take place within a budget defined by time, and with economic resources exposed to the ravages of an economic change called "inflation." Each of these decisions, taken at various points in government at various points of time, requires the foregoing of other decisions which interrelate with a series of other productive choices as well.

The problems of time management are seldom expressed in temporal terms, but each can be understood only within the exigencies of synchronization, sequence, and rate. The optimal decision is an ideal construct. Striving toward optimal decisions in the real world involves the co-ordination of many ministries, acting unilaterally, often in ignorance, and with a myriad number of competing responsibilities. Most development programs overlap many ministries; the degree of commitment and urgency to

81. See, for example, Government of Pakistan, Planning Commission, *Final Report* of the Committee on the Review of On-going Schemes (Karachi, 1961), pp. 31–36.

the whole program and each component project varies. The development of a consumer durables industry can be held up by a decision of a Reserve Bank in releasing foreign exchange—a delay that might have repercussions on the absorption of technical workers and the priorities for transportation facilities. The problems of synchronization, sequence, and rate are further complicated by the relationships of budgeting officers, planning commissioners, and ministries of finance in sanctioning expenditures. These can spell "delay." A delay at one point in time might well render fruition of a project at another point in time tenuous. But the problems are complicated by other factors as well. In a federal system or when local governments are necessary for cooperation, synchronization depends on a series of decisions by administrators with different loyalties and different time perspectives. In developing countries, decisions are also vulnerable to the timetables of governments which give them aid. A delay in the Congress of the United States to approve an aid appropriation might have an adverse multiplier effect throughout the economic program of a developing nation. All of this is also contingent on the "production" of time-oriented civil servants. This, too, is a question of investment with a long gestation period.[82] Governments—foreign, federal, state, and local—are not the only units that must be aware of time in order to achieve results. Citizens' "choices," too, must be synchronized, sequenced, and made at the proper rate. A refusal to install tube wells, to use hybrid seeds, or to shift one's career from law to education can bring to naught the "best laid plans." Wars, political bargaining, and bureaucratic empire building, all further complicate the timing problem confronted by development administrators.

The promise of development, then, is substantially linked with time management in the public sector. It is on this issue that the public administration developed in the industrialized nations is relevant. For instance, an analysis of the recommendations made by American and United Nations consultants on this issue reveals

82. Albert Waterston, "'Planning the Planning' Under the Alliance for Progress," in Irving Swerdlow, ed., *Development Administration: Concepts and Problems* (Syracuse, N.Y., 1963), pp. 141–162.

the centrality of time management. A fairly representative example of this literature is Bernard Gladieux's survey of public administration in Pakistan in 1955.[83] Underlying his recommendations is an important temporal assumption.

[For Pakistan] time is priceless and funds are precious. When essential projects or goals take twice or more as long to accomplish than the planned schedules, and when the administrative costs are far in excess of reasonable standards, then the national objectives themselves are endangered and inflationary trends given further impetus. . . . The war against poverty, disease, and illiteracy demand[s] the very same high standards of performance and accomplishment [as the military]. This can only be achieved with the best personnel and administrative equipment which can be found or devised.

The rest of his analysis is filled with the imagery of progressive time and the need for timing. The inherited administration is "static," "enchained by precedent," and "does not sufficiently stress the action . . . aspects of administration." His recommendations for better time management include a decentralization "to overcome the paralysis of action," a greater stress on technicians as opposed to the generalists who "clog the channels," more self-contained units "which are free to move ahead," and a personnel system appreciating "the significance of this program to the future of Pakistan." Above all, he argues, there is a need for a central planning agency located near the center of political power, to bring "creative social and economic vision to this broad undertaking" through its "co-ordinating" and "energizing" functions. Without this agency of synchronization, "the program may well flounder without direction and stimulation." Among its many functions, the planning board is to provide current information about the progress of the economy, to make projections about future development, to oversee and co-ordinate the federal, provincial, and local development efforts in order "to achieve maximum utilization of resources" and "program balance," and to evaluate performance with "presumed returns." For

83. *Reorientation of the Pakistan Government for National Development* (Karachi, 1955), mimeo. See also Warren F. Ilchman, "Rising Expectations and the Revolution in Development Administration," *Public Administration Review,* XXV (1965), 314–325.

the individual ministries and departments at all levels, he recommends a "micro" planning function to work toward a condition in which these units are so conscious of time and productivity that the function of the central planning board will be only "correlation of the integrated plans of the ministries and provinces, checking them only for overall consistency and balance." He assumes that this "is still some distance away." Modern administration, thus, as seen by this analyst and his professional colleagues, is concerned essentially with controlling the time factor through the agencies of synchronization, sequence, and rate.

Changes in the administrative systems of developing countries cannot be understood without recognition of this new emphasis on time. This emphasis comes at a period in which, for many of these nations, the most significant expenditure is in the field of economic development. Under the pressure of the ideological commitment to controlled development and the problems of managing time to achieve this and with the prodding of such agencies as United States Agency for International Development, the World Bank, UNTAP, and the Colombo Plan, the governments seeking industrialization have stressed the need for time management in their reorganization and modifications of procedures.[84] The most obvious examples can be found in the area of co-ordination. Planning commissions, which seek to hold change under control in order to make better decisions in the present, have become universal. Considerable ministerial reorganization has taken place to permit unified programs in agricultural production, industrialization, and education.[85] Regional councils have been experimented with to co-ordinate federal, provincial, and local government efforts.

Other innovations in time management can also be found. In fiscal institutions, procedures have been altered to permit longer expenditure phases and greater flexibility in the making of contracts. Development expenditures have been separated from

84. See, for example, Sixto K. Roxas, *Organizing the Government for Economic Development Administration* (Manila, 1964).

85. Indian Institute of Public Administration, *The Organisation of the Government of India* (New Delhi, 1958), pp. 119–137, 193–246; Organisation and Methods Division, *Annual Reports* (New Delhi, 1954–65).

"establishment" and other expenditures; and, though as yet unsuccessful, attempts have been made, both in government corporations and in government-wide programs, to apply the concept of program budgeting.[86] To assist the co-ordination of implementing programs, many nations have adopted the device of development working parties, which combine the relevant ministries in a way that is intended to minimize the delays caused by the normal operation of the hierarchies of the participating organizations. Evaluative institutions have been created to assess progress, such as program evaluation organizations, project wings, and committees on plan progress. Organizations to carry out continuous management surveys—O and M divisions—have been established both on a ministry and on a government-wide basis. PERT and "the line of balance" have been applied to projects to maximize temporal advantage.[87] Establishment and strengthening of institutions to gather data for planning projections is also a common feature. Finally, the training of civil servants—post-entry and mid-career—includes now exhortative and theoretical work on development and the demands of time management.[88] This training is supplemented by education for staff persons in European and American universities and the institutes of regional economic commissions of ECOSOC to acquire new techniques of time control, such as linear programming.

"Time Transfer" and Development: Four Hypotheses

The argument to this point has suggested that there arose in the West during a particular period a highly valued conception of linear time. In this conception it was thought that a collectivity would achieve for its members greater and greater amounts of

86. Malcolm B. Parsons, "Performance Budgeting in the Philippines," *Public Administration Review*, XVII (1957), 173–179.
87. Committee on Plan Projects, *The Line of Balance Technology* (New Delhi, 1961).
88. See, for example, M. R. Inayat, *Perspectives in Public Administration* (Civil Service Academy of Pakistan, Lahore, n.d.), especially articles by M. R. Inayat, S. Fida Hassan, and Abdul Qayyum.

material goods and increasing human longevity, this to be achieved through the application of science and technology to the natural and human environment. Further, the essay has argued that the eventual transforming quality of this metaphor, through the choices of its adherents, has recast many of the institutions of the industrial West in its own image. It has been further argued that through various means and by various elites, these values and institutions were imported by the industrializing countries of the non-Western world. Imported were the belief in linear progress, the responsibility of the state to bring about a this-worldly material improvement, the criteria of efficiency and productivity, and the institutions of timing. To suggest that "new time" has begun to affect the "old clocks" of the non-Western world is one thing; but to identify the conditions under which Western linear time and timing institutions will succeed in replacing older views is another. In a sense, that is not the responsibility of this essay. Here the concern is with the administrative systems of developing countries. It is appropriate to assess, in a very preliminary and tentative fashion, the comparative productivity of these administrative systems and to ask what conditions may be relevant to this level.

Productivity is assumed to be a correlate of time values described in this essay. The assumption here is that those administrative systems which have higher levels of productivity are those in which the functionaries and the wider society place a high premium on time as a resource and seek to realize the promise of linear time; that is, the governments and their elites seek to apply human and mechanical technology to achieve higher standards of material life. What, then, are the factors that contribute to a high value placed on time as a resource and account for differences in productive levels?

Four hypotheses will be considered. The first is that administrative structures of timing—those to facilitate synchronization, sequencing, and rate—account for differential levels of productivity. The very existence of these institutions is assumed to indicate a high value placed on time. According to this hypothesis, those administrative systems which are "better organized from a timing point of view," those administrative systems which minimize delay by structural means, are those which have higher levels of productivity. The second hypothesis is that those governments which value development more highly, as seen in expenditure on development or as indicated by the structure of their elites, have a higher level of productivity. The third is the Riggs hypothesis that productivity of administrative systems is dependent upon pluralistic institutions. Finally, the fourth hypothesis is that social factors, especially urbanization and professionalization of roles, contribute to the differential levels. The means used to test these hypotheses, it must be stressed, are gross and can only lead the way to further research. It is also recognized that the sample is small and the data available often misleading.

We face first the fact that productivity is a much-debated concept, and that there seems to be no easy way of measuring it cross-nationally.[89] The assumption used here is that the capacity of the public sector to produce goods and services can be used if increases in output over time is the measure. The more accepted method of comparing input of resources with output faces so many difficulties that it has been rejected in this essay. The data for an input-output analysis is difficult to obtain for developing countries and always raises the problem of cross-national equivalences. In addition, as the preceding section has made clear, the productive efficiency of any one division or ministry really is contingent on decisions made by several other ministries as well. The influence of "delays" caused by decision-makers in these other ministries would make a ministry-by-ministry index impossible.

The "capacity to produce of the public sector," which is the comparative tool for this essay, is an index used to compare the productivity of a sample of fourteen administrative systems of developing countries. It is made up of the production totals over time of the public sector's development efforts: kilowatts of electricity, tons of steel, tons of cement, tons of food grains, miles of

89. Bureau of the Budget, *Measuring Productivity of Federal Government Organizations* (Washington, D.C., 1964).

roads, irrigated acres, teachers, and students in primary and technical schools. These totals were adjusted to take into consideration not only percentage increases in production, but also the size of the country and the size of the base from which increases were measured.[90] A ten-year time series was used whenever possible, and from a much larger sample, only those countries were used for which data on five or more of the items listed above could be found. The original plan was to break down the items to have three indices: public sector industrial productivity, agricultural productivity, and "social" productivity. This was abandoned for a single index when it was found there was little variation in the three indices. A country high in one was high in the other two. A rank order on the capacity to produce was achieved: (1) Yugoslavia, (2) Mexico, (3) Argentina, (4) Chile, (5) Colombia, (6) Thailand, (7) India, (8) Egypt, (9) Philippines, (10) Turkey, (11) Nigeria, (12) Pakistan, (13) Sudan, and (14) Tanzania.

The assumptions behind "the capacity to produce" index and the rank ordering are five. First, all the countries in the sample are interested in development. Second, variations between items —emphasis on one item more than another—would average out in the sample. Third, yearly emphases—a spurt of road building for a single year, for instance—would average out in the total time series. Fourth, the private sector items, such as tons of food grains, are significantly influenced by the public sector. Finally, and most important, the correlation's significance would depend on a much larger sample. Needless to say, an additional major assumption is that correlation does *not* impute causality.

The conventional public administration assumption is that proper structuring will yield higher productivity. To eliminate

90. The formula used:

$$\sqrt{\frac{A}{A \, max}} \cdot \sqrt{\frac{X}{X \, max}} \cdot \frac{Y}{Y \, max} \times 100.$$

A is the measure of per capita production of any nation; A max is the measure of per capita production of the nation which ranked highest in per capita production; X is the absolute increase in production of any nation; X max is the absolute increase in production of the nation which had the largest absolute increase in production; Y is the percentage increase of production of any country; Y max is the percentage increase in production of the country which has the greatest percentage increase in production.

the factors for delay—length of hierarchical chain, overlapping of programs, preventing expertise from having an immediate effect on decisions, and so forth—would conduce to the end of more goods and services. From the large number of administrative surveys and recommendations for reform, several propositions were developed and grouped in three categories. The first category, organizational variables, related to the status and functions of the planning body the number of bodies to which the planning board was responsible, the fiscal and budgetary procedures facilitating development, the expenditure on organization and methods, the proliferation of ministries and autonomous agencies, the number of ministries in the key fields of agricultural and industrial production, the existence of program evaluation institutions, and the capacity of the state to collect direct taxes. The propositions on personnel, the second grouping, related to the pay and perquisites of civil servants the number and treatment of specialists, comparative recruitment facts, and the inclusion in training programs of economic development material. The third grouping, "the level of technological sophistication," dealt with propositions on the existence and use in budgeting and planning of advanced quantitative techniques, such as input-output tables and final demand schedules, the percentage of the budget for statistical services, and a judgment on the adequacy of the national accounting system for planning. Comparing the ranked order of the capacity to produce with the structural variables—organization, personnel, and technological sophistication—gave little confirmation to the conventional public administration hypothesis. An over-all coefficient of correlation for the administrative variables, weighted in a common sense fashion, was .25, indicating a very low chance of direct correlations. This does not rule out situations where the level of productivity that was achieved was due to these structural arrangements or where their further institutionalization will not see an impact on productivity. But, hesitantly and tentatively, it might be argued that the hypothesis of conventional public administration has little merit.[91]

91. For a full discussion of method, data, and results, see Warren F. Ilchman and Allan Samson, "The Capacity to Produce: Prologue to a Controversy" (forthcoming).

But conventional public administrators also insist that the motivation of the functionaries is important. Although no study of bureaucrats' attitudes toward time exists, there is a possible correlate to motivation in the seriousness of development intentions. If the governments expend high relative amounts on development, then they are serious and probably compel the functionaries to seek higher levels of productivity. Two tests of this—one major and one minor—were undertaken. It was impossible to compile an index for per capita expenditure for development in the nations of the sample or on the ratio between military and development expenditures. But, if it can be assumed that much of the expenditure of the government is in the development field, then an index of the expenditure of the central government as percentage of gross national product might be relevant. Here the coefficient of correlation was .45, suggesting a higher relationship with the capacity to produce than was found in the earlier hypothesis. The minor test was undertaken on the hypothesis that military regimes are particularly committed to development and can assure compliance on the part of administrators. The coefficient of correlation between states led during a considerable part of the time series by the military and the capacity to produce is .23. This may, of course, be the product essentially of the sample and not necessarily of the empirical world.

The third hypothesis is that of Fred W. Riggs, according to which productivity of the public sector is variable with the number and strength of non-bureaucratic institutions, especially countervailing political institutions.[92] Although this brief statement does not do justice to the many variations and convolutions of the "prismatic society" theory, it represents a testable proposition. Taking the items listed by Riggs as constituting the pluralistic or diffracted situation and using the judgments employed by the *Cross-Polity Survey*, an index was formed of political development. The coefficient of correlation between these factors and the capacity to produce is .32. It might be argued that all the countries in the sample are "prismatic" and hence the mixed characteristics would yield this variable outcome, but this argu-

92. *Administration in Developing Countries* (Boston, 1964).

ment would only reveal a tautological character in the original hypothesis.

Testing of the fourth hypothesis is not a welcome task. The study of change in developing countries has been marked by an infinite regress of relevant factors. In the economic field, for instance, the causal factors in growth have moved from a savings-investment ratio through innovative entrepreneurship to a need for achievement borne of particular child-rearing practices.[93] This same regression is necessary to find those factors which correlate best with the capacity to produce. The conception here is that those features in the wider society that conduce to a high value placed on time as a resource will create the conditions for public functionaries to value time highly—a stress on productivity which is both mediated by the consumers of public products and through the socialization of the administrator in a time-oriented society. Five conditions seem to correlate rather well. The first is urbanization. As can be easily imagined, cities require a higher degree of synchronization and internalization of a neutral, general time sense than do rural areas. There seems to be considerable independent empirical confirmation of this assumption as well.[94] In the case of the correlation of percentage of population in cities over 20,000 and the capacity to produce, the coefficient of correlation is .75. A second condition favoring a widely held time value is industrialization. Industrial modes of production, as was argued earlier, require high degrees of synchronization, a discipline enforced by a neutral time sense, patterns of consumer temporal discipline imposed by wages and salaries, and individual mobilization that inspires a calculating propensity. Comparing the capacity to produce with the percentage of GNP in non-agricultural production, the coefficient of correlation is .81. A similar test can be made by using the percentage of the work force in non-agricultural work. Here the correlation is .63. The third condition is the extent of the development of mass media. The assumption in this case is that the mass media

93. David C. McClelland, *The Achieving Society* (Princeton, 1961).
94. J. Stoetzel, "La pression temporelle," *Sondages*, XV (1953), 11–23; Leonard Reissman, *The Urban Process: Cities in Industrial Societies* (Glencoe, Ill., 1964), Table 5, p. 177.

are conducive to temporal values in that they presume a synchronization of common interests, an empathetic capacity to envision other roles and their disciplines, a sense of universal immediacy of events, and an awareness of the passage of time.[95] Correlating the capacity to produce with two variables of the mass media—radios per thousand and newspapers per thousand —produces the correlations of .85 and .84, respectively.

A fourth condition in the wider society is education. The assumption here is that formal education requires a temporal disciplining—periods, examinations, the development of the capacity for deferring gratification, and the inculcating of a calculating propensity to improve life chances. On the further assumption that the relationship of education to the capacity to produce is most relevant at the point of higher education, the coefficient of correlation between national higher education per 100,000 and the capacity to produce is .62. A final condition is what might be called professionalization of roles. The assumption behind the correlation is that a society with a higher percentage of professionals per 100,000 is one in which temporal values are held by a significant population, for the educational and career patterns of professionals are conducive to an individual calculating propensity and a capacity for discipline through the deferring of gratification. Data on professions are difficult to find. If the reader will permit an otherwise unpardonable extrapolation, the index for comparison is composed of doctors and teachers per 100,000 population. Information on engineers and lawyers is too fragmentary to be used. A composite index of teachers and physicians was constructed and compared with the capacity to produce. The coefficient of correlation is .80. In all five, a higher correlation exists than can be found in the administrative, ideological, and political variables. These correlations suggest that an increasing capacity of the public service to produce might depend on the industrialization, urbanization, and the expansion of higher education, professional roles, and the mass media. A melancholy prospect indeed. Old clocks might break down!

The intention of this essay was threefold: to show the rise of

95. Daniel Lerner, *The Passing of Traditional Society* (Glencoe, Ill., 1958).

the conception of linear time and the institutions of timing in the West, to see the tentative and incomplete adoption in non-Western nations of these values and institutions, and to speculate on the conditions for these values and institutions to begin to result in higher productivity in the public sector. There is, one hopes, persuasive evidence in relation to the first two, though volumes could be written to expand what were paragraphs in this essay. The persuasiveness of the third intention, like most work on social change, remains an open question.

But a further open question is present. It is the normative and aesthetic implications raised by the triumph of progressive time and timing. As the traditions of social science and comparative administration neither seek to understand the implications of this triumph nor are capable of judging them once they are identified, the best I can do is to suggest, with Dante, that Paradise is: "Là ove s'appunta ogni Ubi ed ogni Quando."

Chapter 6

Developmentalist Time, Development Entrepreneurs, and Leadership in Developing Countries

Hahn-Been Lee

It is not future time that is long,
but a long future is a long expectation of the future.
Nor is past time long,
but a long past is a long memory of the past.

The Confessions of St. Augustine,
Book 11, Chapter 28.

Social scientists have theorized that time orientation is one of the most basic orientations of man, and that in a society the distribution and ordering of alternative time orientations is closely related to the rate and direction of change.[1] This essay is an attempt to develop in a speculative fashion a relationship between time perspectives and attitudes toward change in developing countries. The main objective is to identify the optimum time orientation for development and to specify the incidence of such an optimum time orientation among different potential elites —this with a view to integration of resources toward the goal of national development.

The term "national development" is used interchangeably with "modernization." It is thus defined as a process of improving a nation's social, economic, and political systems to enable them to absorb continuous changes and meet increasing and different

1. Florence Rockwood Kluckhohn and Fred L. Strodtbeck, *Variations in Value Orientations* (Evanston, Ill., 1961), p. 10.

demands.[2] It is, therefore, a composite term comprising such interrelated goals as an open society and sustained political and economic growth.

The study is based both on research in the literature on such matters as the psychology and sociology of time, innovation theory, development politics, and development administration, and on reflections from experience, the latter pertaining chiefly to the author's service as a senior civil servant in the Government of the Republic of Korea during the decade of the 1950's and beyond.

Change and Time Consciousness

In the history of a traditional society, there is a time when the modern world knocks at the door. It may take various forms: a visit of "black ships" from a foreign power demanding the opening of trade relations; transmission of a new religion accompanied by new knowledges and technologies; foreign invasion; and liberation from a closed colonial control as the result of an international war. Whatever form the opening of the society may take and in whatever sequence and with whatever recurrence the crucial events may take place, the advent of the modern world is a traumatic time of national introspection. It opens up new temporal dimensions to individual men and to the society.

For our purposes we shall think of time as presenting and developing two dimensions: one which orients man and the society toward the world; and another which orients man toward himself and the society toward its history.[3] We shall call the former the "external time" and the latter the "internal time."

External time is "objective" time. It confronts man and society with *change*. Change is indeed the dominant characteristic of the external time of modernization. The change that a developing nation undergoes is a general change which is complex in nature,

2. See S. N. Eisenstadt, *Modernization: Growth and Diversity* (Bloomington, Ind., 1963), p. 5.
3. For different uses of time as an analytical tool, see Max Heirich, "The Use of Time in the Study of Social Change," *Am. Soc. Rev.*, XXIX (1964), 386–397.

rapid in tempo, and profound in impact. Changes occur in concert, in succession, and in conflict. Some of the main components are:[4] (1) Demographic change—a population explosion, population movements (e.g., war refugees, rural exodus), qualitative changes of population (e.g., growing proportion of younger and educated generation); (2) Sociocultural change—increasing literacy and formal education, a renaissance and spread of indigenous written language, agrarian reform, decline of the extended family, expansion of the military establishment, urbanization; (3) Ideological change—the spread of ideas of nationalism, egalitarianism, democracy, the welfare state, a planned economy; (4) Technological change—including changes in manufacturing, transportation, communication, the mass media, the military; (5) Economic change—monetization, inflation, income redistribution; and (6) Political change—the institution of national and local elections, the organization of national and local legislative and executive organs and courts, the development of political parties and interest groups, the entry of the intellectuals and the military into the central political arena, possible coups and revolutions.

Not only is the complexity of the intertwined external changes great, but their tempo is swift as well. Many of the changes occur simultaneously or one after another in a relatively short span of time. More changes may take place during a decade in a contemporary developing country than during generations in a now-developed country at similar stage.

Due to the complexity and speed of change, its impact is also profound. After one or two decades of sweeping changes, a change in sheer quantity turns into a change in quality.[5] Such

---

4. A classic inventory of change in the administrative environment is John M. Gaus, "The Ecology of Government," chap. 1 in his *Reflections on Public Administration* (University, Ala., 1947), pp. 1–19.

Recent literature on the components of social change which I have found particularly valuable includes: Richard T. LaPiere, *Social Change* (New York, 1965), chap. ii; Neil J. Smelser, "Mechanisms of Change and Adjustment to Change," in B. F. Hoselitz and W. E. Moore, eds., *Industrialization and Society* (The Hague, 1963), pp. 32–33; and Eisenstadt, *op. cit.*, pp. 2–5.

5. This idea is developed in Heirich, *op. cit.*, pp. 390–391.

qualitative change is revolutionary in character, yet it is seldom so perceived by the society which undergoes it.

Attitudes toward Change and Time Perspectives

The opening to the modern world begets a sense of breaking with the country's past, attenuates and threatens the sense of unbroken descent from and continuity with a legendary founding of the nation. The "eternal order" suffers from "a sharp decline or a virtual collapse."[6] With the fading of the dimension of eternity, time confronts man with overwhelming change. To a man confronting such change, time offers both opportunity and pressure: time is at once a friend and a foe. In this situation, man's attitude toward change may take three basic forms: positive, negative, and ambivalent.

To those with a positive attitude toward change, time opens up a wonderful opportunity. It challenges them to increase the scope of their knowledge and to try to catch up with the modern world, or even to attempt to outmodernize the latter, which is often envisaged in the form of a reference country.[7] To those who view change as an opportunity, time is linked to the idea of progress. As John A. Vieg points out, progress requires, among other things, a conception of time in which "men think in terms of a potentially ascending line or spiral."[8] It requires a belief that time is a helpful instrument available to man in his struggle for a better future. Individuals and groups possessing such positive orientation "trust" time and the future. We shall call this positive, forward-looking time orientation *developmentalist.*

When change is viewed in a negative way, on the other hand, time becomes a burdensome pressure. It presents itself in a succession of "sub-changes" so rapid, so unintelligible, and so uncontrollable that the individual feels lost and helpless. In this situation of relentless change, the valued past is perceived as being

6. Hans Meyerhoff, *Time in Literature* (Berkeley and Los Angeles, 1955), p. 89.
7. The reference country may be the one from which the country in question received an actual or perceived aggression.
8. *Progress Versus Utopia* (Bombay, 1963), p. 9.

ground to pieces and senselessly used as raw material in the fabrication of an unthinkable future.[9] Individuals and groups possessing such a negative view of change distrust time and the future. The outcome of distrust of time and the future is an attitude of escape, escape primarily into the past. We shall designate such a negative, backward-looking time orientation *escapist*.

A third attitude toward change is possible and occurs frequently. It is an ambivalent attitude: the individual refuses to escape into the past and yet he cannot commit himself to a positive view of the future.[10] The resulting response to the pressure and tension of change is an attempt to maximize short-run returns through manipulation of the existing circumstances.[11] The individual becomes primarily present-oriented. We shall designate such ambivalent, present-bound time orientation *exploitationist*.

To summarize, a negative attitude toward change looks back toward the past and yields an escapist time orientation; an ambivalent attitude toward change concentrates upon the immediate present and yields an exploitationist time orientation; and finally a positive attitude toward change looks forward to the future and produces a developmentalist time orientation. Chart I presents the relationship between the different attitudes toward change and the different time perspectives, resulting in different time orientations.

This chart should not lead to the misunderstanding that all future-oriented time perspectives are necessarily developmentalist, or all past-oriented ones escapist, or all present-oriented

9. Mircea Eliade's *The Myth of the Eternal Return,* trans. W. R. Trask (New York, 1954), chap. iv, "The Terror of History," is a good analysis of the plight of the historical man severed from the eternal past.

10. E. H. Erikson relates man's time conception to his problem of personality identity by suggesting that the positive time conception sponsors a process of identity, whereas the negative time conception produces a crisis of identity. He further suggests that creativity occurs when an overwhelming negative conscience is linked with the sensitivity and the power drive of a positive conscience. See *Young Man Luther* (New York, 1958), pp. 217, 221.

11. For elaboration of this attitude, see LaPiere, *op. cit.,* pp. 96–99, "Incongruence and the Vitiation of Social Elements." Erikson calls this attitude "dominance by the *id*," which corresponds with an inner space-time oriented toward "wish fulfilment" (*op. cit.,* p. 218).

ones exploitationist. These are the dominant time orientations with respect to the three temporal perspectives, but there are residual time orientations in each perspective. In order to ascertain the residual ones, we shall examine in greater detail the structural relationship among the three time perspectives, i.e., the past, the present, and the future.

Chart I. *Dominant Time Orientations*

TIME PERSPECTIVE				
	future			developmentalist
	present		exploitationist	
	past	escapist		
		negative	ambivalent	positive
		ATTITUDE TOWARD CHANGE		

Psychologically and practically, time experience begins with a single time based on an appreciation given by nature of an irreducible minimum of time. This is the experience that men call the "present." Appreciation of longer periods depends on *memory* as the efficient cause and has the achievement of *purpose* as its final cause. Thus, the development of the concept of the past depends on memory and that of the future on purpose.

The past is of great importance in man for present action. It is the storehouse of his knowledge, and his present activity is guided more or less by the memory of past experience. As Mary Stuart put it, "an individual or society robbed of the sense of the past is lost."[12] The future, on the other hand, is an unfulfilled purpose which is conscious of its aim. The definiteness of this aim in part depends on memory. Our anticipations are, in the main,

12. For an exposition of time experience, see her *The Psychology of Time* (London, 1925), pp. 20–28. This quotation is from p. 22.

composed of elements provided by memory, since past experience will lend precision to our aim, even though the existence of an aim is not due solely to past experience.

In order to obtain purposeful action on the part of individuals and the society, it is of utmost importance that memory and purpose, the past and the present, be integrated toward the future. When such integration of time experience occurs, *developmentalist time* appears. When this fails to occur, either *escapist time* or *exploitationist time* obtains. Development is a difficult task precisely because the proper integration of time experience is the exception rather than the rule. We shall consider various residual time attitudes in this light.

Escapist time, though oriented primarily to the past, can also take the form of an escape into the future or a refuge in the present. It can manifest itself in such out-of-time fantasies as "futurism" or "millenialism" and "presentism" as well as "archaism."[13]

The dominant escapist time is retrospective, harking back to the "good old days." When it seems to man beyond his strength to face the pressure of rapid change, it remains for him to take refuge in a time-space where he will find the realization of his desires with less effort. To individuals, retrospection, the solace of nostalgia, may mean a return to the early childhood on the farm, or to some ancestral glories of the family. To a nation, it usually involves "archaism,"[14] the idea of duplicating a golden age in the nation's history. If such a retrospective orientation produces actions, they are directed toward restoring people—individually or collectively—to the style and level of life in the "good old days."

The time of refuge in the present is erratic. This is related to a sharp "shrinkage" of the past and especially to the decline of the family. The erosion of the family or man's severance from it entails loss of a sense of continuity and belongingness. The indi-

13. A systematic analysis of the various attitudes of refuge is provided in Paul Fraisse, *The Psychology of Time* (New York, 1963), pp. 184–198.

14. For a discussion of archaism, see Mary Matossian, "Ideologies of Delayed Industrialization: Some Tensions and Ambiguities," in John H. Kautsky, ed., *Political Change in Underdeveloped Countries: Nationalism and Communism* (New York, 1963), pp. 252–264.

vidual's life is now confined to a much narrower span of time than
when he consciously felt himself a link between several generations. He is increasingly isolated within the present moment.[15]
The time of refuge in the present is, therefore, either lonely or full
of purposeless activity: such time breeds a ritualistic action pattern, namely, the routine. This time orientation is prevalent
among war refugees,[16] and, in the administrative context, may
characterize bureaucrats caught by rapid social and political
upheavals.

The flight into the future presents an overexclusive anticipation
of what is yet to come. It is a utopian orientation. The dream of
utopia is born not out of confidence in the general trend of things
in a society, but rather revulsion against the present and perhaps
even—paradoxically—out of fear of the future. Proclamations of
utopia tend, therefore, to be signs of wishful thinking rather than
guarantees of miracles about to be performed. "Futurism" or
"millenialism" is therefore not only deceptive but also damaging
to human aspiration and achievement. It can mean an appeal for
the realization of the desired goal at one full stroke. It can be
a "desperate" time orientation and can produce desperate actions.

Exploitationist time is pre-eminently a time of the present. It
shuns both past and future and would exclude them from the
present in order to make the most of every hour. Obviously, this
is a hedonistic attitude. It is the aim of a man who is content to
feel himself alive, when the present hurts him less than a past
laden with suffering and remorse or a future fraught with anguish
through its very uncertainty. There is no thought of sacrificing
any part of the present for the future: maximum gratification in
the present is the motto.

15. A good illustration of such a "presentist" individual is given in a portrait of
Benjamin Constant, the 19th-century Swiss romanticist, who, in the words of
Georges Poulet, "n'avait jamais eu d'enfance, ni d'habitudes, ni de sentiment de la
tradition" (*Etudes sur le temps humain* [Edinburgh, 1949], p. 240). Poulet quotes
a passage from Constant's diary which vividly shows the terror-stricken mentality
of such an uprooted soul: "Une impression que la vie m'a faite et qui ne me quitte
pas, c'est une sorte de terreur de la destineé. Je ne finis jamais le récit d'une
journée en inscrivant la date du lendemain sans un sentiment d'inquiètude sur ce
que le lendemain inconnu doit m'apporter" (p. 242).

16. Erikson's article entitled "Identity and Uprootedness in Our Time" in his
collection of lectures, *Insight and Responsibility* (New York, 1964), pp. 83–107, is
a good analysis of the psychology of the uprooted refugees.

The exploitationist time also has its residual variations in the past and the future. When applied to the past, it turns into a regretful orientation,[17] a remorse over the missed past which, the individual feels, should have been enjoyed then but which adverse circumstances hindered him from realizing. Such a time orientation tends to produce actions which try to recoup some of the lost past, and hence results in irregularities and enormities in social and political behaviors as the outcome.

A "missed past" can be shifted to the future, just as the utopia of the past is related to the utopia of the future. When so shifted, it becomes an imaginary missed future, a future which, as the individual feels, should be enjoyed but appears so threatened that it may never be realized, unless he takes a pre-emptive or presumptive action. The exploitationist time of the future is thus hasty. The outcome of such hasty time orientation may be erratic and even violent action.

What are then the manifestations of developmentalist time in the three temporal perspectives? The dominant developmentalist time occurs in the future. When applied to the future, it is prospective: it plans ahead and is ready to take reasonable risks. Such a time orientation yields vision, the vision of progress. To a man who plans ahead, "time is viewed as the supreme value,"[18] because other values can be realized only in the course of and as the result of time.

Such a prospective time orientation gets support from residual time attitudes in the present as well as in the past. When this attitude permeates the present, it generates the willingness to defer gratifications in the present for returns in the future. Developmentalist time of the present thus generates savings.

Applied to the past, developmentalist time is eager to inherit it, i.e., to use the past as a valuable resource. In the modernizing context, it searches in the nation's past history for clues for future progress. There is no attempt merely to restore the past, but rather an effort to build a future using the creative elements from the history of the nation. Thus inheriting the past yields legitima-

17. Fraisse, *op. cit.*, p. 190.
18. Meyerhoff, *op. cit.*, p. 102.

tion in the present and this in turn indirectly facilitates the thrust into the future. Used selectively and constructively the past can sanction innovations (as by the glorification of entrepreneurial individuals and groups) and promote national solidarity.[19]

Developmentalist time is essentially integrated time: in it all three perspectives of man's time experience are attended to; memory and purpose are unified and directed toward the future. The vision of the future is given purpose and precision through the constructive use of the past. The realization of the vision is further accelerated through the sacrifices made in the present. In turn, the vision enables the past to recover its proper meaning and give the present purpose and direction.

Chart II is a recapitulation of the various residual time orientations as well as the dominant ones manifest in the three perspectives of time.[20]

Time Orientations, Elite Roles, and Program Orientations

Having developed a schema of time orientations, the next step is to consider the implications of the different time orientations for development administration.

19. Matossian, *op. cit.*, p. 262.

20. The main source of hints for the development of this schema was George Gurvitch's suggestive work, *The Spectrum of Social Time* (Dordrecht, Netherlands, 1964). Gurvitch's spectrum contains the following eight varieties of social time: (1) enduring time—where the past is dominant and projected into the present and the future; (2) deceptive time—an enduring time masking crises and surprises, where a rupture between the past and the present occurs; (3) erratic time—a time of uncertainty, where the present appears to prevail over the past and the future, with which it finds it difficult to enter into relations; (4) cyclical time—a mystic time, where the past, present, and future are mutually projected into one another; (5) retarded time—a delayed time whose unfolding is awaited so long that although the future is actualized in the present, it is not efficient; (6) alternating time—where the realization of past and future compete in the present, and delay and advance struggle endlessly with equal strength; (7) time pushing forward—where the future becomes present; and (8) explosive time—where the present as well as the past are dissolved in the creation of the immediately transcended future. See pp. 30–33.

The nine time orientations in Chart II do not match Gurvitch's eight social times, but approximate correspondences can be established between the retrospective-escapist time and the "enduring time," between the utopian-escapist time and the "explosive time," between the prospective-developmentalist time and the "time pushing forward," etc. Gurvitch's "erratic time" comes close to the erratic-escapist time, whereas his "deceptive time," "retarded time," and "alternating time" have exploitationist characteristics, although these do not individually correspond with the three versions of the exploitationist time.

Chart II. *Dominant and Residual Time Orientations*

TIME PERSPECTIVE	future	-utopian	-hasty	Developmentalist -prospective
	present	-erratic	Exploitationist -hedonistic	-saving
	past	Escapist -retrospective	-regretful	-inheriting
		negative	ambivalent	positive
		ATTITUDE TOWARD CHANGE		

Some students of development administration have suggested the desirability of constructing a typology of program orientations for different administrative systems. Edward Weidner's "Suggested Typology" is a case in point.[21] It is the thesis of this paper that the different time orientations developed in the preceding section could be applied fruitfully in constructing such typologies. Chart III is a crude attempt to relate the dominant time orientations presented in Chart I to elite roles and their program orientations.

Chart III. *Time Orientations and Elite Characteristics*

ELITE CHARACTERISTICS	TIME ORIENTATIONS		
	Escapist	Exploitationist	Developmentalist
Role pattern	retreatist	waster	innovational
Leadership style	authoritarian	bureaucratic	entrepreneurial
Program orientation	law and order	consumption	production

1. Escapist time is related to a *retreatist* role pattern. The term "retreatist" is used to denote a state of mind in which individuals perceive a sharp decline in their status and undergo relative

21. Edward W. Weidner, "Development Administration: A New Focus for Research," in Ferrel Heady and Sybil L. Stokes, eds., *Papers in Comparative Public Administration* (Ann Arbor, Mich., 1962), pp. 92–115, esp. 108 ff.

withdrawal from assertive activity.[22] Such a role pattern is prevalent among the traditional elites, i.e., tribal and clan chiefs and members of a landed aristocracy. Elites originating in such backgrounds find the new environment of change and flux threatening to their status, which is based on their past. They perceive actual or imaginary "withdrawal of status respect." Many members of the independence movement during the colonial days who become the political leaders of the new state after liberation from colonial domination are apt to fall into this category.[23] These first-generation nationalist leaders are eminently the symbol of the past. Their glory lies in the past, in the independence movement, a struggle to recover a long past that had been lost. Though sensitive to the task of nation building, their dominant time orientation is nostalgic. They easily become annoyed at the demands of modernization. In fact, they may become frustrated and infuriated at the revelation that they are not quite equal to the new tasks of modernization. Torn between the self-system based on their past and their visible ineptitude at new present tasks, they become increasingly authoritarian in their leadership style.

The program orientation of such an elite is toward law and order. This stems from their retrospective time orientation and paternalistic-authoritarian role pattern. Restoration of the past is their main wish. They have little concern for the future and pay little real attention to the problem of industrialization. Theirs is a program which tries in a vague fashion to restore conditions to

22. Two terms used here to denote different elite role patterns, "retreatist" and "innovational," are drawn from Everett E. Hagen's suggestive work, *On the Theory of Social Change: How Economic Growth Begins* (Homewood, Ill., 1962), Part III.

23. For a study of the social background of Korean political leaders of the post-colonial period, see Bae-ho Hahn and Kyu-taik Kim, "Korean Political Leaders (1952–1962): Their Social Origins and Skills," *Asian Survey*, III (1963), 305–323. In the Korean context, these first-generation political leaders were strongly imbued with Confucianism, which was the dominant traditional ideology in the country, and which had a strongly nostalgic bent. The concordance of Confucianism with "archaism" is systematically analyzed in a recent article by a Korean scholar. See Byong-ik Koh, "Yukyo Sasang e issosoui Chinbo-kwan [The Concept of Progress in Confucianism: With Reference to the Causes of the Failure for the Concept to be Formed]," in Tong-so Pak, ed., *Balchon-ron Sosol [Introduction to the Theory of Development]* (Seoul, 1965), pp. 57–82, esp. 64 ff.

the level of a certain base period, and day-to-day measures are designed to make people temporarily content.

2. The exploitationist time is related to a *waster* role pattern. A bureaucratic-political elite emerges at the heel of the first-generation nationalist leaders, as the latter group fades away before the complexity of the problem of nation building, economic development, and government administration. The social background of this second-generation elite is characterized by a combination of upper class (mainly landed aristocracy) family origin, colonial education, and legalistic-bureaucratic occupational grounding. Members of this elite do not themselves possess any substantial amount of charisma but are eager to bask in the glow of their nationalist predecessors, and do not hesitate to maximize power and control in the charismatic shadow of the latter.

Side by side with legalistic-bureaucratic politicians, a cadre of colonially trained civil servants reigns in the post-colonial civil administration. Their training has been subordination to and imitation of their masters. In the words of Lucian Pye, they have been indoctrinated "in the spirit of the clerk."[24] Their office lore is full of episodes of clerical feats in minor offices of the colonial days. They are skeptical of the ability of the younger generation of civil servants who join their ranks, insisting that "the new generation is no match to theirs."[25] In spite of their experience, they lack the will and the skill to meet their country's complex problems effectively. Conscious of their status, but incapable of meeting new situations, they become hedonistic in their time orientation and wasteful in their official conduct.

In their programs, this elite is highly *consumption-oriented.* They are fond of the official regalia, and are prone to ostentatious public expenditures on all fronts without specific rational priorities. This sets in motion a vicious circle: their high expenditure programs cause inflation, which in turn prompts consumption rather than saving throughout the society.

3. Developmentalist time is related to an *innovational* role pat-

---

24. Lucian W. Pye, *Politics, Personality, and Nation Building: Burma's Search for Identity* (New Haven, 1962), p. 216.
25. *Ibid.*, p. 227.

tern. The important quality of vision and forward-planning is
spread thinly among a relatively small number of politicians and
administrators sharing a reformist outlook. The innovational leaders are *entrepreneurial* in their leadership style. They are eager to
put ideas into practice. They are keenly interested in planning for
the future. For this future they advocate sacrifices and deferred
gratifications in the present. For this future they are also willing
to take risks, although they try to minimize them by careful
forward planning. With their outlook geared toward the future
and their resources marshaled and invested for long-run returns,
the entrepreneurial elites stress *production.*

In any regime, there are some, though few, politicians with a
relatively forward-thinking and task-oriented outlook. The relative weight of such an outlook within the regime depends on the
general makeup of the governing elite as well as the internal
power position of such elements. When such task-oriented elements are closely associated with (and perhaps overlap) the
effective leadership, a developmental thrust is obtained, whereas
when these task-oriented leaders are dissociated from the locus of
effective power or the "solidarity makers," a "breakdown of modernization" occurs.[26]

Task- or production-oriented politicians sometimes find their
most congenial allies among the younger civil servants, in whom
developmentalist time tends to be manifest. Gradually young
men with a new education and a new outlook, who have been
trained at universities both at home and abroad during the post-
colonial period, join the ranks of the new civil service. Some of
them move up the bureaucratic ladder fast through the channel
of competitive examination. Within the bureaucracy, a cadre of a
new type of administrator gradually takes shape, composed
chiefly of those who are relatively young, who are responsive to
modern ways, and who share a merit and reformist outlook.

As the ambitious young administrators struggle up the ladder
of bureaucracy, they come into proximity with the channels of
political decision-making, i.e., the cabinet and the legislature.

26. S. N. Eisenstadt, "Breakdowns of Modernization," in *Econ. Dev. and Cult.
Change,* XII (1964), 345–367, at 354.

This key location, coupled with the special resources they command in terms of information and new ideas, provides these reform-minded civil servants with opportunity for the role of policy counselor as well as that of program formulator.[27] Also, when the political decision-makers are interested in their service, these "specialists" can provide the expertise needed for programs of administrative reform. Of course, the presupposition is the existence of entrepreneurial elements among the political leaders genuinely committed to programs and reforms.

We have hinted that in the politico-administrative setting of a developing country the time orientation of the elite can rise diagonally (Chart I) from the *escapist,* through the *exploitationist,* to the *developmentalist* box with the implication that their program orientation can also develop from *law and order* through *consumption* toward *production.* But this is by no means an automatic trend, for as John A. Vieg rightly maintains, it is only possible depending on the availability of the "two sufficient conditions for progress," i.e., political leadership and administrative competence. In Vieg's words,

Given a favourable environment, meaning one in which the possibilities of deliberate and constructive change are taken for granted, the highest function of the politicians is to help the people dream great dreams and to decide, broadly speaking, what they want, when, where, and how. As for the administrators it is their role . . . first to advise the politicians regarding practical considerations so that popular expectations may be held within reason and then to "make the great dreams come true."[28]

Loci of Potential Development Entrepreneurs

We have so far confined the discussion of elites to political and administrative elites. In this section, we shall consider

27. See Fritz Morstein Marx, "The Higher Civil Service as an Action Group in Western Political Development," in Joseph LaPalombara, ed., *Bureaucracy and Political Development* (Princeton, 1963), pp. 90 ff. In my view, Morstein Marx's observations are equally pertinent to the new bureaucracies in developing countries.

28. *Op. cit.,* pp. 10–12.

three groups that are potential sources of "development entrepreneurs."[29] They are (1) the intellectuals, (2) the military, and (3) the businessmen.

The Intellectuals

We here use a narrow definition of intellectuals, the "core" intellectuals, i.e., scholars, authors, men of arts, and journalists.[30] The typical time orientation of the intellectuals is the utopian version of escapist time. Many of them are committed to modernization, but modernization at a great speed. They wish to bring the future immediately to the present.[31]

In spite of their utopian predilection—which disqualifies them for many roles—they have an important influence on the course of a nation's modernization. Modernization involves changing values, and in the task of changing values possessed by people, the intellectuals play a decisive role. The work of a nation's modernization would, therefore, be seriously hampered without adequate support from, and active participation by, the intellectuals.

A discussion of the intellectuals in a developmental setting would not be complete without consideration of the students from whose ranks the intellectuals rise and who themselves form part of the intellectual class in developing countries.[32] Above all, the students represent the younger generation, which combines

29. This term was suggested by Professor Weidner in one of the seminar sessions in which he served as a visiting consultant.

30. See Robert A. Scalapino, "Political Modernization and the Intellectual," in the *Report* of the International Seminar on the Problems of Modernization in Asia, Korea University, Seoul, June 28–July 7, 1965, pp. 502–509.

31. A recent empirical study of the values of Korean professors in conjunction with those of farmers and businessmen suggests the futuristic-escapist attitude of the intellectuals in Korea. Some pertinent points: among the three groups under survey, the professorial group is found most skeptical about the "self-conception of the Korean character" (the Korean character is bad because of poverty), and most pessimistic in terms of the "attitude toward success in society" (it is hard for a man to succeed in Korea even if he is able and works hard). See Sung-Chick Hong, "Values of Korean Farmers, Businessmen, and Professors," in the *Report* of the International Seminar on the Problems of Modernization in Asia, pp. 789–799, Tables 7 and 8.

32. Edward Shils, "The Intellectuals in the Political Development of the New States," in Kautsky, *op. cit.*, pp. 203–205. See also, William A. Douglas, "Korean Students and Politics," in *Asian Survey*, III (1963), 584–595. A similar study on the university students in India is provided in the chapter on "Students" in Myron Weiner, *The Politics of Scarcity* (Chicago, 1962), pp. 158–185.

idealism and creativity with rebellion. At this stage the impulses of self-assertion and the striving for individuality and creativity are at their height. Furthermore, youths have a special, more direct relation with the ultimate common values of the society than have adults: the youth is more strongly collectivity-oriented than the adult.[33] In short, students possess an explosive, utopian time. They are most eager to bring the future into the present at one stroke. But precisely because of this they are potentially creative, for as Gurvitch so revealingly suggests, the "explosive time" is the "time of creation," although it endures "for a very short, too short an instant."[34]

How can this potential source of creativity, i.e., the intellectuals and the students, be tapped for the cause of development? This question poses a great challenge to a modernizing leadership, but one for which there is no easy response.

The Military

In many developing countries, the military have emerged as a significant candidate group for modernizing roles. Many explanations are given in the recent literature on the causes of such military ascendancy.[35] In the main there are two lines of analysis and comment: first, the modernization of the military organization itself; second, the lag of civilian recognition of the military modernity as perceived by the military.

As Lucian Pye points out, nearly all of the new countries have taken the World War II type of army as their model. In so doing, they have undertaken to create a form of organization that is typical of and peculiar to the most highly industrialized civiliza-

33. S. N. Eisenstadt, *From Generation to Generation: Age Groups and Social Structure* (New York, 1956), pp. 269-323.

34. *Op. cit.,* p. 51. A philosopher's view of "the flash of creative intellect" in the student uprising in April, 1960, in Korea is provided in Chong-Hong Park, "Sasang kwa Haengdong [Ideas and Action]," *Sasangge Monthly* (Seoul), Jan., 1961, pp. 44-53.

35. Two excellent general accounts are: Lucian W. Pye, "Armies in the Process of Political Modernization," in John J. Johnson, ed., *The Role of the Military in Underdeveloped Countries* (Princeton, 1962), pp. 69-89; and a pamphlet by H. Daalder, *The Role of the Military in the Emerging Countries* (The Hague, 1962), pp. 12-17.

On Korea, see William A. Douglas, "The Current Status of Korean Society," in *Korean Affairs*, I (1962), 390-397, esp. 396.

tions yet known. As the armies of the new states have striven to approximate their industrial-based organization models, they have had to establish all manner of specialized skills and functions that are only remotely related to the command of violence. These skills include not only such military techniques as weapons use and tactics, but also such organizational and managerial techniques and concomitants as supply management, communications, intelligence, staff and command functions, and economic and manpower mobilization procedures. These lead on to such matters as the formulation of long-range programs and plans, national policies and strategies.[36]

But such modernization within the military establishment does not earn a ready recognition from the rest of the society. This is particularly the case within a culture where the traditional value scale has an unfavorable bias toward the military profession. In such a case tension arises, and this tension grows when the modernization in the military is not matched by parallel movement in other spheres. Moreover, since the military is one of the most effective channels for upward social mobility, young officers from lower social strata who move up to positions of greater power and responsibility via the army ladder may carry with them hostilities toward those with greater advantages and authority in civilian society. The tendency for the military elite to question whether the civilian elites achieved their stations by merit adds another conflict to civilian-military relations in most underdeveloped countries. In periods of acute social unrest, this conflict mounts. Some officers may see in the situation "civilian failure," and may decide to come to the fore of the polity in the form of overt action.

The military officer corps in developing countries is generally future-oriented. By nature of the military discipline, their time is never utopian. Thus it remains to range between the presumptive exploitationist and developmentalist. The exact nature of the time orientation of the military if and when they arrive at the center of the polity depends largely upon whether the thrust is

36. A feature story in the *Pacific Stars and Stripes* (Nov. 20, 1956) by David E. Halvorsen on "ROK National Defense College" is a good illustration of the depth of military training in Korea during the latter half of the 1950's.

steered by a clique imbued with a "fraternal time"[37] or whether it is based on the modernizing outlook of the officer corps at large. Too often, the former incidence prevails; a hasty time attitude is presented which, in Gurvitch's language, "does not find a passage towards the future and only projects the present towards it." Can the developmentalist time of the modernized military organization at large be effectively used for the cause of national development? This question also presents a challenge to a modernizing leadership.

The Businessmen

In a developing country, the merchant class should not be minimized as a source of industrial entrepreneurs.[38] If the state is not to be the universal entrepreneur, private entrepreneurs must be deliberately cultivated, and these are most likely to be drawn from among businessmen who have some capital and some managerial experience. But businessmen in developing countries are handicapped. Almost overnight, instead of operating a shop they find themselves running a modern factory; and since they have not had time to accumulate experience, this leads to inefficient use of the new facilities. Nor have they had opportunity to change their orientation from concentration on a quick profit to the development of a continuing organization concentrating on production.

In spite of their possible exploitationist attitude, it is primarily from among the businessmen that the modicum of investments and capital formation (even with public loans) develop. The act of investment looks forward to the future. As business is linked with technical patterns, procedures, and inventions, not to speak of the market, some innovational elements are inherent in the process.[39] Thus, although the businessmen do not automatically

37. See Gurvitch, *op. cit.*, p. 81. The "fraternal" characteristics of the junta leaders in Korea in the period 1961–63 are extensively analyzed by William A. Douglas in his article, "South Korea's Search for Leadership," *Pacific Affairs*, XXXVII (Spring, 1964), 20–36, esp. 27.

38. Clark Kerr *et al.*, *Industrialism and Industrial Man* (New York, 1960), pp. 34–37.

39. See Gurvitch, *op. cit.*, p. 82, for the time attitude of the "groupings of economic activity." Hong's survey, "Value of Korean Farmers, Businessmen, and Professors," bears out these pertinent characteristics of Korean businessmen: among the three groups under survey, the businessmen are least traditional

make an entrepreneurial class, through the discipline of the widening market, through their linkage with technological innovations, and through their contacts with innovating entrepreneurs in other spheres, they can become the source of an active entrepreneurial elite.[40]

We have suggested that *potential* "development entrepreneurs" exist not only among the task-oriented politicians and reform-minded administrators but also among the intellectuals, the military, and the businessmen. Chart IV is a recapitulation of the relative loci of the different groups on our schema of time orientations.

Chart IV. *Loci of Potential Development Entrepreneurs*

		negative	ambivalent	positive
TIME PERSPECTIVE	future	intellectuals →	military →	DEVELOPMENT ENTREPRENEURS
	present		politicians & administrators ↗	businessmen ↑
	past			charismatic political leaders ↑
		negative	ambivalent	positive
		ATTITUDE TOWARD CHANGE		

Development Entrepreneurs as Innovators

Underlying theorizing about potential development entrepreneurs are the assumptions that no group has a monolithic time

family-oriented, most positive toward money relative to status, most willing to take risk (prefer a son-in-law who is interested in enlarging wealth to another interested in maintaining it—the other two groups showed reverse preference), and most positive in their attitude toward success (a man can succeed in Korea if he is able and works hard). See "Values of Korean Farmers," Tables 1, 3, 4, 8.

40. David McClelland suggests, on the basis of a comparative survey of social class background of managers in Turkey, Mexico, Italy, the United States, and Poland, that "the best place to recruit business managers is from the middle classes because they are more apt to have higher *n* achievement from that background than if they come from a lower or an upper class background." See *The Achieving Society* (Princeton, 1961), p. 279.

orientation; and that developmentalist time, which is innovational and entrepreneurial, is not a fixed possession of some special individuals or groups but is capable of being developed out of related and adjacent time orientations depending on the creation of proper conditions. For, as H. G. Barnett theorizes, "every individual is basically innovative."[41] Carl R. Rogers elaborates this theory further in these words:

> The mainspring of creativity appears to be the same tendency . . . as the curative force in psychotherapy—man's tendency to actualize himself, to become his potentialities. By this I mean the directional trend which is evident in all organic and human life—the urge to expand, extend, develop, mature—the tendency to express and activate all the capacities of the organism, to the extent that such activation enhances the organism or the self . . . it exists in every individual and awaits only the proper conditions to be released and expressed. . . .[42]

It is precisely the creation of such conditions for the release and expression of human creativity that is the supreme task of leadership. But before we enter a discussion of leadership, a discussion of the linkage between developmentalist time and innovation is in order.

Hagen differentiates two steps in the process of innovation: (1) arriving at a new mental conception, and (2) converting it into action or into material form. He equates creativity with the first and entrepreneurship or "innovation" in the narrow sense with the second step.[43] Other analysts of the diffusion of innovation usually differentiate three functions or roles: the "innovators," the "advocates," and the "adopters" of innovation.[44] We shall identify the "innovators," or more exactly the "original innovators," with Hagen's first step, i.e., creativity, and the "advocates" and the "initial adopters" with his second step, i.e., entrepreneurship. It will be noted that developmentalist time corresponds specifically to the "advocates" in the task of diffusion of innovations.

41. *Innovation: The Basis of Cultural Change* (New York, 1953), p. 19.
42. "Toward a Theory of Creativity," in Harold H. Anderson, ed., *Creativity and Its Cultivation* (New York, 1959), p. 72.
43. Hagen, *op. cit.*, pp. 86–87.
44. Barnett, *op. cit.*; E. M. Rogers, *Diffusion of Innovations* (New York, 1962); and LaPiere, *op. cit.*, chaps. iv–vi.

The "original innovators" create for the sheer joy of creating something new. They are "deviant," "non-conformist," "hyper-motivated," "egocentric," and "socially insensitive." They are not particularly susceptible to incentives, except that the society must be sufficiently flexible for the emergence of their creative talents. They are there to be discovered. The requisite strategy with regard to the creative elements in the society is simply to recognize them and protect them, so that the release and expression of their creative energies can be facilitated. Among the potential development entrepreneurs, individuals with explosive time orientation, namely the intellectuals, fall within this category.

A pertinent theory on the formation of innovation is that of "innovating enclaves."[45] These enclaves may be found in different spheres and take various forms. In developing societies, they may be some universities, research institutions in some banks, particular government bureaus, some special military educational units, some religious sects, etc. Often some of the members of these enclaves possess not only the quality of original innovators but that of the advocates as well. A society that takes care to permit an autonomous growth of such enclaves takes an important step ahead on the road to modernization.

The advocates are more amenable to incentives: they are more often motivated by prestige and wealth—hence their susceptibility to positive recruitment. As noted, some members of the innovating enclaves are either at once innovative and advocative or more advocative than innovative. At any rate, some of them with an organizational sense tend to come into contact with others of like minds and a process of cross-fertilization begins. Some finally come out of the enclaves to play more active roles, sometimes in co-operative but often in competing roles among themselves. Once out of the enclaves they engage themselves, whether within the ruling elite strictly speaking or among the competing elite groups, in "advocacy," in trying to put into practice the new ideas

45. S. N. Eisenstadt, "Social Change, Differentiation and Evolution," *Am. Soc. Rev.*, XXIX (1964), 375–386.

developed in the enclaves. They cease to be mere visionaries: they become "development entrepreneurs."

As an increasing number of development entrepreneurs emanate from the innovating enclaves, there emerge growth centers or leading sectors of entrepreneurial energies. In this process, the entrepreneurs often develop their own "protestant ethic." This process is aptly described by Albert Hirschman:

> . . . those who have been caught by progress . . . will easily convince themselves, and attempt to convince others, that their accomplishments are primarily owed to their superior moral qualities and conduct. It is precisely this self-righteousness that will tend to produce its own evidence: once these groups have spread the word that their success was due to hard work and virtuous living, they must willy-nilly live up to their own story, or at the least will make their children do so. In other words, there is reason to think that the "protestant ethic," instead of being the prime mover, is often implanted *ex post* as though to sanctify and consolidate whatever accumulation of economic power and wealth has been achieved. To the extent that this happens, a climate particularly favourable to further growth will actually come into existence in the sectors and regions that have pulled ahead. . . .[46]

What is the requisite strategy for insuring the emergence of these potential development entrepreneurs from the innovating enclaves and the growth centers? Rostow cites two conditions besides the internalized value system: first, "the new elite must feel itself denied the conventional routes to prestige and power by the traditional less acquisitive society of which it is a part"; second, "the traditional society must be sufficiently flexible (or weak) to permit its members to seek material advance (or political power) as a route upwards alternative to conformity."[47] In short, a strategy must insure that social mobility of this type exists. It must also insure the possibility that a new entrepreneurial elite can rise from the middle or lower-middle strata of the society, which are, as McClelland suggests, the prime source of potential entrepreneurial talents.[48]

46. *The Strategy of Economic Development* (New Haven, 1958), pp. 185–186.
47. W. W. Rostow, *The Stages of Economic Growth* (Cambridge, 1960), p. 51.
48. *Op. cit.*, pp. 256, 280.

In this connection, Eisenstadt's idea of "free-floating resources" is particularly relevant.[49] For the continuing growth of a political system, he argues, the political sphere has to create or facilitate the conditions necessary for the constant development of various types of free-floating resources. This means that various strata and groups in various fields—economic, social, and cultural—must be permitted some measure of autonomous activity. Obviously this implies tolerance in the political sphere, particularly on the part of the ruling elite. The antithesis of this is "monolithic aspirations," i.e., attempts to direct and control all social developments and all avenues of social and occupational mobility within the ruling political group and to monopolize all positions of power and allocation of prestige. Eisenstadt suggests that, under the latter circumstance, a "breakdown of modernization" sets in.[50]

In our schematic representation of time orientations, *potential* advocates are adjacent to the developmentalist box: included are politicians and civil servants, the military, and the businessmen. Enterprising intellectuals also are in the adjacent area. The task set is to identify and promote the entrepreneurial elements in these several categories. Promotion involves not only recruitment into the ruling elite but also permitting some scope of autonomous activity. Obviously this requires a high degree of imagination, tolerance and even risk-taking on the part of the political leadership. But should the political leadership be spared the need to possess one of the fundamental qualities of development entrepreneurship, namely, risk-taking?

Innovations become operative only when they are adopted. According to Everett Rogers, the adoption process has the following five stages: (1) awareness, (2) interest, (3) evaluation, (4) trial, and (5) adoption.[51] The crucial stage appears to be the evaluation stage, in which the individual mentally applies the innovation to his present and anticipated future situation, and then decides whether or not to try it—a "mental trial." The

49. S. N. Eisenstadt, *Political Systems of Empires* (London, 1963), chap. xii, esp. pp. 312–316.
50. *Ibid.*, pp. 360–361.
51. *Diffusion of Innovations* (New York, 1962), pp. 81–86.

adoption of innovation is perceived by the individual as a risk. For this reason a reinforcement effect is needed at this stage to convince the individual that his thinking is on the right path. Information and advice from others is likely to be sought at this point, and this process should be facilitated.

In this connection, the nature of "initial adopters" may be crucial for the successful widespread adoption of an innovation. Ideally, adoption should be by those in established positions of authority in the area of life that is affected by the innovation. Examples of such "prestigious adopters" are highly desirable and effective. The term "prestigious adopters" implies a popular recognition of some established status which in turn stems from memory of some past merit or performance; therefore, we get the reassuring effect upon adoption, which involves the "fear of the unfamiliar." In this sense, "initial adopters" are also development entrepreneurs.

Where are such "initial adopters" to be found? One potential source is the charismatic nationalist leaders who can bring forward the inheritance of the past for constructive use in the future. This is an area where the bottom right box in our time schema *can* have meaning. The attitude of inheriting the past as a resource is a positive one. Modernizing leadership should actively cultivate potential "initial adopters" in this category in order to facilitate diffusion of innovations. Modernization will gain momentum when the modernizing elite can secure among their ranks a significant number of such "initial adopters." Chart V is a recapitulation of the relative incidence of "original innovators," "advocates," and "initial adopters" in our time schema.

Conclusion: Integration of Time Orientations as the Function of Leadership

Developmentalist time is a dynamic forward-looking orientation. Potentially it is in every man, although in the milieu of rapid environmental change the individual is more apt to be inclined in an escapist or exploitationist direction. Inasmuch as the germ of developmentalist time resides in every individual, and potential "development entrepreneurs" can be located in different groups whose time orientations are related and adjacent to developmentalist time, individuals and groups possessing a proper time orientation can be identified and marshaled. The active locating and promoting of these "development entrepreneurs" is pre-eminently the function of political leadership.

Chart V. *Incidence of Innovators, Advocates, and Adopters*

TIME PERSPECTIVE		negative	ambivalent	positive
	future	original innovators →	potential advocates →	advocates
	present		potential advocates	↑ potential advocates
	past			↑ initial adopters
		negative	ambivalent	positive
		ATTITUDE TOWARD CHANGE		

This presupposes, first of all, the presence or emergence of a leadership that undertakes such task. Edward Shils tersely points out, "No new state will modernize itself in the present century without an elite with force of character and intelligence. No new state can modernize itself and remain or become liberal and democratic without an elite of force of character, intelligence, and high moral qualities."[52] The function of political leadership lies in channeling the nation's talents, energies, and resources into the task of modernization, with a view to securing the process and shortening the time span of transition to modern status.

In the temporal context, channeling resources means channeling various time orientations *toward developmentalist time*. This is the central task of leadership in development administration. This task has three aspects.

First, it is imperative that the political leadership itself possess

---

52. *Political Development in the New States* (The Hague, 1962), p. 86.

a developmentalist attitude. A developmentalist leadership must steer clear of both utopian and exploitationist time orientations. Utopianism hopes to avoid hard choices by a flight into futuristic visions, whereas exploitationism pursues short-run expediencies at the expense of principle and with inadequate consideration of the ultimate consequences. The former begets wishful thinking, whereas the latter breeds drift and irresponsibility. Leadership must be reliable and responsible.

Responsibility consists in part in giving a sense of direction, pace, and sequence.[53] This involves an integration of ideas and programs. In operational terms, this requires that the leadership visualize both the agenda and stages of national development.

"Agenda" implies a list of sub-goals which will be instrumental in the realization of the ultimate goal of national development. Current literature on nation building and modernization highlights the following items: (1) securing domestic law and order and international position; (2) mobilizing and/or reconciling various political forces for modernization; (3) creating new values and building institutions; (4) accumulating capital, both human and physical, for economic development; and (5) securing an efficient administrative system for program implementation in order to obtain a sustained growth.[54]

To be operational, the agenda must be organized into sequence, staged and phased. Three stages of development administration suggested by Weidner provide at least a rough schema: (1) take-over, (2) experimental, and (3) program control.[55]

Obviously the law and order item precedes other agenda items,

---

53. For discussion of sequence and synchronization, see Pitirim A. Sorokin, *Sociocultural Causality, Space, Time* (Durham, N.C., 1943), pp. 172–173; Wilbert E. Moore, *Man, Time, and Society* (New York, 1963), pp. 45–50. Also, Mary Parker Follett's concept of understanding "the moment of passing" may be equated with the concept of sequence. See Henry C. Metcalf and L. Urwick, eds., *Dynamic Administration: The Collected Papers of Mary Parker Follett* (New York, 1940), p. 263.

54. See Milton J. Esman, "The Politics of Development Administration," in J. D. Montgomery and W. J. Siffin, eds., *Approaches to Development* (New York, 1966), pp. 59–112. See also, Howard Wriggins, "Foreign Assistance and Political Development," in *Development of the Emerging Countries: An Agenda for Research* (Washington, D.C., 1962), pp. 181–214, esp. 185–209.

55. Edward W. Weidner, *Technical Assistance in Public Administration Overseas: The Case for Development Administration* (Chicago, 1964), pp. 233–239.

for only in an environment of relative stability can development begin. But of necessity political modernization, sociocultural transformation, and capital formation have to progress simultaneously in newly developing countries; however, this may complicate the problem of maintaining law and order.

Too often economic development strategies assume autonomy of the economic sphere and disregard the need for prior or parallel developments in the political and social spheres. This may occur because of a lack of historical understanding: in countries in which modernization took place in earlier centuries, social and political developments preceded the industrial revolution. But for the presently developing countries, what is necessary is synchronization of development efforts in all three spheres, given the relative urgency and wider exposure to the modern world.[56]

Second, the function of channeling talents and resources requires the leadership to search for "development entrepreneurs" from among the potential sources. This implies seeing men in a different light, seeing them in their potentialities, then recruiting and promoting the innovational talents for entrepreneurial roles. This is a process of integrating men and ideas. It is itself a creative role.

Creative leadership is able to release energy and to elicit sacrifices for a common purpose. In this regard, modernizing leadership must have a concern for conflict resolution. It must be able to release conflicting energies and integrate them.[57] This requires imbuing with a common purpose. It requires a "broadening of the

56. A classic example of synchronized policy vision in the Korean context is "kyongyon Honch'aek" (Privy Policy Recommendation) in 1583 by Yi Yulgok, the celebrated scholar-official of Yi Dynasty. The three-point policy recommendation made nine years before the Hideyoshi Invasion of A.D. 1592 included: a Decade of Saving; a Decade of Education; and a Decade of Defense Build-up. Unfortunately, this recommendation was not adopted. For detail see Kyong-tak Kim, *Yulgok ui Yongu [Study of Yulgok]* (Seoul, 1960), pp. 121–124.

An excellent current discussion of the need for "political and social infrastructures" for economic development is an article by Warren F. Ilchman and R. C. Bhargava, "Balanced Thought and Economic Growth," in *Econ. Dev. and Cult. Change,* XXIV (1965), 385–399.

57. Brooks Adams was a forerunner in thinking along this line when he remarked: "Administration is the capacity of coordinating many, and often conflicting, social energies. . . ." See *The Theory of Social Revolutions* (New York, 1914), p. 207.

framework," by which the conflicting parties become involved in issues other than the current ones which engender conflict. To do this is a challenge to creativity, involving the transformation of men and groups into "participants" who have a certain stamp, sensitivity, and commitment.

This is, broadly and ultimately, an educational process. To build up national purpose, the political leadership must not only dream a great dream but also infuse day-to-day behavior with long-run meaning and purpose. It does this in significant part by perceiving and setting examples of developmentalist thought and role patterns and finding modes of communication that will inculcate such thoughts and patterns. In this way, the leadership will be able to elicit sacrifices and secure deferred gratification among the people, which will help create a better future for the nation.

Finally, political leadership must, in addition to possessing a developmentalist time orientation and locating and promoting development entrepreneurs, create conditions under which developmentalist time or development entrepreneurship can germinate and thrive. It must create a flexible and secure climate so that free-floating resources can be created and accumulated. Basic to such a climate is *trust*. And in operational terms, trust is the outcome of security, solidarity, and legitimacy. Prospective adopters of innovation must feel secure when their consent is sought to new directions. And for the leadership to inspire trust among the followers, it must have its foundation upon legitimacy and morality. This is the foundation for creating conditions that will make possible in the future what is excluded in the present. As Chester Barnard remarked nearly a generation ago,

Morality . . . is deeply rooted in the past, it faces toward the endless future . . . the quality of leadership, the persistence of its influence, the durability of its related organizations, the power of the coordination it incites, all express the height of moral aspirations, the breadth of moral foundations.[58]

58. Chester I. Barnard, *The Functions of the Executive* (Cambridge, Mass., 1938), p. 284.

For any country, and especially for a developing country, the crucial question is this: is a leadership possible that can integrate for the task of national development both "a long expectation of the future" and "a long memory of the past," as was meditated by St. Augustine?

Chapter 7

Leadership, Organizations, and Time

Frank P. Sherwood

Time was, is past; thou canst not it recall;
Time is, thou hast, employ the portion small;
Time future, is not, and may never be;
Time present is the only time for thee.

Anonymous

The relationship of time and leadership in complex organizations has received little scholarly attention. It would seem to be deserving of more. Such a relationship becomes highly relevant as societies adopt, or seek to adopt, modernizing value systems.

Time then assumes symbolic significance as a scarce resource, and the social system itself is regarded as purposive. In these circumstances the leader, occupying a position of formal authority, is held accountable for accomplishment in time by the organization. Thus the introduction of optimizing values broadly recasts the nature of the leadership function. In an earlier period the leader could devote himself to position maintenance; his concern was to strengthen such power relations as would secure the continuation of the rewards of status. As modernizing values are infused into a social system, however, the maintenance of position—though still a prime goal—cannot be so narrowly and directly pursued. For position maintenance becomes dependent, in part, on the extent to which the leader is perceived as facilitating the movement of the collectivity toward whatever expectation levels are widely shared. In short, the modernizing leader has to work harder, and he depends more on the whole social system to assure his continuation in power.

Time is now something that must be "used" by a leader, and the limitations of time have become more pressing. Even the most physically durable people have need for sleep and relaxation; and even if they did not, time would still be finite. Since the coin of time no longer floods the market place, its value rises. The leader now faces many time choices: how much of his time income to allocate to his organizational, public role; how to choose among alternative uses, and on what bases; and how to develop a time perspective that will maximize present gratification without materially harming future prospects.[1]

Changing time perspectives and referents of leaders would seem to have particular importance to the study of comparative administration and development administration.[2] Certainly many of the failures in inducing change in developing countries have been laid to faulty "leadership." Though in most instances it is impossible to determine whether the accusation is directed toward a person or a system, it is, nevertheless, a fact that leadership is perceived as a major problem in developmental efforts and that time perceptions, orientations, and uses are deeply involved. Thus, to the extent that any study can help shed light on leadership and time in highly complex, managed change processes, the effort would seem worthwhile.

The Leadership Concept

Let us first be specific about leadership. My interest is in a definite category of leaders: those who occupy formal positions in

1. David C. McClelland, *The Achieving Society* (Princeton, 1961), develops rather substantial evidence that (*a*) concern about time is related to high achievement motivation and (*b*) high *n* achievement is an essential ingredient of economic growth and development. See particularly pp. 324 ff.

2. Sune Carlson, whose study of time as used by Swedish executives was a pioneering venture, has argued the value of comparative study. He wrote, "While studying the work of the chief executives of 'Au Printemps' in Paris I had the opportunity of observing executive behavior in a different environment, and this experience indicates that comparative research on this point may be fruitful" (*Executive Behavior* [Stockholm, 1951], p. 117). "Time" may prove to have considerable importance as a data-ordering and retrieval factor.

complex organizations. Such a specification permits us to avoid some of the system variables that may condition the behavior of a Ghandi in pre-independence India as opposed to a Nehru as Prime Minister and head of a government. In the latter case, Nehru occupied a position at the top of a large, formal hierarchy. His position was organizationally, rather than individually, created; and although other occupants might have perceived the behavioral requirements of that position in different ways, all would have seen it as a formal leadership position in a particular organization.

Our point is that a study of the behavior of actors in leadership roles in formal organizations says more about the system than it does about the individuals—a point well known in social psychology, but nevertheless one worth emphasizing. My argument is that the conceptual separation of the role and the actor only is meaningful in the specific, individual case. Rather rapidly, when we study several leaders in a formal system, individual personality differences cancel themselves out; and the significant data remaining are specifications of system imperatives with regard to the position occupied.

In their major studies of leadership, Shartle and Stogdill operated from the general premises suggested here. In pursuing their investigations of leadership processes, they studied the behavior of the actors in formal systems. A leader was formally defined, ". . . as a person who occupies a position of high level responsibility." They also pointed out that although they did not expect all leaders to act alike, ". . . such differences can be classified and analyzed."[3]

In short, the concern here is with the nomothetic, rather than the idiographic; the washing out of individual differences is, we believe, in accord with the goals of comparative study. But there is a tendency to dwell upon the idiosyncratic in leadership behavior. We are greatly impressed by the entrepreneurs who buck the system, by the Churchills and De Gaulles who breathe new

3. Ralph M. Stogdill, Robert J. Wherry, and William E. Jaynes, "A Factorial Study of Administrative Performance," in Stogdill *et al.*, *Patterns of Administrative Performance* (Columbus, Ohio, 1956), pp. 40–41.

meaning into old enterprises (or old meaning into new enterprises), and by the martyrs. All cultures need their heroes (even their anti-heroes). Nevertheless, the functioning of a society in total is less the work of the hero than of the unsung maker and influencer of small events. Thus, it is the way the culturally bound and organizationally positioned leader perceives his situation and orients his behavior that should command our chief research attention. This is particularly true in development administration. It is all very well to hope that a hero will miraculously appear to induce changes sought; but we hedge our bets better when we view leadership as a non-heroic social process which can never be far removed from its moorings.

Of Time and Leadership

When disenchantment with trait studies of leadership developed, analysis turned to power distribution. Leadership was seen as a social process in which there was a need for initiating, directing, and motivating; the focus changed from the individual to the system, or at least to the individual in and interacting *with* the system.

Undoubtedly the best known early studies of power distribution were the efforts inspired by Lewin at the University of Iowa, as a result of which authoritarian, democratic, and laissez faire leadership became a standard part of our social science fare. Since that time much of the work of Likert, McGregor, Thelen, Maier, and others has been concerned with the consequences of various forms of power distribution. Alex Bavelas has perhaps epitomized the power-distribution approach by pointing out that the critical question is not "Who is the leader?" but "How are the leadership functions distributed in this organization?" He continues,

The way in which a management distributes the responsibility for making the set of choices it has thus claimed to itself defines its structure. What organizational leadership is and what kinds of acts it constitutes are questions that can be answered only within this framework of scope and structure. In these terms leadership consists of the continuous choice-making process that permits the organization as a whole to proceed toward its objectives despite all sorts of internal and external perturbations.[4]

Bavelas's basic point that leadership involves power and influence in a context hardly seems arguable. But further relevant questions remain. Once we know *who* exercises power, even how much of what kinds of power, we need to know what leaders do to maintain and amplify their power.

Of course, this is not a new question. It is the subject of a mass of administrative literature, most of it speculative or anecdotal. Chester Barnard argued somewhat ambiguously that the "essential executive functions" are "first, to provide the system of communication; second, to promote the securing of essential efforts; and, third, to formulate and define purpose."[5] The emphasis is on co-operative rather than individual effort. Thus, in the discussion of purpose formulation Barnard comments, "It is more apparent here than with other executive functions that it is an entire executive organization that formulates, redefines, breaks into details, and decides on the innumerable simultaneous and progressive actions that are the stream of syntheses constituting purpose or action."[6]

As this citation from Barnard indicates, even the seminal writers have left us with a good deal of uncertainty as to what the individual leader really does in this intensely human process. It is in this context that the appeal of time studies is particularly great. For time not only provides a useful reference point for defining activity, it also helps to measure emphasis. Ideally, the identification of a successful leader and the inventorying of his use of time should put us well on the way toward a communicable body of knowledge about the nature of good or effective executive behavior. In practice, however, the complications have been far greater than this simplistic paradigm would suggest. All leadership study has been plagued by inability to establish cri-

4. "Leadership: Man and Function," *Adm. Sci. Quart.*, IV (March, 1960), 491–498, 496. First sentence of quote italicized by Bavelas.
5. *The Functions of the Executive* (Cambridge, Mass., 1947), p. 217.
6. *Ibid.*, p. 231.

teria of success or non-success. The development of prescriptive statements has consistently foundered on this problem.

But even a simpler, descriptive model has posed difficulties. If we study use of time, its use must be charged against one or more activities. What are they to be? And how does their choice and definition affect the conclusions one reaches about behavior? Of course, it is possible to secure a mass of data about time expended in such work processes as telephoning and in certain subject matter considerations such as personnel. These, however, have only a limited meaning unless they are placed in a broader conceptual scheme.

It is clear, too, that most of putatively descriptive efforts have not been descriptive alone. There has been the implication that executives ought to look at themselves because they are doing things they should not be doing and not doing things they should be doing. This prescriptive aspect was typically expressed by Comstock Glaser in describing the purpose of a time-use analysis in a government agency in which there had apparently been a substantial increase of workload. "There had been no elaboration of the organization structure nor extensive delegation of administrative authority. The result was that the major executives became bogged down with routine and were unable to give time to constructive planning and broad observation."[7] Note particularly the approving adjectives assigned to planning and observation.

One of the major efforts to employ time-use analysis for empirical research purposes was in the leadership studies conducted by Shartle and Stogdill at Ohio State University. Various research strategies were employed, but one of the major ones was an executive activity analysis. Shartle reports: "Executives in business and military organizations were studied in terms of the activities they performed. *Work patterns* were developed and given statistical analysis to determine various types of work performance. The research was started by using job analysis; executives were questioned and observed to determine *what* they did."[8] The basic approach was to ask the various leaders what per

7. *Administrative Procedure* (Washington, 1947), p. 32.
8. Carroll L. Shartle, *Executive Performance and Leadership* (Englewood Cliffs, N.J., 1956), p. 82.

cent of time they spent on activities in three broad categories: (*a*) work with other people; (*b*) individual effort; and (*c*) major responsibilities. Category *c* was apparently exclusive of the other two and involved delineation of separate management processes, such as planning, co-ordination, evaluation, inspection, and so forth. Shartle argued that the fourteen processes found to constitute category *c* were empirically derived and represented some departure from traditional theory of the executive activity. He pointed out, for example, that ". . . investigation and research are not often thought of as executive functions."[9]

The basic question asked in many of the Ohio State studies is whether the work activity of a leader, measured in terms of time use, is significantly influenced by a variety of situational variables of a positional, organizational, or interactive character. Conducted over a ten-year period (from 1946 to 1956), the Ohio State effort certainly has made a contribution to our knowledge of leadership.[10] Yet, although one can be complimentary of the over-all contribution, it is clear that these studies have not dealt successfully with two major problems: (*a*) the less obvious (e.g., cultural) factors that influence executive time strategies; and (*b*) the development of a broad (i.e., comparative) framework within which the various executive functions might be timed and classified. Perhaps this was too much to expect. What the Ohio State studies do show is that executive activities vary far more intra-organizationally than extra-organizationally. Within the organization, the level of the leader and the nature of the work flow around him have a rather clear effect on his behavior. Further, the differences between jobs were shown to be greater than those between organizations; specifically, differences within Navy units were shown to be greater than the differences between Navy and industrial organizations.

Conceptually, the best executive time study to date is that of Swedish businessmen, by Sune Carlson.[11] This study, which was

9. *Ibid.*, p. 84–85.
10. See as examples of research reports in which the analysis of time is particularly utilized: Stogdill *et al., op. cit.*, and Stogdill, Ellis L. Scott, and William E. Jaynes, *Leadership and Role Expectations*, Research Monograph No. 86 (Columbus, Ohio, 1956), p. 186.
11. *Op. cit.*

published in 1951 and which has been widely quoted in the literature of management as the authoritative statement on executive use of time, owes an intellectual debt to Chester Barnard and Harold Lasswell. Barnard provided a conceptual base by suggesting the executive's pivotal function as communicator; and Lasswell indicated the utility of contact analysis as a means of understanding executive communications.[12] Carlson himself was very reserved with regard to the significance of his research, and he went to great pains to point out that he had raised more questions than he had answered. There was need, he said, for behavioral norms against which executives might compare themselves. Since he had no such standards, Carlson contented himself with traditional time-saving, i.e., efficiency considerations; and, as a result, this is probably the most disappointing part of his effort. Executives *are* different from bricklayers. The exercise of influence cannot easily be subjected to "one best way" efficiency tests.

The Ohio State and Carlson studies appear to be the only two research enterprises that have dealt seriously with executive time analysis, and it is clear that these ventures thus far have not set off any explosion of knowledge about the leader and his use of time. The category problem remains the single most major constraint on such efforts; and when one introduces Carlson's concerns about norms, the difficulty mounts.

Time as a Factor in Administrative Reform: An Empirical Analysis

Since the Seminar in 1965, I have been involved in a modest effort to develop more empirical data on time as a factor in the administrative process. In this connection two doctoral dissertations have been produced with a major emphasis on temporal dimensions; and a Research and Development laboratory has been the object of personal inquiry as a future-oriented, specialized society.

12. Harold Lasswell, *The Analysis of Political Behavior* (New York, 1949), pp. 279 ff.

One of the dissertations, authored by Kleber Nascimento, concerned the strategy of administrative reform in Brazil. Pointing out that governmental reform efforts had been virtually continuous since Getulio Vargas came to power in 1930, Nascimento raised the basic question why the grand plans that have been projected have had relatively little effect on system behavior.[13] His hypothesis was that the plans and attempts to implement them had taken relatively little account of Brazilian behavior patterns. To test the validity of his hypothesis, Nascimento secured data on two facets of Brazilian and American administrative behavior: (*a*) time—its value and usage; and (*b*) authority. He found substantial differences in the two cultures, thereby suggesting the necessity to modify reform strategies in accord with each situation.

Briefly, Nascimento argued that administrative reform in Brazil had been abstracted from the culture. It was instrumental in the sense that Weberian bureaucracy was seen as a value-neutral vehicle, as easily implanted in the South American society as in pre-World War I Germany. It was assumed, for example, that there were no blocks to a high synchronization of activity, to the use of time for work-related activity, and to an emphasis on rapid (expedient) administrative action. This approach, Nascimento suggested, embraced three basic elements of strategy: (*a*) *Change Scope*: It was "wholistic" in the sense that the strategy envisaged change in the totality of the government and had major implications for co-ordination and scheduling. (*b*) *Language Style*: Its verbal symbolism was prescriptive, in the assumption that the basic problem was to tell people how to readjust their behavior. (*c*) *Obstacle Mapping*: Its concern was with cognitive impediments, in the anticipation that the membership of the bureaucracy shared the same definitions of rationality and simply had to be made to understand the reasons for the changes.

Over-all, the emphasis in the reform efforts was placed on formal processes, particularly on organization structure. In con-

13. Kleber Tatinge do Nascimento, "Change Strategy and Client System: Administrative Reform in Brazil" (doctoral dissertation, University of Southern California, 1966), 446 pp.

trast, Nascimento saw administration as largely a "behavioral event" which could not be taken from its societal context. He sought, therefore, to demonstrate how the "behavioral profile" of the Brazilian executive differed from Weberian-dictated assumptions about the bureaucrat. Unable to develop data on all dimensions of such a profile, he settled on the temporal factor as illustrative, along with authority behavior and attitudes.

A questionnaire was developed and administered to a population of 115 Brazilian and 137 American public executives. In each case, the respondents must be regarded as a population, not a sample, inasmuch as it was economically impossible to provide for the randomness required to speak with authority about each of the two societies. Nevertheless, the size of each respondent population was appreciable, all levels of government were represented in both countries, and all respondents held responsible positions in government. Some bias might have been introduced by the administration of the questionnaires at training sessions in both countries.

It should be noted that Nascimento's assumption was that instrumental strategies of administrative reform *had* worked in the United States, which is certainly open to some question. If we accept this premise, however, the point and promise of the comparative inquiry become evident: Brazilian similarity with the American behavior profile would suggest the utility of common strategies; differences in the behavior profile would seem to demand variant strategies.

The message from the data seems clear. There *are* major differences in the way time was perceived by the executives of the two cultures. On virtually every dimension, Nascimento found statistically significant differences between the Brazilian and American responses.

In his analysis he relied heavily on the conceptual scheme developed by Moore.[14] His categories of analysis were: (*a*) Rate—which obviously refers to frequency but has other implications as well. The perceived pace of progress, for example, suggests an environment of change; and rapid change tends to accentuate the

14. Wilbert E. Moore, *Man, Time, and Society* (New York, 1963).

market value of time. (*b*) Synchronization—which relates primarily to the co-ordinated timing of interrelated events. The industrialized society, with its real and symbolic production lines, is typified by high synchronization. The greater the synchronization, the more precise time units tend to become. (In his unindustrialized country, one student has reported, there are only three daytime units: morning, afternoon, and evening; and appointments are made according to these time units.) Put another way, the more important a minute becomes, the greater the value a society places on synchronization. (*c*) Sequence—which involves not only the order in which time is applied to various tasks but also relates to the amount of time given to them. Thus, it is possible to develop insight on the operating values of the executive by looking at his time allocations.

Rate

For the purposes of the Nascimento analysis, rate was seen as largely a perceptual question. That is, a feeling of urgency about the work situation was taken as indicative of activism and a change orientation. David McClelland's conclusion that the perception of time as a scarce resource correlates with high achievement motivation was also viewed as a dimension of rate.[15] Two questions were asked, and both revealed statistical significance at the 1 per cent level, according to the Chi Square test. Asked how frequently they felt hurried or pressed on their government job, 80 per cent of the American respondents placed themselves on the upper half of a frequency continuum, whereas only 47 per cent of the Brazilians did. A second question solicited an impression of the extent to which government employees sought to accomplish as much as possible in their available work time. In this case, the differences were even sharper, with 72 per cent of the American respondents rating the work pace on the upper half of the time maximizing scale and only 16 per cent of the Brazilians doing so.

The importance of data of these kinds in fashioning a change

15. *Op. cit.*, pp. 324 ff.

strategy seems considerable. As Moore has noted, "where change is more valued than permanence, rate becomes instrumental in heightening the concern about time as a scarce resource."[16] The reverse is very likely true: Where time is not regarded as scarce, it is probable that permanence is valued more than change. Brazil's bureaucracy, with apparently little concern for time as a scarce resource, neither seems ripe for change nor congruent with a basic assumption of the "instrumental model" used by Nascimento.

Synchronization

In his analysis of the experience of administrative reform, Nascimento also laid great emphasis on the importance of synchronization. Centralization, for example, depends heavily on scheduling capacity. During the Vargas period, a major effort was made to direct reform through a central department of general administration (DASP). Among other difficulties, the department foundered because of synchronization problems, as Nascimento points out:

The temporal requirements that resulted from the centralization approach of the reforms were made much more compulsive because of another characteristic of the change strategy that has prevailed in the Brazilian experience, namely, wholism. Since the reformers were only a handful of experts in administration, a small elite, and since the reforms involved the whole bureaucracy, it became impossible to have delegates of the central agency, with a common technical background and value orientations, perform the role of change agents in the field. As pointed out before, the forces of change never came to form a constellation within the context of the Brazilian bureaucracy; rather they gravitated in, and around, one solitary star, the DASP. This increased the dependency of the central agency not only on the scheduling ability and prompt action of the field agencies, but equally on the prevalence of an organizational, rather than personal, criterion of priority in the individuals' allocation of their working hours.[17]

Levels of synchronization in the two cultures were probed primarily in terms of the making and keeping of office appoint-

16. *Op. cit.*, p. 50.   17. *Op. cit.*, p. 357.

ments. It was hypothesized that synchronization is advanced by an orderly workday, in which most appointments are made in advance and proceed on schedule. The value placed on synchronization was to be identified by the extent of concern over disruption in this process, both in terms of unanticipated contacts and in terms of failure to keep on schedule.

One surprise was that the American public executive is significantly more apt to receive a person without a prior appointment than his Brazilian counterpart. Perhaps as a result, the Brazilian sees his workday as more orderly and predictable; indeed, 20 per cent of the Brazilians said their workday "always" went according to scheduling. None of the Americans felt able to say that.

In retrospect it was probably naive to assume that such a question would yield very useful information. (One can imagine a bureaucrat sitting in his office living a completely orderly life and having no unscheduled visitors, as the city burns around him.) Nascimento did find an acute "position-orientedness" in the Brazilian system that, rather than promoting the rational purposes of Weberian bureaucracy, utilized status as a means of personal gratification.

Further, there can be differing interpretations of an orderly workday; at least in part, the scale of the time units reflects such perceptions. If the morning is seen as one time unit, it is quite easy to stay on schedule. But, say, in the world of television, where one minute is a big and highly valued time unit, synchronization demands are infinitely intensified. Therefore, Nascimento's datum on promptness in keeping appointments is of particular interest. Over 50 per cent of the American respondents used time units of less than ten minutes in duration to define lateness in meeting an appointment; less than a quarter of the Brazilians (22 per cent) did so. Furthermore, 21 per cent of the Brazilians employed a time unit of more than twenty minutes. Specifically, most North Americans thought a person late if he did not appear within nine minutes of the appointed time; the great majority of Brazilians thought a longer time appropriate.

The implication of interest in these data is that perceptions about the length of time units may be the real key to achieving greater synchronization within a system. If arrival at a conference within thirty minutes of its scheduled beginning is considered "on time," there will be no perception of a problem if arrival is a half-hour later. On the other hand, if the expectation is that 9:00 A.M. means 9:00 A.M., arrival at 9:30 will be regarded as big trouble indeed. In the Brazilian situation there is apparently a perception of orderliness and schedule because time units are larger than in the United States; and the real task is to convince the Brazilian executive he must use smaller time units, thus leaving him to feel his own problem of synchronization. In short, the reformer must impose his values as to the appropriate length of a unit of time over those presently operating in the Brazilian culture. But that, obviously, is no easy task.

Sequence

A third major area of concern was allocations of time, as a reflection of priorities operating in the public administrative system. Evidence is substantial that Brazilian public administrators are neither expected to, nor actually do, spend as much time at their government work as do American public administrators. Data from the study are as follows: (*a*) Seventy-eight per cent of the Brazilians—but none of the North Americans—reported an official work week of less than 40 hours. (*b*) Seventy-four per cent of the Brazilians said they actually worked less than 40 hours per week on the job, as compared with 6 per cent of the American respondents. Further, 59 per cent of the Brazilians reported they worked less than 30 hours per week, as compared with 1 per cent of the American officials. (*c*) Dual employment is common in Brazil, very uncommon in the United States. Eighty per cent of the Brazilian respondents said it was common or very common as contrasted with 5 per cent in the United States. (*d*) Where two employers are served, it was estimated by 39 per cent of the Brazilian respondents that executives spend less than half their work time on government tasks. The majority of the American respondents (79 per cent) thought the government got more than 75 per cent of the dually employed official's time, as compared with 19 per cent in Brazil.

Patently, Nascimento thus secured considerable evidence that administrative reform based on a rationale of scarce manpower and valuable time will encounter a most fundamental problem. But to anyone familiar with the Brazilian situation, the findings are not surprising. Even where major programs have been undertaken, government offices have often remained empty in the morning hours, with all the obvious consequences not only in marshaling manpower for the necessary tasks at hand but for securing the required co-ordination. Further, the problem is not a simple matter of better time-keeping to insure sufficient commitment to the government job. Over a great many years, compensation levels have been adjusted to reflect the part-time character of government employment. Economic survival has customarily come to require the holding of another job; hence, efforts to secure full-time service from presumably full-time employees have typically foundered on the problem of salaries. To secure the kind of time commitment known in the United States, the public payroll would have to reflect very major increases in individual compensation levels.

But the chain does not end at this point. Although it is likely that a given number of employees working full-time are able to produce more than a greater number of part-time people (i.e., holding total compensation stable), the imperatives of a system wedded to "welfare bureaucracy" make this an unacceptable alternative. Welfare bureaucracy as a system thus becomes an important allocator of time, producing attendant dilemmas for any architect of administrative reform. Time devoted to public pursuits is highly fragmented, facilities are strained for a few hours of each day, and synchronization problems are heightened by the relatively few hours workers are in offices.

Time Perspectives

Finally, Nascimento was interested in differences in time perspectives, an area of inquiry that does not neatly fit within the Moore categorization, though it might be regarded as an aspect of synchronization. Chris Argyris has particularly argued the saliency of the time perspective in administration, his "mix model" making time one of six basic dimensions. Each of the dimensions is conceived as a continuum ranging from the minimum of organization health for survival to a high of "positive" organization health. In the case of time, the spectrum of organizational health moves from the situation in which core activities are "largely determined by the present to a state in which the present core activities are continually influenced by considerations including the past history, the present, and the anticipated future of the organization.[18]

In an earlier work, Argyris related the concept of maturity to lengthened time perspective. Immaturity implies a heavy discount of the future; maturity includes the capability to defer gratifications in the anticipation of greater ones in the future. The hierarchical system, he argued, is related to immaturity-maturity because control by superiors deprives the individual of an opportunity to predict and make his own future: ". . . individuals have little control over their working environment. Concomitantly, their time perspective is shortened because they do not control the information necessary to predict their future."[19]

Nascimento found the Brazilians' perceptions of governmental decision-making somewhat more heavily weighted toward the past and present than the perceptions of the American respondents. Although respondents in both countries saw present official policy as the fundamental criterion of decisions, the degree of emphasis was considerably higher in Brazil. In decision-making the Brazilians were more apt to rely on past precedents; future implications counted more heavily with the North Americans.

Other data also suggested a somewhat greater future orientedness on the part of the American respondents. Forty-five per cent of the North Americans felt there was concern for the future in American government behavior, as contrasted with 38 per cent in Brazil. When respondents were asked about the dominant temporal orientation of their own jobs, 86 per cent of the Brazilians said their jobs involved the past or the present, as compared with

18. *Integrating the Individual and the Organization* (New York, 1964), p. 154.
19. *Personality and Organization* (New York and Evanston, 1957), pp. 60–61.

68 per cent of the North Americans. Perhaps more significantly, two-thirds of the American respondents reported they wanted a job whose basic concern was with the future, as compared with one-third of the Brazilians.

On the other hand, two-thirds of *both* Brazilians and North Americans thought the primary concern of their government *should* be with the future. What conclusions are warranted? The North Americans want to live in the future-oriented world they feel appropriate for the government as a whole, and their behavior seems to reflect this; in a formal sense the Brazilians are also future oriented but are significantly less inclined to be "participants," to make their official behavior reflect their formal commitment.

Job content, of course, is only one element in a lengthened time perspective. Of greater significance is the individual's view with respect to his own life space. In this respect a very major difference seems to exist between the two cultures. In answer to a query about the degree to which the respondent thought ahead about his job and career, 38 per cent of the Brazilians reported they never think about the future; and 93 per cent said they do not look beyond the next year. In contrast, nearly two-thirds of the American officials (65 per cent) declared they were planning and thinking about themselves at least three years into the future.

The practical implications of a lengthened time perspective for the administrative process are considerable. It appears, for example, that the reformer must deal with powerful demands for immediate gratification by the actors in the Brazilian system. Changes that promise long-run benefits to the participants or to the society would therefore not possess high value. In this sense, behavior is likely to be immature.

There may be implications also for specific organizational strategies. For example, the predominant tendency in Brazil's administrative reform efforts has been toward centralization, thereby reducing decisional autonomy at the lower levels. Such a strategy may have operated to shorten further the time perspectives of the Brazilian public official by depriving him of information and increasing his dependence on higher authority. The alternative would obviously be to force initiative and decision responsibility downward, which in many ways seems as compatible with Brazilian culture as does centralization. Theoretically (i.e., following Argyris), the decentralization approach would lengthen time perspectives and move the system toward greater organization health.

Synchronization is also affected by length-of-time perspectives, a factor which may be especially important in developing societies such as Brazil. In such nations there is understandable official concern for making maximum use of scarce resources; and plans and planning have become a central part of administrative thinking and the administrative process. The common view is that the key to such planning is goal setting and allocating resources. But in fact the critical problem is "follow through" and meeting time schedules. Brazil has produced many beautiful plans, the majority of which have had only very modest societal consequences. One cause of failure may have been a heavy discounting of the future. At the moment of action, the present exigency has triumphed over promised rewards.

Summary

Nascimento concluded:

Brazilians and Americans differ significantly from each other as to their time orientations. Differences are sharper in the case of perceptions of actual behaviors than in expectations or values about time related behaviors. In general, Brazilians hold less optimizing and more personal orientations toward time, as contrasted with Americans.

The findings of the present study indicate that the prevailing time patterns in the Brazilian bureaucracy are antagonistic to those which are required by the strategy of change that has guided the attempts to reform that bureaucracy.[20]

Administrative reform efforts in Brazil have appeared to take little account of the people in the administrative system and their

20. *Op. cit.*, p. 415.

values. These efforts have assumed that there exists a commitment to change, that there is inherent co-ordinating capability, that a full marshaling of manpower can be achieved, and that the strategy will result in greater organization health. Each of these assumptions can be tested, at least in part, by probing the temporal perceptions of executives. To establish a type of benchmark by which difference might be measured, Nascimento made a comparative study of Brazilian and American public executives.

The contrasts between the two populations were notable. The Brazilians were less inclined to see time as a scarce resource, and inferentially less inclined to value change; apparently had significantly less co-ordinating capability because they used less precise time units; had a somewhat shorter perspective, particularly as they viewed their own jobs; and spent significantly less time on the job. A reform strategy which would take full account of these variables in the behavior profile of the Brazilian public executive, it was argued, would have a far greater chance of achieving long-term effect in the society.

Conclusions

The Nascimento study provides further evidence of the complexity of the leadership process, even when it is simplified in some degree by a focus on those who occupy formal positions of managerial responsibility. For this reason, it will be useful if approaches to inquiry are developed that confront the problem less globally. There is a specificity about "clock" time which makes it a useful departure point for, or instrument of, research; further, perceptions toward, and use of, time may be reflective of a much larger range of individual values and behavior about which we need to know more. Why, then, is the temporal perspective found so little in analyses of the executive?

Possibly the biggest problem has been our long preoccupation with a generalized, abstract model of the executive. The intent of such efforts has primarily been prescriptive; we have wanted to develop data which would allow a leader to compare his behavior against some idealized norm. As we have seen in the Nascimento study, however, leadership cannot be abstracted from its cultural and institutional bases.

Concentration on the idealized executive has perhaps resulted in an exaggerated emphasis on accounting for time use, a too literal reading of the "time is money" dictum. Time is a resource, but it is not money; and in *some* senses it is scarce for everyone. Hence, there are definite limitations in treating it as a budget entry. The problem becomes particularly vexing when we ask how such an accounting system can be made operational. Does the leader himself really know when he is engaged in planning and/or strategizing? If he doesn't, who does? And how?

The comparative approach provides a degree of liberation from some of these problems. The data concern real people responding to differing personal and environmental imperatives. The comparative study of executive time is less an accounting exercise and—if properly pursued—more a broad indication of the assumptions and values of the leader, more revealing of the systemic constraints operating on a leader in a given environment. Studies that are cross-cultural reveal significant factors that studies—even if comparative—within a single culture do not reveal. The Nascimento and the Ohio State studies present an enlightening contrast in this respect.

Nascimento's conclusions were probably to be expected. Certainly it is often observed and well documented that cultures differ in their temporal norms. Yet, despite this, the orientation of reform theory continues to be universalistic and mechanical. Cultural variables are often treated as only modest constraints on the application of a grand strategy. As a result, the contradictions between theory and practice have sometimes been dramatic. In the Brazilian case, great stress has been placed on centralization despite the fact that formal leaders place relatively low value on synchronization; and great emphasis has been placed upon planning in a society whose public executives discount the future heavily in their temporal orientations.

While cross-cultural research has obvious importance, the comparative study of time and leadership within a single culture should by no means be discounted. The opportunities it presents may not at first be apparent because temporal values seem so widely shared. In the United States it would seem that a deep commitment to scarce time values has become a virtual requirement for success in any major enterprise, public or private.

Yet it is significant that the Ohio State group found marked differences in time use among leaders occupying different roles within the same organization. The Chief in Organization A differed, for example, from his Deputy. On the other hand, actors in similar roles but in different organizations behaved quite similarly. Thus the Deputy in Organization A was apt to use his time like the Deputy in Organization B, rather than like his Chief. Obviously something happens within these social systems to cause such relative uniformity of behavior; and that something is very likely hierarchy, which structures our work organizations in roughly similar ways and thus imposes common expectations on specific role occupants. In this respect the differences found by the Ohio State group were illustrative of the ability of a contrived social structure to dominate individual behavior. Furthermore, it is to be observed that the uniformity suggests a general congruence with the temporal values of the larger society.

What happens when these more discrete structures collide with the dominant value system? This was a question to which Nascimento addressed himself, in seeking to develop strategies for the modification of administrative behavior in Brazil. If the norms set by the immediate organization are powerful determinants of individual behavior, then it is important to recognize that structure, broadly conceived, has implications beyond the mere patterning of relations. In Brazil, the use of the instrumental model of Weberian bureaucracy simply reinforced already established shortened time perspectives, dependence, and resistance to change. Could a matrix approach that emphasizes interdependence elicit behavioral responses in the opposite direction?

My own research suggests that the Ohio State conclusion that the temporal dimensions of executive behavior are roughly similar across organizations needs refinement. In some cases new combinations of structure and function have clearly produced organizations that differ appreciably from the "common model." The research and development laboratory, as one element in the fast-growing "knowledge industry" in the United States, is one example of the differing organizational systems that are emerging within the culture. Its function is the production and application of new knowledge. Its structure must be such as to promote independence of thought, innovation, and creativity.

My studies at Westlab, a pseudonym for a large government R & D installation of nearly 5,000 employees, suggest that such enterprises are congruent with their general culture matrix at some points, and variously incongruent at others. The greatest congruence comes in the *synchronization* commitment. Though it is far removed from the production line, Westlab operates on the basis of extremely precise time units, and highly sophisticated scheduling is the most fundamental part of the organization's control process. The greatest incongruence comes in regard to *sequence* factors; the loosening of traditional controls and the emphasis on self-responsibility are perhaps best to be seen in the discretion provided the individual to use and organize his own time. Westlab is also modestly incongruent in the value it places on rate. Its function has caused it to place greater value on change than is probably characteristic in the change-oriented society as a whole; the "crash program" is virtually a way of life.[21]

Such analyses are at best primitive and preliminary. However, there is the indication that organizational adaptation is taking place in the United States, either as a result of the imperatives of function or because of more intensely managed, conscious efforts to modify structure to accommodate new values. I suspect it is a combination of both.

The relationship of formal leadership and organization is obviously so close as not to deserve further comment. However, it may be useful to insert the reminder that much of my interest in the temporal dimensions of leadership has developed because of the changing missions and roles of organizations.

In the developing societies of the world, it is still possible to

21. Frank Sherwood, "The Clock and the Specialized R and D Society," in Evelyn Glatt and Maynard Shelly, eds., *The Research Society* (in press).

observe public organizations that are purposive only in the sense that they serve their membership. They are not effectively held accountable for larger societal tasks. In this situation we are most apt to find the position-oriented executive. His personal security does not depend on the over-all performance of the organization but rather on his ability to do the individual things needed to hold his post. In this situation time is often used as a status symbol. The boss arrives late and leaves early to make it clear to everyone what the authority situation is, and this is quite rational, in context, because there are relatively few leadership tasks that demand his time.

As expectations of performance are placed on the organization, the leadership imperatives change. At this point, personal security comes not so much from providing cues about the authority structure as it does in constructing a co-operative system that is prized by its environment. Generally, this means "doing a job." Thus, as organizations become purposive, leaders have a common problem. They need to exercise influence over the systems they head. By definition the leader is not himself the system; he must have followers. How the leader advances his influence is, in my judgment, substantially a function of how he spends and orders his time. The leader must consider time a scarce resource; and he must test his time allocations in terms of their utility in exercising influence. Presidents as well as bureau heads may have some lessons to learn from this type of self-scrutiny.

Influence strategies, and therefore use of time, will vary according to the organization and its function. In the industrialized, production-oriented society, the leader deals with the relatively stable environment of an hierarchically structured organization. His influence is directed toward a relatively small group of subordinates who can fan out and bring impact to bear upon the organization as a whole. The thrust is toward continuity and control. In the post-industrial society, this picture is changing rapidly. The environment is one of swift change; and the organization, seeking to adapt, is less predictable and more temporary in its structure of relationships. The leader must struggle with high levels of ambiguity; yet he is still viewed as responsible, and his personal security continues tied to the performance of the organization.

The emerging picture of leadership in the post-industrial society is far closer to that of the political figure in conflict resolution than to the military and industrial hero of the past. Analyses at Westlab indicate, for example, that formal leaders spend tremendous amounts of time in problem-solving, involving almost constant interpersonal contact. Professional specialization plus the "temporariness" of the system raise more jurisdictional issues, call for more idiosyncratic solutions, and require far greater access to the leader.

Yet it is important that these conditions of immediacy and ambiguity not be taken as any indication of the lessening significance of the leader. Indeed, there is a pressing requirement for imaginative and innovative approaches to the study of leadership. One possible direction involves the linking of comparative method with temporal perspective. In my own thinking, research undertaken since the Seminar in 1965 has served only to reinforce the potential of this approach. Furthermore, in numerous training programs, I have found a great receptivity on the part of practicing administrators for "time" data and ideas. It seems clear that time provides a useful perspective on theoretical-scientific problems and on the real-world dilemmas of executive behavior.

Chapter 8

Time and Development under Communism: The Case of the Soviet Union

Kenneth T. Jowitt

> Development as a mode of thought and action involves the
> emergence of an orientation towards time and change . . .
> where the future is understood not only as a dimension of
> existence and a boundary of life, but as an object of inten-
> tional action which can be anticipated, controlled and made
> to conform to goals devised in the present.
>
> John G. Gunnell

Our object is to consider the matter of time and development
with special reference to communism. Specifically, our analysis
focuses on the Leninist model of development as it has been
employed in the Soviet Union.

The framework for this analysis consists mainly of two elements. One relates to alternative but not necessarily mutually
exclusive ways in which elites may conceive of time; the second
involves the notion of developmental stages. In considering how
an elite conceives time we shall use Wilbert E. Moore's tripartite
schema: rate, sequence, and synchronization. According to
Moore, rate refers to "frequency of events," sequence to "actions
follow[ing] one another in a prescribed order," and synchronization to the simultaneity of actions "or at least their presence at a
particular time."[1] For our treatment of "developmental stages"
our perspective is shaped by Philip Selznick's idea of problems

---

1. *Man, Time, and Society* (New York, 1963), p. 8.

that "are set for an organization by the stage of growth in which it finds itself and which are to be distinguished from problems posed by the task at hand or from problems which do not call for organizational changes."[2]

At a general level, we shall be interested in trying to discover and analyze the relationship between certain conceptions of time and certain problems associated with particular developmental stages. However, we are equally interested in specifying the *particular* form and content of such problems in the case of a given organization. To understand the dilemmas currently confronting the Soviet elite in its attempts at continued development, we feel it is essential to understand both the *general* set of problems which confront this organization at a specific stage of growth (i.e., those associated with the creation of a complex economy) and the *distinctive* form and content assumed by such problems in the Soviet environment. Our premise is that neither a stress on the universal aspects of development nor an emphasis on the uniqueness of a particular case of development is sufficient; that the two approaches must be joined to advance general understanding and the understanding of a unique situation.[3]

"Relative Backwardness"

It has been stated that the emergence of a developmental orientation to time found its "paradigmatic expression in modern Western society." However, any attempt to analyze development in anything other than a modern Western society must begin with an appreciation of the context within which elites concerned with development must operate, of the alternatives available to a developmentally oriented elite, and of the constraints which shape and limit such alternatives. Alexander Gerschenkron's formulation is perhaps the most familiar and useful. He points out that:

2. *Leadership in Administration* (White Plains, N.Y., 1957), p. 103.
3. On the relation of distinctive solutions to "universal" problems see Reinhard Bendix, "Concepts and Generalizations in Comparative Sociological Studies," in *Transactions of the Fifth World Congress of Sociology* (Louvain, 1963), pp. 532–539.

... in a number of important historical instances industrialization processes, when launched at length in a backward country, showed considerable differences as compared with more advanced countries, not only with regard to the speed of the development (the rate of industrial growth) but also with regard to the organizational and productive structures of industrialization which emerged from these processes. Furthermore, these differences in the speed and character of industrial development were to a considerable extent the result of application of institutional instruments for which there was little or no counterpart in an established industrial country. In addition, the intellectual climate within which industrialization proceeded, its "spirit" or "ideology" differed considerably among advanced and backward countries. Finally, the extent to which these attributes of backwardness occurred in individual instances appears to have varied directly with the degree of backwardness and the natural industrial potentialities of the countries concerned.[4]

Within a context of perceived relative backwardness the sense of urgency expressed by both Lenin and Stalin and their stress on rate over sequence and synchronization becomes meaningful, and lends support to Heirich's contention that "the ways in which a theory uses—or ignores—time often reflect the nature of the problem calling for solution and the kind of answer given to it."[5]

To differentiate developmental responses according to degrees of backwardness, however, is not enough. It is also necessary to appreciate the specific nature of a developmentally oriented elite's ideology, which not only reflects an environment of "relative backwardness" but also *defines* the latter in politically relevant terms.

When Stalin said, "The question of a fast rate of development of industry would not face us so acutely as it does now if we had such a highly developed technology as Germany . . . ,"[6] he was responding to a condition of "relative backwardness" in political terms. And it is impossible to understand the nature of Soviet development without appreciating the politically oriented per-

4. *Economic Backwardness in Historical Perspective: A Book of Essays* (Cambridge, Mass., 1962), p. 7.

5. Max Heirich, "The Use of Time in the Study of Social Change," *Am. Soc. Rev.*, XXIX (June, 1964), 391.

6. Joseph Stalin, "Industrialization of the Country and the Right Deviation" (*Pravda*, No. 273, Nov. 24, 1928, reprinted in *Works*, Vol. II, Foreign Languages Publishing House [Moscow, 1954], 255–302. Speech delivered at the Plenum of the CC, Nov. 19, 1928), in Nicolas Spulber, ed., *Foundations of Soviet Strategy for Economic Growth: Selected Soviet Essays* (Bloomington, Ind., 1964), p. 269.

ception of Soviet backwardness with which Lenin and Stalin operated. According to Lenin, "owing to the present circumstances, the whole world is developing faster than we are. While the capitalist world is developing, it is directing all its forces against us."[7] Stalin's statement concerning relative backwardness becomes more meaningful when his following comment is added: "The question of a fast rate of development of industry would not face us so acutely if we were not the only country . . . of the dictatorship of the proletariat."[8] Patently, the sense of urgency so characteristic of Leninism reflected both the relative economic backwardness of the Soviet Union and the political world-view possessed by Lenin and institutionalized in his party.

The "Leninist Reversal"[9]

The observation that in effect Lenin turned Marx on his head has been made numerous times. A review of this "reversal" will contribute to an understanding both of the mode of development which has occurred in the Soviet Union and of the types of problems that confront the Soviet elite today.

As against Marx, Leninism is characterized by a *lack of trust*— of history, of the proletariat, and of any social-political force outside the Party's control. When the Party came to power and addressed the problem of industrialization, such an orientation had a certain justification. As Esman—not a Marxist commentator —has noted, "some interests need to be muffled if the integrity of the new nation is to be protected and innovative measures are to have a reasonable opportunity to be carried out."[10] Further, he argues, a competitive party system, one "which accords a virtual

7. V. I. Lenin, *Selected Works* (Socialist Construction, NEP) (New York, 1937), IX, 268.

8. Spulber, *op. cit.*, p. 269.

9. This term is used by Robert A. Feldmesser in an excellent article, "Social Classes and Political Structure," in Cyril E. Black, ed., *The Transformation of Russian Society* (Cambridge, Mass., 1960), pp. 235–253.

10. Milton J. Esman, "The Politics of Development Administration," in John D. Montgomery and William J. Siffin, eds., *Approaches to Development: Politics, Administration, and Change* (New York, 1966), pp. 59–112, 73. The quotation following is from p. 93.

veto power over change to many vested interests and has difficulty mobilizing or sustaining a sense of national purpose, is a
dubious instrument for changes of the scope required for deliberate modernization."

Complementary to the sense of urgency which characterizes
Leninist elites, the lack of trust facilitates the avoidance of time-
consuming "pay-offs" to non-Party accountability groups.[11] Blau
makes a similar point in terms which are congruent with the
perspective of this article, arguing that: "the most general cost
incurred in supplying any social reward is the time required to do
so in social associations. Since the significance of this time depends on the alternatives foregone by devoting it to a given
exchange relation, it may be considered an opportunity cost."[12]
The lack-of-trust characteristic of Leninism may with some reason be considered a eufunctional factor vis-à-vis development in
a context of relative backwardness insofar as it minimizes the
commitments or "social rewards" that are to be distributed, and
consequently the number and range of strictly "development"
alternatives that would have to be sacrificed.

The second aspect of the Leninist reversal relevant to our topic
is the way in which this reversal has been and is today legitimated. At the most general level this was done in terms of
leadership. The old mot that Marxism is not so much a theory of
politics as a doctrine of economics is relevant here, for Lenin
certainly injected a strong political element with his doctrine of
Party. If, as Esman put it, "far reaching and purposeful social
change usually requires the sustained initiative of relatively small
energetic and cohesive groups,"[13] the party devised by Lenin may
be viewed as most appropriate. At the most concrete level, Lenin's reversal has been legitimized in terms of successful industrialization. The 1961 Program of the CPSU observed with obvious
satisfaction: "Socialism is the road to freedom and happiness for
the peoples. It ensures rapid economic and cultural progress. It

11. See David E. Apter, *The Politics of Modernization* (Chicago, 1965), pp.
243–245, for a discussion of "accountability groups," i.e., groups which for
material and/or ideal reasons are able to exert claims on governmental decision-
makers.
12. Peter Blau, *Exchange and Power in Social Life* (New York, 1964), p. 101.
13. Esman, *op. cit.*, p. 72.

transforms a backward country into an industrial country within
the life-time of one generation and not in the course of centuries."[14]

For present purposes the most interesting aspect of the legitimation of Party power relates to its assumption of *total responsibility* for sustained and rapid development. Appropriately, Stalin
best expressed this: "Since we have come to power and taken
upon ourselves the task of transforming the country on the basis
of socialism, *we are responsible for everything, the bad as well as
the good. . . . And only we Bolsheviks can do it.* But in order to
accomplish this task we must systematically achieve a fast rate of
development of our industry."[15]

The following statement by Stalin brings together all of the
major themes dealt with thus far—concern with development,
relative backwardness, world-view, sense of urgency, Leninist
reversal, and the Party's assumption of total responsibility:

We are fifty or a hundred years behind the advanced countries. We
must make good this distance in ten years. Either we do it, or they
crush us. This is what our obligations to the workers and peasants of
the USSR dictate to us. But we have other, still more serious and more
important obligations. They are our obligations to the world proletariat . . . we place them higher.[16]

The substitution of Party for Class, of Organization for Consciousness, was to be legitimated by the assumption of responsibility for all decision-making; and, to be real, total responsibility
had to be combined with total control.

The Party and Development

The specific organization which assumed total responsibility
for the rapid development of the Soviet Union was of course the
Communist Party. It is essential to understand the nature of the

14. From Jan F. Triska, ed., *Soviet Communism: Programs and Rules* (San
Francisco, 1962), p. 57.
15. In Spulber, *op. cit.*, p. 268. Emphasis added.
16. From "The Tasks of Business Executives," in *Leninism* (London, 1940), p.
366.

Party if one is to appreciate the character of Soviet development: political, administrative, and economic.

A striking analogy may be drawn between the Party and what Frank P. Sherwood has called the "specialized R & D society."[17] Both organizations are characterized by an orientation toward "change as purpose." In both cases this orientation has led to a "greater acceptance of the crash program."[18] Furthermore, both organizations emphasize rate relative to their emphasis on either sequence or synchronization. Neither organization can entirely neglect the latter two, however, particularly synchronization, for as Sherwood notes: "It would be hard to imagine how an organization could commit itself to a high rate of change and at the same time ignore the necessities of coordination." As Jerry Hough has so ably argued, the Party has not neglected the task of co-ordination; in fact, one of its primary and most effective roles is that of co-ordinator.[19]

The consequences of this orientation in the R & D organization and in the Party are similar in one very important respect. In both instances "he who has power is he who has capability to disrupt the fulfillment of a deadline. . . ."[20] If one agrees with Crozier and Krupp that a situation of uncertainty is one of indeterminate power, then in a system where rate is highly valued, responsibility concentrated, and distrust an ideological element, there is certain to be an emphasis on control in order to prevent any dilution of responsibility, lowering of rate, or loss of power. In this context, the concept of the "command economy" and Bendix's notion of "dual bureaucracy" become relevant, for the "command economy" is an attempt to prevent the appearance of areas of uncertainty through the use of detailed directives, and the function of the "second" or Party bureaucracy is to prevent any decrease in rate.[21]

17. "The Clock and the Specialized R and D Society," in Evelyn Glatt and Maynard Shelly, eds., *The Research Society* (in press).
18. *Ibid.*
19. "The Soviet Concept of the Relationship between the Lower Party Organs and the State Administration," *Slavic Review*, XXIV (June, 1965), 215–241.
20. Sherwood, *op. cit.*, p. 21.
21. See Sherman Krupp, *Pattern in Organizational Analysis* (New York, 1961), pp. 168–185; Michel Crozier, *The Bureaucratic Phenomenon* (Chicago, 1964);

The Party's role as defined by its leadership is conceived in terms of rapid and continuous change, with the emphasis to date on mobilization rather than distribution, on potentiality for a future rather than present equity.

Potentiality vs. Equity

David Apter's formulation of a Leninist elite's orientation once in power cogently expresses the attitudes of such elites toward development. According to Apter, "the communist [form of government] emphasizes the fulfillment of potentiality." "Individuals for example are perceived as nothing more than potentials. Structurally, the political community is the means of translating potentiality into some sort of reality." In such a system, "instrumental values are elevated to the level of consummatory values, with the result that the goals of the state, particularly those of modernization and industrialization become sacrosanct."[22]

In Max Heirich's terms, Leninist elites are more concerned with "becoming" than "being,"[23] and this concern is reflected through the stress on rate and potentiality. Thus, Stalin pointed to the "special merits and advantages of the Soviet system of economy," and stressed the fact that such an economy "bears within itself the colossal potentialities necessary for overcoming any and all difficulties."[24]

This stress on rate and potentiality by a Party similar in orientation to an R & D corporation has had and does have definite consequences for the character of administration in the Soviet Union. Reinhard Bendix has pointed out that in Weberian terms, "An ideally functioning bureaucracy . . . is the most efficient method of solving large-scale organizational tasks [but] only if these require the orderly administration of public affairs under

Gregory Grossman, "Notes for A Theory of the Command Economy," *Soviet Studies,* XV (Oct., 1963); and Reinhard Bendix, *Work and Authority in Industry* (New York, 1956), pp. 375–378.

22. *Op. cit.* The quotations are from pp. 12, 31, and 359, respectively.

23. *Op. cit.,* p. 387.

24. "The Results of the First Five Year Plan," Report Delivered at the Joint Plenum of the CC and the CCC of the CPSU (1/7/33), in *Leninism,* p. 439.

the rule of law." Bendix has also noted that ". . . a continuous and dependable operation which combines efficiency with a more or less stable norm orientation is usually obtained at the price of some inflexibility for the sake of maintaining the rule of law and achieving an equitable administration of affairs."[25] However, in a regime in which the elite is primarily concerned with rate and potentiality rather than "being," synchronization, and equity, it is precisely inflexibility, i.e., routinization, which is to be avoided. Such routinization is also to be avoided insofar as it raises the dual threats of "backsliding" and "restoration."[26] With these considerations in mind, Weber's point that what "appears irrational from one point of view may well be rational from another" (Bendix) is applicable to the character of Soviet administration. The Soviet elite's attempt to realize the potential of the Soviet economy rapidly and its assumption of responsibility for the success (or failure) of such an attempt led to such institutional arrangements as a "dual bureaucracy" and the "command economy," as well as to certain behavioral orientations on the part of the Party, particularly that of intrusiveness in all spheres.

It is important to appreciate the positive as well as the negative aspects of such a constellation of values, structures, and behaviors for development in the Soviet Union. True, total responsibility assumed by the political elite resulted in the concentration of power in its hands, but as Huntington has argued (similarly to Esman), "in an early stage, modernization requires policy innovations and hence the concentration of power. . . ."[27] Nevertheless, although concentration of power may be a necessary condition of policy innovation, it is not a sufficient condition for development. For "positive development" to occur (i.e., in Riggs's terms, increasing differentiation plus social performance),[28] effective political leadership must be in evidence, and there is no more impor-

---

25. "The Cultural and Political Setting of Economic Rationality in Western and Eastern Europe," in Gregory Grossman, ed., *Value and Plan* (Berkeley, 1960), pp. 245–261. The two quotations are from p. 257.
26. See Henry Roberts, *Russia and America* (New York, 1956), pp. 47–49.
27. Samuel P. Huntington, "The Political Modernization of Traditional Monarchies," *Daedalus*, XCV (Summer, 1966), 763–788, 770.
28. Fred Riggs, "Administrative Development: An Elusive Concept," in Montgomery and Siffin, *op. cit.*, pp. 225–256, 242.

tant consideration for a Leninist elite than effective performance of its leadership functions. One of the critical functions of leadership is to define the goals of an organization and to direct the organization toward the fulfilment of these goals. The success of Soviet industrialization would seem to indicate that the Soviet elite has been capable of meeting these demands of leadership, securing compliance to its commands through a combination of coercive, utilitarian, and normative sanctions.[29] There are several factors that have contributed to the success the Soviet leadership has enjoyed. One of them involves the Soviet elite's "developmentalist" time orientation. Hahn-Been Lee has suggested that "when applied to the future [such a time orientation] is innovational and entrepreneurial: it plans ahead and is ready to take risks." In his essay, Hahn-Been Lee has suggested that such a time orientation yields vision, the vision of progress. Several dimensions of the Soviet elite's particular developmentalist time orientation can be discovered.

The first involves the leadership's awareness of the need to specify its goals and to do so in a way that elicits support from its followers. In fact the success of the Party was seen as being dependent on the clear statement of its goals in operationally relevant terms. Note Stalin's comment: "Finally, the results of the Five-Year Plan have shown the Party is invincible if it knows its goals, and if it is not afraid of difficulties."[30] The latter part of this statement displays the risk-taking orientation which Lee finds essential in an orientation toward development.

The second dimension is the leadership's awareness of the need to control the bureaucracy. Riggs states that "bureaucrats serve as efficient agents of their principals . . . when the principals know what they want and are able to impose their will upon their agents."[31] In a context in which such a bureaucracy as may exist is oriented toward the routine performance of tasks and in which the political elite is confronted with a situation it defines as one

29. See Amitai Etzioni, *A Comparative Analysis of Complex Organizations* (New York, 1961), *passim,* for a discussion of modes of compliance and types of sanctions.

30. Stalin, in *Leninism,* p. 440.

31. Fred Riggs, *Administration in Developing Countries* (Boston, 1964), p. 265.

demanding change rather than stability or preservation, the elite must insure the responsiveness of the administrative structures at its disposal. The Soviet elite has never neglected this control function. The existence of a Party apparatus paralleling the state bureaucracy, control over personnel selection, and the maintenance of Party cells in all ministries, such means have resulted in effective (not merely formal) political control of the bureaucracy.[32]

The third dimension of a developmentalist time orientation that has contributed to such success as the Soviet elite has enjoyed—particularly concerning economic development—has been the ability of the Party to recruit a sufficient number of motivated personnel to assume entrepreneurial roles. Again, according to Lee, political leadership must "create conditions under which developmentalist time or development entrepreneurship can germinate and thrive." As is evident from the context of his statement, Lee did not have the Soviet case in mind; yet the Soviet leadership did just this. As Schurmann says: "The Soviets wanted a solid phalanx of managers to direct industry. No Weberian-type bureaucracy was contemplated. . . ."[33] The reason for this was not simply the lack of a sufficient legal-rational bureaucratic tradition in Russia. The major reason lies, rather, in the difference which exists between alternative leadership styles, and in related alternative perceptions of goals and means. "Bureaucrats strive for routinization, for the creation of stable predictable environments . . . managers live in a changing world and accept change as the norm."

Given the Soviet elite's concern with rapid development on the one hand and the avoidance of inflexibility, routinization, and stagnation on the other, the greater emphasis placed on managers is quite understandable. The success of Soviet industrialization, in turn, must be attributed to a generally successful performance by these managers and to the effective relationship which existed between them and the Party.

32. Bureaucra*cies* would be more correct.
33. Franz Schurmann, *Ideology and Organization in Communist China* (Berkeley, 1966), p. 236. The quotation following is from p. 166.

The Soviet case obviously poses a leading theoretical and empirical problem. We put it in the form of a statement: what has been often (customarily?) considered a sign of administrative development, the creation of a Weberian-type bureaucracy, may be dysfunctional to an elite concerned with rapid industrialization. Certainly the Soviet example demonstrates that "men may increase the zeal and rationality of their work effort while they are systematically led to distrust one another and in certain respects are deliberately prevented from knowing what to expect."[34]

Finally, the success which the Soviet elite has enjoyed vis-à-vis the goals of modernization and industrialization has resulted from another facet of the Party's "intrusiveness." Diamant, in his essay, suggests that ". . . the new states tend to be preoccupied with questions of rate and neglect the imperatives of synchronization and sequence." But in the first place, as we noted earlier, a preoccupation with rate does not preclude a great deal of attention to synchronization. In the second place, the new states generally are not so much guilty of neglect of this aspect of development as they are unable to deal with it given their lack of an effective instrument for doing so.[35] For the Soviets, one of the strengths of the CPSU has been its performance of social and economic co-ordinative functions. To the extent that these have been successful, the intrusiveness of the Party in all spheres has made possible the management of the "unintended consequences" produced by the overriding emphasis on rate.

"Diminishing Backwardness"

We must confront now the fact that the situation in which the Soviet elite today finds itself differs from that which it faced in the 1920's and 1930's. The Soviet Union has entered a new stage

34. Reinhard Bendix, *Nation-Building and Citizenship* (New York, 1964), p. 158.
35. In this connection see Aristide Zolberg, *Creating Political Order: The Party-States of West Africa* (Chicago, 1966), *passim*. See also Hough, "The Soviet Concept."

of growth which might be described as one of "diminishing backwardness," a stage which is, in large part, a consequence of the Soviet elite's successful program of industrialization. In this new stage, new *types* of problems have emerged, and these new problems call into question the solutions that have "worked" in the past. Gerschenkron has summed up the relationship of industrialization, diminishing backwardness, and new problem areas as follows: ". . . the process of industrialization is also a process of diminishing backwardness. In its course, factors that were lacking formerly tend to become evident and acquire increasing importance within the body economic."[36]

It is important to stress, as Gerschenkron does, that the "new problems" facing the Soviet elite are not necessarily unprecedented in their past experience; the point is rather that these problems now assume a heightened importance and that the handling of them has become critical to the maintenance of the system's character.[37] These problems concern the Soviet administrative system, the economic system, and particularly the relationships of both to the Party.

At the most general level one can say that even before Stalin's death, and certainly increasingly since, there have been an increasing number of anomalies evident in the Stalinist developmental paradigm.[38] In terms of our schema for time, we might say that the stage of growth now confronting the Soviet elite is one in which relatively greater emphasis must be placed on synchronization and sequence as against rate. The ways in which the post-Stalinist elite has reacted to the increasing anomalies and to the general question of substantial system transformation can only be

36. "Russia: Patterns and Problems of Economic Development," in *Economic Backwardness*, p. 123.

37. Selznick's distinction between routine problems, for which an organization has solutions, and new, critical problems, for which it does not, is relevant here (*op. cit., passim*); see also Karl W. Deutsch, *Nerves of Government* (New York, 1963), for his discussion of "integrity and dignity," pp. 131–132.

38. See Thomas S. Kuhn, *The Structure of Scientific Revolutions* (Chicago, 1962). Kuhn's conceptualization of change through the emergence of anomalies within a paradigm is relevant to the development process. For specific anomalies associated with the Stalinist paradigm and a discussion of such, see Gregory Grossman, "The Soviet Economy," *Problems of Communism*, XII (Mar.–Apr., 1963), 32–41; and "The Structure and Organization of the Soviet Economy," *Slavic Review*, XXI (June, 1962), 203–222.

understood through reference to the Stalinist legacy, i.e., to the historically specific set of "substitutions"[39] which have shaped and defined the character of Soviet development. The two most important "substitutes" employed in the process of Soviet industrialization have been the command economy and the dual bureaucracy. Both of these phenomena are related to the type of party which has provided leadership for the industrialization process. Both of these phenomena demonstrate this leadership's assumption of total responsibility for development in all spheres and its total control over and within these spheres of activity.

The Party's Dilemmas

In sum, the set of "substitutions" employed by the Party in the industrialization process is the primary source of the Party's present difficulties. These "substitutions" are not simply expendable instruments of development. Rather they have become an integral part of the definition of the Soviet system, particularly of the Party and its self-conceived role in that system. In short, these substitutions have become "infused with value." They can be changed "if at all only at the risk of severe internal crisis."[40]

On close view, there are two interrelated problems with which the Soviet elite must deal. One is a technical problem—really a complex of interrelated problems—which concerns increasing need for *innovation* of one kind or another.[41] The other is a problem in institutions and values, and concerns the ability of the Party to dissociate its identity from the specific institutional forms it has employed in the past, forms which are presumptively dysfunctional for the new innovative needs.

39. See Gerschenkron, on substitutions (*op. cit.*, pp. 51, 116, 123–124, 129, 135, 358–359, 362). The concept of "substitution" refers to strategies of development used by modernizing elites which differ from those strategies associated with development in England and the United States.

40. The language quoted here is from Selznick, *op. cit.*, p. 40. Selznick's discussion is a general one of "institutionalization," change, leadership, etc., not a discussion of Soviet phenomena. However, it seems to us highly relevant to present Soviet problems.

41. On this matter see Gregory Grossman, "Innovation and Information in the Soviet Economy," *Am. Econ. Rev.*, LVI (May, 1966), 118–130.

Of the various problem areas confronting the Soviet elite, we shall focus on five. First of all, there is the "within culture" conflict over time orientation. This is expressed in the contrast between the continued "combat" or mobilization orientation of certain segments of the Party, and the orientation of personnel engaged in certain economic and administrative pursuits. The orientation of the latter under "developed" conditions corresponds to a great extent with the concepts of calculability and formal rationality, and is appropriate to their present more or less "bureaucratic" occupational status. During the stage of "relative backwardness," the Party's opposition to a bureaucratic orientation was eufunctional in terms of economic development and political coherence. But in a stage of "diminishing backwardness," the Party may no longer be the sole or even primary possessor of a "progressive" orientation.

A second problem area involves the question of trust. We have pointed out that the Leninist reversal and the assumption of total responsibility by the Soviet elite are ultimately based on distrust. However, in the current developmental stage, with its need for innovation, progress is dependent on an increasing demonstration of trust by the Party toward personnel and toward structural arrangements which are critical in handling the problems created by an increasingly sophisticated and complex economic and administrative system.

A third dilemma confronting the Party relates specifically to the question of synchronization. In the current stage of development, there is a pressing need for co-ordination and integration of the various economic, administrative, and social elements critical to the maintenance and growth of the Soviet system. However, the ability of the Party to perform these co-ordinating and integrating functions under present conditions is in question, whatever its successes in this area under the old conditions of relative backwardness. As has been convincingly argued, one of the reasons for this early success was the authority which the Party possesses at all levels of the Soviet system. This authority is in part a reflection of the *institutionalization* (to use Selznick's terms) of the Party in the Soviet Union. There is, however, a negative consequence attached to the Party's having become, through its institutionalization, "infused with value." For if Kassof is correct, the Party not only uses its authority to facilitate its co-ordinating and integrating tasks but is ". . . impelled by a belief not only in the practical desirability, but the moral necessity of planning, direction, and coordination from above in the name of human welfare and progress."[42] In short, the Party approaches co-ordination as a consummatory value, not as an instrumental one. This may have very important implications regarding the Party's capacity to adopt forms of co-ordination which stress a "regulative" as opposed to "authoritative" relationship between Party and system. We shall expand this point shortly.

A fourth dilemma facing the Party is an intra-Party problem. It arises from the desire of certain sectors of the Party to reform the system, particularly to achieve greater autonomy at the enterprise level. Such a move has as object the enhancement of the capacity of the Soviet system to handle new and increasing demands. However, such a restructuring of the Soviet economic and administrative systems would threaten the newly gained corporate identity of the Party, reflected in the present oligarchic nature of the central leadership and the power of regional first secretaries. Nove has described this dilemma in the following terms:

. . . the reformers wish to create order at the microeconomic level and to provide macro-economic criteria . . . if this is so, the reforms do not threaten the functions of the party at the centre nearly so much as they affect the powers of local party organizations. It is the oblast party secretary and those beneath him whose raison d'etre very largely consists in interfering with economic processes. Therefore we must expect the strongest resistance to change to come from the party's local functionaries, and of course from those at the centre whose mentality reflects their interests and who love to interfere personally in detailed economic problems.[43]

A final problem area facing the Party stems from resistance to the lowering of expectations, if not always goals. Certainly the

42. Allen Kassof, "The Administered Society," *World Politics*, XVI (July, 1964), 558.

43. Alec Nove, "The Politics of Economic Rationality: Observations on the Soviet Economy," in *Was Stalin Really Necessary?* (London, 1964), p. 65.

Khrushchevian era was one in which the major concern of the most powerful individual in the Party was rate of development (although again the relevance of synchronization to rate was never completely forgotten).[44] Rate was particularly important inasmuch as legitimation of the regime assumed a predominantly economic character;[45] the maintenance of a high rate of growth in the economic sphere was considered a necessary element in the self-justification of the elite's position and values. The importance of rate was threefold: (*a*) in terms of economic pay-offs, (*b*) in terms of regime legitimacy vis-à-vis the population, and (*c*) in terms of regime legitimacy vis-à-vis the elite itself.[46]

The relation between aspiration level and achievement[47] is a critical concern in analyzing the responses which the Soviet elite has made and is making in its current stage of development. A legacy of ambitious goals, high rate of development, and lack of institutionalized means of resolving power struggles all contribute to the difficulty of the Party in dealing with the problems of "diminishing backwardness."

At a slightly higher level of analysis, we may approach the question of continued Soviet development in terms of sets of "conflicting imperatives."[48] Before enumerating them, it is important to make clear that the elite does have an area of choice as it seeks to deal with these conflicting imperatives. Responses may include attempts to "maximize," and to achieve systemic transformation through a number of comprehensive reforms, as well as attempts to "satisfice" or find minimally acceptable answers to problems.[49] Also, it is important to avoid defining solutions to the problems confronting the Soviet elite in our own terms, so that responses lacking a democratic orientation have no chance to

44. See S. Strumilin, quoted in *Current Digest of the Soviet Press* (Feb. 4, 1959), X, no. 52 (from *Literaturnaya Gazeta*, Dec. 2, 1958, pp. 1–2).
45. See Richard Lowenthal, "The Revolution Withers Away," *Problems of Communism*, XIV (Jan.–Feb., 1965), 10–17.
46. For statements containing these three elements see N. Khrushchev, *Current Digest of the Soviet Press*, XI, No. 2 (1959), 1.
47. On this matter see Richard M. Cyert and James G. March, *A Behavioral Theory of the Firm* (Englewood Cliffs, N.J., 1963), p. 115.
48. For an excellent discussion using such a perspective see Reinhard Bendix's *Max Weber: An Intellectual Portrait* (New York, 1962), Part III.
49. On organizational strategies and alternative goals see James March and Herbert Simon, *Organizations* (New York, 1958), pp. 140–141.

succeed, to avoid defining the dilemma(s) the Party faces in a way that intentionally or unintentionally biases the "answer" to the "dilemma(s)."

Perhaps the most important set of conflicting imperatives which the Soviet elite faces, relevant to the question of economic, political, and administrative development, is that of authority vs. regulation. Parsons distinguishes between the two as follows:

(Authority) This is the case which focuses on the disposability of human services in the context of organization for a definite collective goal. The important point is the legitimation of the right to make decisions which are binding on the members of the collectivity. By regulation, on the other hand, I mean a set of controls over activity where the regulating agent, to be sure, exercises functions of leadership, but specifies only limits of acceptable action of the part of the units under his control.[50]

An orientation of total responsibility and control, i.e., of "authority," obviously is different from and may conflict with one of "regulation." As we have observed earlier, there is a conflict between the Party's "intrusiveness" and the need for increased autonomy by economic-administrative subunits over decisions affecting sequences, operational control, and so forth. However, one must be careful not to conclude that this necessarily means the removal of the Party from the economic-administrative spheres, any more than an increasing emphasis on "regulation" as opposed to "authority" necessarily means the end of Party rule. True, a stress on "sequence autonomy" would mean a greater area of choice for the heads of enterprises, and this would have consequences for the Soviet system's structures and values. But this does not necessarily entail a comprehensive transformation of the system's character. In Schurmann's terms, such a move would increase the operational autonomy of lower level units without necessarily lessening the policy role of the higher Party organs or the co-ordinating role of regional Party organs (in fact such a role might well be enhanced). Also, it is interesting to note, if the Party institutionalizes such a relationship between control and

50. Talcott Parsons, "The Principal Characteristics of Industrial Societies," in Cyril E. Black, ed., *The Transformation of Russian Society* (Cambridge, Mass., 1960), p. 29.

producing units, the Party system will resemble the R & D organization even more.[51]

Finally, there is conflict between the concentration and the
expansion, if not dispersion, of power in the Soviet system. This
conflict also relates to the nature and degree of Party control,
posing troublesome problems in the relations between the Party
and Professionals. To contemplate what may be implied by the
concentration, expansion, or dispersion of power is to facilitate an
appreciation of the complex relations which develop between
these two sectors in a setting of diminishing backwardness.

One of the more important characteristics of such a setting is,
of course, the increased importance of expertise. Experts with
specialized knowledge become more indispensable and thus more
powerful in areas relevant to their knowledge (even though such
indispensability is checked in varying degrees by the increased
availability of such experts). Therefore, it is incorrect to say that
in adapting to the current situation the Party can simply co-opt
such experts formally, with *responsibility* shared by the Party and
its expert agents, and with *power* remaining entirely in the Party's hands. Power would have to be and in fact is shared. However, the critical consideration is: power over what? In a formal
sense, experts can demand power within their respective professional domains and be granted such by the Party without redefin-
ing or demanding a redefinition of the political character of the
regime. Two points might be raised. In the first place, the nature
of expert demands will vary with the responsiveness of the political elite to such demands and to the problems which it perceives.[52] In the second place, certain experts will be listened to
more readily than others and at certain times more than at others.
For example, scientists, planners, managers, and administrators
might receive attention in that order.

It would appear from present evidence that the Party is capable of allowing an expansion of professional autonomy within
specific spheres of activity, including the administrative, thereby

51. See Sherwood, *op. cit.*; and also note the similarity in conceptual orientation
to Apter's categories of norms, structures, and behavior.

52. Perhaps a better word would be *conceives*, for it is the conception of
problems held by an elite which is of relevance.

demonstrating a capacity for adaptivity and development without qualitatively altering the identity of the political system. This
is not to conclude that the process of power expansion may not
produce unintended consequences in terms of the Party's ability
to control change. But it may be that the Soviet elite is capable of
political, economic, and administrative development at this stage
of growth without resorting to dispersion of power in political
rather than professional terms.

To gain a better sense of alternatives and probabilities, it might
be useful at this point to consider two historical examples of the
way in which the Party has attempted to deal with the requirements of adaptivity and mobilization, and of synchronization and
rate.[53]

Khrushchev and "Exploitationist Time"

In an interesting article on "Time and Cool People," John
Horton quotes Max Weber on elite time perspectives. Weber
pointed out that "it is the powerful and not the powerless who are
present-oriented. Dominant groups live by maintaining and expanding their present."[54] The reasons behind the focus on the
present may, however, differ according to elite types and as a
function of an elite's environment. Revolutionary elites with their
stress on the future may strongly emphasize the present insofar as
it is perceived as an obstacle to goal achievement, and thus a
source of frustration casting doubts on the positive nature of the
future.[55] A specific condition which might generate such a concern with the present would be a crisis of leadership within a
"future-oriented" revolutionary elite, such as the Soviet one. We
deepen our understanding of the nature of the Khrushchevian era

53. Interestingly enough, in a recent article Merle Fainsod has formulated the
tasks confronting the Party in exactly this language. See "Transformations in the
Communist Party of the Soviet Union," in Donald W. Treadgold, ed., Soviet and
Chinese Communism: Similarities and Differences (Seattle, 1967), pp. 42–73.
54. Trans-action, IV (Apr., 1967), 9.
55. For the relation of time perspective to anxiety and for a discussion of the
relation between emphasis on present and future in the terms mentioned here see
Milton Rokeach, The Open and Closed Mind (New York, 1960), pp. 51–53, 56,
63–64, 79–80, 366–375.

if we note (*a*) the situation of elite conflict which existed, (*b*) the distinctive stress on rate of development and concern with the "future" which continued to characterize this elite, and (*c*) the interaction of these two elements as expressed in the behavior of Khrushchev.

Khrushchev possessed what Hahn-Been Lee would term an "exploitationist" orientation toward time. According to Lee (in his essay above), "exploitationist time" is basically hedonistic and present-oriented. It is capable of being past- or future-oriented, however, and when directed toward the future it becomes an imaginary missed future, "a future which, as the individual feels, should be enjoyed but appears so threatened that it may never be realized, unless he takes a pre-emptive or presumptive action. The exploitationist time of the future is thus hasty. The outcome of such hasty time orientation may be erratic and even violent action." It is interesting to note how closely this statement approximates the accusations leveled against Khrushchev by his opponents and successors.

Khrushchev's behavior was an attempt to resolve the question of development in terms of continued high rate together with an increasing emphasis on synchronization and sequence. The reasons behind the sporadic and "harebrained" behavior demonstrated by Khrushchev include his inability to break or remove commitments which he had made to the Party in his rise to power. Viewed from a systemic perspective, the dilemma the Party confronted was as follows: In order to achieve a decisive restructuring of the Soviet system to meet the new demands which were being placed on the system, a set of innovative decisions was called for. Such decisions required a concentration of power in the hands of a leader, i.e., Khrushchev. But the Party had only recently—after Stalin's death—regained its corporate identity. Therefore, the Party resisted any of Khrushchev's moves which appeared to threaten that identity.[56] Ultimately, the Party was willing to sacrifice leadership (of a certain type) for identity (expressed by oligarchic leadership).

In the situation in which he found himself, Khrushchev's re-

56. See the excellent analysis offered by Lowenthal, *op. cit.*

sponses to problems were often "utopian." According to Selznick: "Utopian wishful thinking enters when men who purport to be institutional leaders attempt to rely on overgeneralized purposes to guide their decisions. But when guides are unrealistic, yet decisions must be made, more realistic but uncontrolled criteria will somehow fill the gap. Immediate exigencies will dominate the actual choices that are made."[57]

Khrushchev not only failed to redefine the Soviet system, he exacerbated certain of its problems, as for example in the administrative realm, where his contribution was a negative one in terms of creating anything like a framework of stable expectations.

Brezhnev and Kosygin and the "Retreat to Technology"

According to Brzezinski, the current Soviet leadership is made up of a "younger generation of bureaucratic leaders to whom orderliness of procedure [is] instinctively preferable to crash campaigns."[58] Assuming Brzezinski is correct, this might well appear to be an indication of administrative development insofar as it involves a growing disposition on the part of political leaders not to "intrude" into administrative matters. In Riggs's terms, this would mean the beginning of structural as opposed to sectoral differentiation with regard to the relationship beween the administrative and political spheres.[59]

Nevertheless, the prospects for Soviet administration are not all positive. To begin with, the Soviet system has increasingly been bureaucratized. To the extent that the individuals now occupying bureaucratic roles were socialized in their roles during the Stalinist period, their administrative responsiveness to social demands cannot be expected to be very great. Without the interference of the Party, bureaucratism in the negative sense of irresponsiveness

57. Selznick, *op. cit.*, p. 148.
58. Zbigniew Brzezinski, "The Soviet Political System: Transformation or Degeneration," *Problems of Communism*, XV (Jan.–Feb., 1966), 4.
59. "Administrative Development," pp. 233–234.

and arbitrariness may develop to new heights. And to the extent that, in Brzezinski's words, "a regime of clerks cannot help but clash over clerical issues," administrative development *insofar as it is to be defined reciprocally with political development* will be negative. This is so for the following reason. An orientation on the part of the Soviet political elite to "clerical issues" is a good example of what Selznick has termed a "retreat to technology," the definition of problems in terms of technique rather than values. Rather than signifying the End of Ideology, an orientation to "clerical issues" may well involve, on the part of the Soviet elite, a response to a situation which generates anxiety. To the extent that this is true, a focus on "clerical issues" involves ". . . an evasion of . . . real commitments by paring . . . responsibilities."[60] Stated in terms relevant to our concerns, such an elite orientation within the Party will contribute to a lack of leadership in the political sphere and a corresponding lack of control over the administrative. The mechanism whereby this situation might be created is that of "opportunism." To draw on Selznick once more:

When an enterprise is permitted to drift, making short-run, partial adaptations, the greatest danger lies in uncontrolled effects on organization character. . . . There is also the likelihood that character will not really be transformed: it will be *attenuated and confused*. Attenuation means that the sought for distinctive competence becomes vague and abstract, unable to influence deeply the work of staff and operating divisions.[61]

The loss of Party identity or attenuation of the latter resulting from an opportunistic orientation by a Party elite which defines critical issues in terms of technique may result in the lack of effective leadership for the administrative (and other) subsystems.

If nothing else, one must understand that it is difficult to prescribe any specific "reform" in the Soviet Union with the idea that it will produce nothing but intended and positive (from the

---

60. Selznick, *op. cit.*, p. 79. See Brzezinski, *op. cit.*, p. 7, for statement on "clerical issues."
61. *Op. cit.*, pp. 144–145. Emphasis in original.

point of view of the prescriber) consequences for Soviet development. It is more important to understand that analyses which implicitly or explicitly see democracy or democratic developments as a condition of continued Soviet development may be very wide of the mark. In fact "democratic developments" may, as indicated, jeopardize continued Soviet development. Finally, it is most important to understand that the concrete solutions offered by the Soviet elite to the demands associated with their current developmental stage will be very heterogeneous, with mixed consequences for the capacity of the Soviet system, and that a priori this does not imply the stagnation of the system or its inability to adapt.

Two current approaches to the question of Soviet development which seem to be particularly, though not inevitably, prone to seeing democracy or democratic developments as a condition of continued Soviet development are those involving the notion of "constricted development" and of "adaptation."

The Notion of "Constricted Development"

Dwight Waldo at one point noted that "one of the merits of focusing upon development as a 'process' in relation to certain 'types' of goals is that it avoids an excessive ethnocentrism. . . ."[62] Whether or not this is true, however, depends to a great extent on the conceptual apparatus one employs to make the general orientation of development analytically specific.

Perhaps the most widely accepted definition of development today rests on the notion of "capacity." According to Weiner: "When we speak of political development . . . we are concerned first with the expanding functions of the political system, secondly with the new level of integration thereby required to carry out these functions, and, finally, with the capacity of the political systems to cope with these new problems of integration."[63]

62. "Comparative Public Administration: Prologue, Performance, Problems and Promise," *Indian Journal of Political Science*, XXIV (July–Sept., 1963), 215.
63. Myron Weiner, "Political Integration and Political Development," in Jason Finkle and Richard W. Gable, eds., *Political Development and Social Change* (New York, 1966), p. 553.

In order for a given system to increase its capacity to handle new and increasing demands associated with increasing complexity and differentiation, the areas of rationality must expand.[64] In Parsons' terms, there must be a shift from authority to regulation, in order to assure what Riggs calls "social performance." In the Soviet case this would suggest that the questions of labor mobility, money, and markets would be critical ones.[65]

As a way of stating the type of problem that confronts the Soviet elite, such conceptualizations can be useful. However, the conclusions that might be—and have been—drawn from such conceptualizations are often based either on a seriously incomplete analysis or on analyses which contain implicit or explicit democratic biases.

An example of incomplete analysis is that offered by Field in his essay on "Soviet Society and Communist Party Controls: A Case of 'Constricted Development.'" According to the author:

The party has done a fairly good job of surviving and keeping itself in power; it has been able, when necessary, to adjust its structure in order to admit into its ranks those members of society who were most important in reaching the goals defined by the party. It has been to some degree responsive to the demands of professional, industrial workers and (lately) the peasants. But these responses are necessarily in terms of party interests, party ideology and party power.[66]

In the first place, a "fairly good job" is, in the opinion of most students of organization, the most that any elite can do most of the time. In the second place, despite the Party's "selfishness," it may be able to continue expanding its responsiveness. This may entail unintended consequences for the Party in terms of its ability to maintain its identity and control over the system. However, "selfishness" per se is unlikely to lead to its demise. In the third place, the Party is not merely "selfish" in terms of the consequences which its "intrusive" role in society has for system maintenance. In terms of the type of society the *Soviet elite*

64. See Riggs, "Administrative Development," p. 248.

65. See Grossman, "The Structure and Organization of the Soviet Economy," p. 208.

66. Mark G. Field, "Soviet Society and Communist Party Controls: A Case of 'Constricted' Development," in Treadgold, *op. cit.*, pp. 210–211.

values, the Party has performed the leadership function quite adequately.[67]

A relation between analyses which focus on a system's capacity to handle change and a "democratic" bias may not be a necessary one, but it is frequently evident. A clear example is offered by Parsons. Parsons argues: "The basic dilemma of the Communists is that it is not possible in the long run either to legitimize dictatorship of the Party or to abolish all governmental and legal control of behavior as the withering away doctrine would have it. Political democracy is the only possible outcome—except for general destruction or breakdown."[68]

Almond and Powell in their recent work reach similar conclusions when they note that the "responsive" capability of highly differentiated totalitarian systems will be very difficult to develop "*regardless* of the personal desires and ideological commitments of the political leaders. . . ."[69] due to the "gigantic bureaucracy-party organizational complex characteristic of these societies." Their conclusion, in fact their prediction, is "that systems of this class will continue to show a limited range of responsiveness as long as subsystem autonomy remains low and differentiation high." Examples of subsystem autonomy include political parties, pressure groups, courts, and the like. Although neither Riggs nor Almond and Powell are quite so explicit as Parsons in defining the prerequisites for continued Soviet development in terms of political democracy, the notions of "structural differentiation" (as opposed to sectoral differentiation) and "subsystem autonomy" are very easily confused with concrete pluralist democracies and civic cultures.

In fact, more than anything else it seems to be the lack of fairly clear cut subsystem autonomy which leads observers such as Barghoorn to remark in his work on Soviet political culture:

67. See J. F. Hough, "The Soviet Concept"; and "A Hare-Brained Scheme in Retrospect," *Problems of Communism*, XIV (July–Aug., 1965), 26–33.
68. "Communism and the West," in Amitai and Eva Etzioni, eds., *Social Change* (New York, 1964), p. 397.
69. Gabriel A. Almond and Bingham Powell, Jr., *Comparative Politics: A Developmental Approach* (Boston, 1966), p. 325. The two quotations following this come from the same page.

"Indeed it is an assumption of this paper that the Soviet type of social revolution produces only a quasi-modern polity. . . ."[70]

To introduce a comparative perspective, a rather lengthy but relevant statement by two British sociologists on this question merits attention. Nettl and Robertson argue in what is to us a very persuasive fashion that "the structural differentiation model as it stands at present is limited in respect of the societies to which it can be fruitfully applied." According to them, "in the use of the theory of structural differentiation in the conventional manner we find one of the main reasons for the equation of modernity with Western liberal economies. . . . In fact, cultural boundedness in conceptualization and economistic tendencies are both prominent features of the intellectual uses to which structural differential has been put."[71] In support of their contention the authors note that:

Using the degree of structural differentiation (in terms of the specialized and interdependent separation of major social sectors and their respective collectivities and role complexes) as an index of modernity, analysts have designated authoritarian or totalitarian societies as premodern. This on the ground that the manifested degree of differentiation is low in relation to that of many Western societies.

Of greatest interest, however, is the conclusion which they draw. Stating quite explicitly that they accept as an "empirically discoverable process" "redifferentiation" or structural homogenization in authoritarian or totalitarian systems, Nettl and Robertson argue for a reconceptualization of the meaning of such a process, rather than concluding that such a process signifies either a pre-modern development or a distortion of modernity itself. In their words:

. . . we would prefer to speak of "compressed structural differentiation," notable in reference to Communist societies. By "compressed

70. Frederick C. Barghoorn, "Soviet Russia: Orthodoxy and Adaptiveness," in Lucian W. Pye and Sidney Verba, eds., *Political Culture and Political Development* (Princeton, 1965), p. 495.
71. J. P. Nettl and Roland Robertson, "Industrialization, Development or Modernization," *Brit. Jour. of Soc.*, XVII (Sept., 1966), 274–291, 282. All succeeding passages attributed to Nettl and Robertson are also on p. 282 of their article. Emphasis added.

structural differentiation" we mean the process whereby differentiation (particularly in the economic and political sphere) occurs under
intensive and extensive elite surveillance. In such a process the (necessarily bureaucratic) elite "compresses" both time and the social
order.

The consequences of so viewing the process of structural
differentiation are much more useful to those concerned with
comparative analysis than the consequences associated with a
conceptualization of structural differentiation based on a rather
concrete image of specific Western democratic systems. As Nettl
and Robertson point out in their discussion of the notion of
"compressed structural differentiation": ". . . whilst the members
of the political elite assume and/or indirectly control strategic,
frequently multi-role positions in all 'key' areas of society, *this
does not mean the proliferation of specialized political and economic tasks does not continue apace. Nor does it mean that concrete organizations cease to multiply.*" As suggested earlier, the
"payoff" of a conceptualization which attempts to avoid defining
development in terms of the specific experience of certain Western
systems is that one is both less likely to define systems which offer
distinctly different solutions to the process of differentiation as
unique and more likely to perceive and appreciate similarities in
systems which are customarily placed in quite different categories. Thus, these authors state, "It may well be argued, for example, that in accordance with such a definition of compressed
differentiation, contemporary Britain in some respects is more
akin to the Soviet Union than conventional wisdom suggests."[72]

The Adaptive Party

Any argument concerning the prerequisites of development in
a period of "diminishing backwardness" has to deal with the type
of leadership required in such a situation. Fainsod has offered one
of the better statements with regard to the question:

72. See the discussion of Britain's elite culture in Eric A. Nordlinger, *The
Working-Class Tories* (Berkeley, 1967), pp. 13–45, and *passim*.

While it would be incorrect to suggest that the party has abandoned its mobilizing role, some modification is apparent . . . there is much greater reliance on economic incentives to induce responses which the party leadership deems essential. The result has been to introduce a strong adaptive ingredient into the party's mobilizing role. As the diverse interests which the party seeks to manipulate begin to exercise greater leverage, the party leaders find themselves mediating and balancing the claims of the functional and professional groups whose synchronized efforts are required to maintain the system's forward momentum. Whether the transformation of a mobilizing party into an adaptive party will operate as a threat to the system's dynamism is not easily determinable. It may well be that the successful management and direction of a complex and sophisticated industrial society offer no other alternative.[73]

It is particularly important to realize that for the CPSU to become primarily an adaptive party in the absence of certain other fundamental systemic changes would be dysfunctional in terms of both political and administrative development. Such a conclusion is based on the fact that at present the Party provides the leadership for the entire Soviet system. An adaptive party— or one whose distinctive competence would be in adapting rather than mobilizing—would have great difficulty in providing leadership of this type and would experience equal difficulty in performing the function of integration, which is currently a major aspect of the Party's role.

A number of more specific points might be noted in this context. There is to begin with Blau's point. Namely, a party which had for the most part substituted a concern with distribution and equity for that of production and potentiality would incur a number of high opportunity costs insofar as allocating social rewards involves loss of time. Moreover, it is a fact that an adaptive party would also tend to resort to an unequal distribution of services. This is particularly so in a society such as the Soviet which is very highly stratified and where the distribution of political resources is grossly uneven. The consequences of such a situation, with reference to goal achievement *and* equity within the system, are hinted at by Riggs's comment that if in allocating

73. Fainsod, *op. cit.*, p. 68.

a given service, an elite "must determine the status of the applicant, the amount of time and energy consumed rises."[74] A shift then in orientation on the part of the Soviet elite from potentiality, "becoming," rate, and production toward equity, "being," synchronization, and distribution might well obstruct the Soviet system's ability to act effectively on either goal: potentiality or equity.

Then, of course, a devolution of power to non-Party elements in Soviet society does not necessarily promise an increased capacity on the part of that society to deal with new and increasing demands. Once again, one must consider the character of that society, which in turn is the result of the specific historical development it has experienced. In his work on managers in the Soviet Union, Jeremy Azrael makes this point with high salience. Managers, as a product of industrialization, might appear to be more capable of dealing with the new problems confronting Soviet society. However, the term "manager" involves several dimensions. Contained within this role there are cultural and political as well as technical premises. On Soviet managers Azrael notes: "Their rise to a position of significant influence or power might eventually lead to a 'degeneration' of the political system, but it would almost certainly not lead to a vigorous and purposeful reorientation of the system to accommodate new demands and solve new problems."[75]

One of the most important prerequisites of an effective comparative approach is appreciation of the historical distinctiveness in each of the units being compared. A failure in this respect often results in an ethnocentric rather than a genuinely comparative analysis. A primary stress on equity and an adaptive party in the Soviet context at the present time would in all likelihood result in a high incidence of particularism on the part of administrative agencies, rather than in an increase in achievement-universalistic orientations and procedures. Such a stress would also

---

74. *Administration*, p. 269.
75. Jeremy Azrael, *Managerial Power and Soviet Politics* (Cambridge, Mass., 1966), p. 150.

contribute to the existing crisis of leadership which exists within the Party.

Any analysis of the continuing development of the Soviet Union which sets as the preconditions for "development" the appearance of democratic, or what are conceived to be democratic phenomena (i.e., an adaptive party or in Apter's terms a "party of representation"), and which characterizes Soviet development as "constricted" because the Party resists such phenomena narrows—prematurely, unnecessarily, and unwisely—the degree of understanding which it is possible to acquire about the topic of Soviet development.

Chapter 9

Governmental Problems Arising from the Use and Abuse of the Future—the Last Colonialism?[*]

Edwin A. Bock

Perhaps the only moral trust with any certainty in our hands is the care of our own times. With regard to futurity we are to treat it like an orphan. We are not so to attempt an improvement of his fortune as to put the capital of his estate to any hazard.

Edmund Burke

We must prepare our people for a new world quite unlike the old. . . . The average animal breeder has shown more concern about the consequences of his act than the ordinary human being about what will happen to his own descendants. The animal breeder looks 10 generations or more ahead; the human breeder not more than two, if that.

Lord Brain, Presidential Address, British
Association for the Advancement of Science, 1966

When one examines the data of comparative administration through an hourglass, as the essayists in this collection have undertaken to do, a subject that springs to prominence is the relationships between present and future and how these relationships affect the operation of national governments, or are affected by them. How strong are the tendons beneath the integument of presumed continuity between present and future? Is the growing

[*] Copyright, 1967, by Edwin A. Bock. This essay is the introductory chapter of a larger study, now in preparation, of futurism and the political problems of present-future relationships.

capability to shape the future, and the rising disposition to use this power that one sees in the United States, Britain, France, and West Germany best understood in terms of an analogy with benevolent colonialism? And what are the larger political, administrative, and constitutional problems raised by the changing relationship between present and future? These are the concerns of this essay.

The possible relevance of this discussion for comparative government and comparative administration is twofold. First, although it applies primarily to the United States, Britain, France, West Germany, and other West European democracies with strong scientific, technological, and industrial capabilities,[1] the problems it deals with occur—in some ways even more intensely as Daniel Lerner and Charles Black have noted—in other countries to whose people "development" and "modernization" are immediately and critically important.[2] Second, this essay considers as two separate and rightfully sovereign states, for example, the government, people, and institutions of the United States in 1950 and the government, people, and institutions of the United States in 1990. I have attempted to apply to the relationship between two temporally separate "states of the same country" some of the kinds of concerns (and, I hope, some of those frequently recommended appreciations of cultural differences) that one would expect of a tolerant but curious comparative administration field-researcher.

A brief word about terms. Strictly speaking, the present is the split second of here-and-now that has already gone-and-passed. It is like the few cubic centimeters of rubber tire that for one spinning instant connect the heavy automobile to the road. Beliefs about the past and future make up most of the weight of the car, most of the controls, and most of the propelling force (rear-wheel drive for the pure traditional society and front-wheel drive for the pure modern society). For this essay, however, the word "present" means today, tomorrow, and the reasonable certainties

1. Or, to use the "fittingest" of the Russet indicators, those countries with high rates of mail per capita.
2. Lerner, *The Passing of the Traditional Society* (Glencoe, Ill., 1958); Black, *The Dynamics of Modernization* (New York, 1967).

of the next six months. "Future" comprehends all of that fair temporal terrain starting on the far side of present-plus-six-months, running past the short-run future (present-plus-four-years) and out toward whatever eternal analgesic coating-action may form the limit of cosmic duration. "Long-run future" is hereby set as anything from four to twenty years. "Distant future" beyond that. Also, when the words "present," "past," or "future" are used, they sometimes refer to abstract states of time, but more often to the people, institutions, and culture existing at those times.

The Usefulness of the Future for the Present

In one form or another a sense of the future is incorporated in most purposive human,[3] organizational, or political behavior.[4] It is inherent in any means-ends chain and in most conceivable forms of decision-making from the severely rational to the rorty incremental. Depending on how one conceives of it, some aspect of the future is wrapped up in almost every part of our present. My purpose in this first section is to identify certain aspects of the future that are essential to individuals, organizations, and the governmental process, if they are to function in the present. The aim is an appreciation of the intensity and the weight of such *present* interests in the future.

The Individual's Needs

Senses of the future appear to be indispensable for the viability of the human being, and by no means only for mastery of the

3. Paul Fraisse, *The Psychology of Time* (New York, 1963), pp. 153–198; Philippe Malrieu, *Les origines de la conscience du temps* (Paris, 1953). But see J. M. Keynes criticism of "this 'purposiveness' with which in varying degrees Nature has endowed almost all of us," in "Economic Possibilities for Our Grandchildren," in *Essays in Persuasion* (London, 1931), p. 370.

4. Karl W. Deutsch, *The Nerves of Government* (New York, 1966), pp. 91 ff., 182 ff.; Bertram M. Gross, *The Managing of Organizations* (Glencoe, Ill., 1964), p. 469 ff. Bertrand de Jouvenel uses consideration of the future as a distinguishing feature of "political" (as opposed to "judicial") decision-making in *The Pure Theory of Politics* (Cambridge, 1963), pp. 5 f., 151–153.

cause-and-effect sequences upon which physical survival depends. For the individual to achieve even rudimentary organization of his personality, he needs to believe that he will continue to live and that there are aspects of himself that will persist over time into the future. The survival of our sense of identity appears to require a conviction that whatever might happen, something in us will remain the same.[5] The present survival of the individual's personality, his present psychic ability to function, and his present understanding of himself depend on his ability to maintain in his present concepts of, and claims upon, the future.[6]

There is also evidence that the individual's sense of well-being, and possibly his core sense of potency, depend on his achieving a structured relationship with time, a condition that causes him to attempt to manipulate and structure his future if only to achieve the present reassurance of orientation.[7] The strong present need of the individual to have a structured relationship with time is alleged to be one reason that the present-day American finds inner satisfaction and a bolstering of his sense of potency when he assumes the thralldom of a large, long-term financial obligation, the repayment of which will structure at least some of his actions for a substantial part of his adult life.[8] However, the need to nourish the core of the personality and protect it from annihilation caused by lack of orientation to the future may be distinguished from the individual's use of hopes and fantasies about the future to coerce himself into the present achieving behavior

5. Kurt R. Eissler, *The Psychiatrist and the Dying Patient* (New York, 1955), pp. 86–89. See also Erik H. Erickson, *Childhood and Society* (New York, 1950).

6. "If we do not know what we may become, we cannot know what we are" (John R. Platt, *The Step to Man* [New York, 1965]); ". . . the future . . . is the dominant mode of time for human beings . . . a man can understand himself only as he projects himself forward" (Rollo May, in May, E. Angel, and H. Ellenberger, eds., *Existence* [New York, 1958]).

7. For the testimony of clinical psychiatrists see E. Minkowski, *Le temps vecu* (Paris, 1933), p. 279 ff., and May, *op. cit.* Some of the recent (1964–66) experiments in "timeless living" in underground caves seem to confirm the assertions of the clinicians. The need to establish a structured personal relationship with time is presumably the explanation for the prevalence of teleological mythologies among primitive peoples and the survival of teleologies in modern societies. See also John Dewey, *The Quest for Certainty* (London, 1930), chap. i, *et seq.*

8. See the account of "The Mortgage Game" in Eric Berne, *The Games People Play* (New York, 1965).

needed to fulfil a substantive want. The latter use of the future as a means of present self-discipline for substantive achievement, or as a source of hope and fascination to sustain one in present periods of stress, deprivation, or monotony, is certainly quite common and deserves recognition in any inventory of present-vested interests in the future.[9] But this use of the future as a winch, or as a balm against present difficulties and dullnesses, frequent and often powerful though it is, probably does not approach, in frequency and intensity, those described earlier, which are fundamental for the existence, growth, and survival of the personality core.

Another aspect of the future that seems necessary for man's present sense of well-being is the ability to feel assurance, in the here-and-now, that his essential needs will continue to be met. In Hobbes's words in *Leviathan,* "the object of man's desire is not to enjoy once only and for one instant of time; but to assure for ever, the way of his future desire." The present need for pleasurable assurance and anticipation about the future may be so powerful that it anesthetizes the individual from the pains and displeasures of present exertions or sacrifices, or even makes them become a source of pleasure, as burying a bone is for a dog. In a "cold cash" sense, the temporal horizon of some individuals is heavily oriented toward the future; their "real world is a world of plans, of expectations, and of anxieties."[10] Like the stock market or the future markets, on their better days, the present feelings of such persons are mainly derived from assumptions about future situations.

The final and perhaps the most poignant item in this inventory is the human being's need to feel that he stands in some meaning-ful—hopefully even a significant—relationship to the future

9. In this inventory it is not necessary to make much of the distinction between the so-called healthy use of hope or aspiration about the future (if only about the possibility of an end to deprivation) as a means of sustaining oneself through periods of adversity or difficulty, on the one hand, and, on the other hand, the "neurotic" use of the future as an escape.

10. William J. Tucker, *The New Reservation of Time* (Boston, 1916), p. 9. See also Norton E. Long's remarks about the efforts of the achievers of one generation to buy security for the non-achievers of the next in "Local and Private Initiative in the Great Society," in Bertram M. Gross, ed., *A Great Society* (New York, 1968), pp. 81–103.

course of the human race and the universe.[11] Evidence of human supplication for something to relieve an otherwise barren or incompletely satisfying present—over and above the short-run future aspects needed for basic personality survival—appears from Khufu to Kissinger, Robespierre to Willie Loman. Protestant or voodoo, achiever or non-achiever, Melanesia or Middletown, the individual shows a powerful present need for a sense of fitting into a long-run future, as a screen against recognition of his transience or possible triviality, or against feeling the terrors of an infant lost in the Christmas rush at the cosmic department store.[12] Present opportunities for meaningful exertions or for pleasurable expenditures are rarely sufficient for the individual to feel the ennoblement he seeks. The inability of the present to satisfy this need may, as the secularization and rationalization of society narrow the possibilities of future sources of present meaningfulness, explain the growing attractions and status of such future-oriented activities as learning, saving, investment, research, and participation in the planning and execution of long-range projects by large and enduring organizations. But such activities may also gratify those present needs described earlier that have been related to the bone-burying syndrome in wolves and dogs. Because they answer powerful present needs, we may expect people to persist in activities of this kind even though they may become dysfunctional for the society.[13]

11. See the possibilities considered by Henrik F. Infield, "Human Needs and the Need for Ultimate Orientation," in Hugo Boyko, ed., *Science and the Future of Mankind* (Bloomington, Ind., 1964), pp. 203–229.

12. For examples of one type, see Samuel G. F. Brandon, *The Judgment of the Dead* (London, 1967).

13. Except for Keynes, *op. cit.*, p. 368 f. ("we have been trained too long to strive and not to enjoy. . . . Perhaps it is not an accident that the race which did most to bring the promise of immortality into the heart and essence of our religions has also done most for the principle of compound interest and particularly loves this most purposive of institutions"), recognition of these general human needs for relationships to the future as constituting a broad set of underlying factors impelling men to continue making some investment in the future, and affecting many other forms of scientific and economic behavior, is surprisingly sparse. Such general factors would affect the assumed process of decision, considered in such economic theories of expectation as those advanced by Shackle, Hurwicz, and others. See George L. S. Shackle, *Decision, Order, and Time in Human Affairs* (Cambridge, 1961); and the other economic theorists dealt with in S. Andrew Ozga, *Expectations in Economic Theory* (London, 1965). Shackle's reference to the factor of "enjoying my anticipation," seems to me to have been significantly amplified by the political scientist J. W. N. Watkins in his

Taken together, the needs and uses inventoried above constitute a powerful set of present-vested interests in the future. They
are at the root of, and are often intertwined with, the substantive
goals that individuals assume, accept, or set. They provide a
strong weight to insure that any relationship with the future,
whatever is said on the surface, will be primarily serviceable to
the functional and survival needs of the individual's personality
in the present.

The intensity of these thoughts and emotions, and the amorphous, projective nature of the future, have often resulted in men
deluding themselves about the future, and about their relationship to it.[14] The extent to which ideas of the future are at the
mercy of shifting present needs and feelings is apparent when we
remember how our own thoughts of the future have shifted with
experience of toothache, fatigue, or airsickness.[15] Present needs of
the future can cause men to maintain expectations and beliefs
about the future against all evidence. The belief that one is
altruistic about the future itself often carries heavy loads of
present self-service. Conversely, the present needs for certain
kinds of feelings about the future may cause one to deny threatening factual evidence. The unwillingness of personnel at Pearl
Harbor to accept the authenticity, and to appreciate the signifi-

---

essay, "Decisions and Uncertainty," in Charles F. Carter, George P. Meredith, and
George L. S. Shackle, *Uncertainty and Business Decisions* (Liverpool, 1957), pp.
114–115. This recognition by Watkins and Shackle is greater than that given in
the important process formulations of Simon and Lerner that bear significantly on
such behavior. Lerner, *op. cit.*, and "Toward a Communication Theory of Modernization" in Lucian Pye, ed., *Communications and Political Development* (Princeton, 1963), pp. 330–335; Herbert A. Simon, "A Behavioral Model of Rational
Choice," in *Models of Man* (New York, 1957).

14. "The 'purposive' man is always trying to secure a spurious and delusive
immortality for his acts by pushing his interest in them forward in time" (Keynes,
op. cit., p. 370). "People often project illusions about their past. But it is far more
difficult to purify one's concepts of the future from group or individual illusions"
(Eissler, *op. cit.*, pp. 287–288). "There have been men who loved the future like a
mistress, and the future wrapped her breath into their breath and shook her hair
about them and hid them from the understanding of their time" (William B.
Yeats, *William Blake and the Imagination, Ideas of Good and Evil* [London,
1903]). See also Bagehot's essay, "On the Emotion of Conviction," in Richard
Holt Hutton, ed., *Literary Studies by Walter Bagehot* (London, 1879), Vol. II.

15. Kingsley Amis has asked what happened to H. G. Wells around 1905. Up to
that point his scientific romances depicted futures of horror and despair, whereas
his later technological forecasts were usually of perfect future societies. See Mark
R. Hillegas, *The Future as Nightmare* (New York, 1967).

cance, of sighting reports of Japanese units before the attack commenced is one example. Corroboration and more detailed study of this type of denial phenomenon may be found in the experimental and field evidence from recent disaster studies.[16]

Governmental Needs

As is the individual, the governmental process is dependent for some of its functional viability on the present usefulness of aspects of the future. In the first place, the individual participants in the process, both those who govern and those who are governed, have *personal* present interests in the future, and the governmental process must accommodate some of these interests directly or indirectly. The pressure of these individual interests may be somewhat attenuated or mitigated by the mediation of corporations and other organizations, which have life spans longer than individuals, which often have long-term substantive goals, and which, by their internal system of rewards described by Chester Barnard and others, may succeed in building individual acceptance of the need for co-operative behavior to achieve these goals. However, organizations also have functional vested interests in making the future serviceable to essential present needs. The most obvious example is that some future goal is necessary to co-ordinate, synchronize, and legitimate the various individual behavior inputs in a large organization. Without positive future purposes accepted in the here-and-now, the organization and its subunits would find survival difficult. The analogy to the functional need for future relationships and conceptions to the survival of the individual personality suggests itself.

Whatever the governmental system gains in being able to take a long-term view from the fact that it deals not only with individ-

16. Roberta Wohlstetter, *Pearl Harbor: Warning and Decision* (Stanford, Calif., 1962). For an example almost exactly 100 years older, see the incredibly optimistic interpretations of Sir William Hay Macnaghten and others preceding the massacre of the British forces in Kabul during the First Afghan War, in Patrick A. Macrory, *The Fierce Pawns* (Philadelphia, 1966). Another example is Jellicoe's refusal to credit reports of the locations of Beatty's Battle Cruiser Fleet and the German fleet at a critical command decision point in the battle of Jutland in 1916. See also George H. Grosser, Henry Wechsler, and Milton Greenblatt, *The Threat of Impending Disaster* (Cambridge, Mass., 1964); Anna Freud, *The Ego and the Mechanisms of Defense* (New York, 1937).

uals but also with organizations needs to be counterbalanced, analytically, by an appreciation of the fact that in the last analysis it is the individual decisions in government that count. Agencies or corporations neither press the lever on the voting machine nor participate directly and continuously in presidential or top departmental decision-making. Moreover, although it is true that the corporation may succeed in enlisting the individual's participation in a continuing long-range goal of its own by the rewards it can muster, the individual may emerge each night from his organizational stint with tensions and unmet needs—including unmet present needs about the future—that he injects into the political process either as demands or as behavior that makes problems for the governmental system.[17]

In surveying some of the present uses of the future in the operation of the governmental process, one must notice first what is probably at once the best known and, in principle, the most deplored phenomenon. This is the use of promises about the future made to satisfy present needs for political power by politicians or officials who know that such promises cannot be kept, or that the keeping of them would require sacrifices or actions that would harm the society as a whole or even the beneficiaries in the long run. What the frequently cited instances of this kind of behavior have in common is the dishonest, deliberately injurious, or reckless exploitation of the future for selfish present purposes. David Apter and Edward Shils have dealt with demagogic "mobilizers" in the modernization process in recent writings, and the phenomenon in American and European government has been so often described that there is no need to say more here to bring it recognition.[18]

There are, however, several broader, less noticed, and less deplorable respects in which one or more of the senses of the future has contributed to the viability of the governmental process.

17. Edwin A. Bock, "Administration's Basic Concepts and the Social Work Curriculum," in New Approaches to Administration and Research in Social Work Education (New York, 1957), pp. 2–17.

18. See Edward A. Shils, "Demagogues and Cadres in the Political Development of the New States," in Lucian Pye, ed., Communications and Political Development (Princeton, 1963).

They all derive to some extent from that "unmade" characteristic of the future that the optimist might perceive as its malleability and the pessimist its uncertainty.[19] This aspect of the future is connected with a sense of liberty and potency as in de Jouvenal's book on "conjecture":

Il est domaine de liberté parce que je suis libre de concevoir ce qui n'est pas, pourvu que je le situe dans l'avenir; il est domaine de puissance parce que j'ai quelque pouvoir de valider ce que j'ai conçu. . . . Et meme il est notre seul domaine de puissance, car nous ne pouvons agir que sur l'avenir.[20]

Thus, the future can be an almost limitless cornucopia of presently comforting projective possibilities and of presently sustaining hopes and aspirations—as long as it remains future. It is like a gigantic thematic apperception test that can offer, in unlimited quantities, and without going through the governmental system, satisfactions tailored to each individual's personal projected needs.[21] But, the future offers these universal personal benefits only so long as its malleability and its protean potentiality are not destroyed by its having been made tangible and specific. Once a piece of the future is made specific, it may satisfy the needs of the relatively few who seek that particular pattern of known future reality, but it is unavoidable to the myriad projective needs of the many other individuals who want an unmade, unspecific piece of it for millions of different private projective purposes.

By virtue of its malleability and responsiveness to the present needs of different organizations, the future has contributed *ventilation* and *spaciousness* to the political process. The possibilities of the future have offered an expansive frontier refuge from the

19. That entirely improbable person who serves as Washington correspondent for *Vogue* magazine confided in the January, 1968, issue that the "Washington definition of an optimist is a person who believes the future to be uncertain."
20. Bertrand de Jouvenel, *L'art de la conjecture* (Monaco, 1964).
21. A sentence in the 1961 Rockefeller Panel Reports, *Prospect for America* (New York, 1961), conveys only a negative impression of this type of projective use of the future for present purposes: "Lacking a secure footing in reality, men tend to project themselves into a non-existent future or else into an irretrievable past." P. 6. This neglects a whole range of legitimate anticipatory feelings and the beneficial consequences of such future projections. See, for example, Robert Merton's writing on "anticipatory socialization" in *Social Theory and Social Structure* (Glencoe, Ill., 1957), pp. 265 ff.

tightnesses and pressures of today.[22] The individual has been able, in his private feelings about the future, to obtain present satisfactions that may have kept him from loading as many demands onto the governmental system as he might otherwise have done and from pushing as intensely for those demands he has made. Until recently, even those actions of government that reached into the individual's sense of the future, usually affected only small parts of it (and these only for a short stretch ahead); and government incursions into the individual's present or future could be better tolerated because they left much of the future open and undetermined.[23]

The pressure under which the governmental process operates has been reduced also by a related serviceability of the future: the provision of a kind of "hold basket" (the desk tray into which one places matters that one does not wish to deal with immediately). A sense of the future has made it possible for participants in the governmental process to put some matters off until a later time. It has been possible to postpone some matters because of a belief in a neutral or friendly future, a feeling that delay would not irrevocably harm the interests of any potentially affected party. The "hold basket" service of the future for the present has given government greater possibilities for handling issues in a less desperate and urgent atmosphere, greater possibilities for face-saving, for wider consultation, more sophisticated bargaining, fuller rationality, and more toleration.[24]

Up to the point where uncertainty has become distressing, the unmade aspect of the future has also contributed zest and entertainment values to the governmental process, as it has to life in general. The "gaming" aspect of government and economic life

22. Thus, Boris Pasternak, living in the tightness of 1948 Russia, wrote (to Nina Tabidze): ". . . love of the future is for me as much a constant and intimate thing as love of a woman, and I can't do without it" (*Letters to Georgian Friends* [New York, 1968]).

23. This does not apply, of course, to government decisions on such extreme issues as the religious controversies of the 16th and 17th centuries or the drafting of citizens for hazardous wartime service.

24. General Marshall described the objective of United States foreign policy in 1948, when America and Russia confronted one another during the Cold War: "to hang on for twenty or thirty years without starting a nuclear war," hoping that the United States and Soviet irreconcilabilities would gradually lessen. Richard Rovere, "A New Situation in the World," *New Yorker*, Feb. 24, 1968, pp. 43–72.

noted by Frank Knight, Norton Long, and others has been possible only because of certain underlying assumptions about the benignity of the future as it affects the understood "rules of the game." (The whole entertainment aspect of government and politics awaits fuller analysis. All that can be said here is that the ways the governmental process is affected by desires for entertainment are likely to be related to the attractions offered in other areas of society, including their future attractions.)

All of the matters just discussed affect the amount and kinds of consensus vested in the governmental process. Other aspects of the future have been more directly useful in this respect. The most familiar is the use of prospects of the future as inducement or balm in securing present obedience, co-operation, deprivation, or sacrifice. Supported by beliefs in the advertised prospects of the future, people have sacrificed or endured a great deal without losing allegiance to the governmental system. This is, on the societal level, the same use of the future as a *winch* to get through present adversity that one finds in individual life. It has been useful even in populations less allegedly optimistic about the future than the American. For even in a country with an arduous present and modest hopes, the prospect of a future terminal date for present unpleasantness can be supportive, just as bomber pilots have been sustained by the knowledge that their exposure to danger will end after a given number of missions.

The ability to manipulate and "time" future prospects to secure needed present behavior is part of the art of government. It is usually a present-oriented art, even though some present purposes may be seen as instrumental for future goals. Two examples may illustrate its variations and complexities. One is the use of planning goals as incentives (or "carrots") rather than as realistic predictions.[25] Another is governmental promulgation of a particular goal, and the scheduling of progress toward that goal, in such a manner that the real costs will not be felt until long after the decision has been taken. Such scheduling will result in the strong-

25. Ely Devons, *Planning in Practice* (Cambridge, 1950), chap. ii. Chap. iii contains an excellent example of present organizational needs resulting in fantasies rather than accuracy, in making estimates of future resource needs. See especially p. 47.

est deprivations being felt years after the decision, by which time, whether because of the size of the investment already made or because habituation has sanctified the goal, the commitment is seen as irreversible. This technique postpones the severest deprivations until beyond the point of no return; the persons who will bear most of the costs have not yet realistically imagined them when the decision is made, if, in fact, they were old enough to be active participants in the governmental process at that time. One example in the United States is the staggered rise in social security taxes over the last thirty years. Another is the apparent inability to mobilize substantial opposition to decisions to develop a supersonic transport until after the airplane has been built and the citizens actually feel disturbed by its sonic booms.

Finally, the governmental system, like the private corporation and the society as a whole, has depended for the present synchronization and ordering of its many parts upon the prevalence and acceptance of certain beliefs about the future. This dependence, over and above the reliance on beliefs about the future as an aspect of legitimation, arises partly because of the need for predictability of the behavior of others in a complex pattern of co-operation and specialization of effort.[26]

Some of these beliefs about the future have been necessary simply to enable the governmental system to function and survive in the here-and-now. If one assumes, as many organizational theorists and psychiatrists do, that the overriding need is to assure the continued functioning and survival of the individual or the organization, then the "values of the future" which are functional for the present survival of the governmental system may be given as crucial as, or even more weight than, the substantive values of the future-oriented goals and issues that form the subject of political debate. Organizations from the League of Women Voters to political parties and trade unions have been known to create or shape future goals primarily to assure their present

26. Wilbert E. Moore, *Man, Time, and Society* (New York, 1963); Michael Banton, *Roles* (London, 1965); Merton, *op. cit.*; Ralf Dahrendorf, *Homo Sociologicus* (Cologne, 1964); Aiden Southall, "An Operational Theory of Role," *Hum. Rel.*, XII (1959), 17–34.

survival and strength, just as demagogues have exploited the future for present purposes.[27]

Changes Affecting Present-Future Relationships

The interest of the present in the future, and the relationships between present and future, have been profoundly affected by occurrences since 1946.

There has been, first, a constellation composed of: (1) greater capacity for technological innovation; (2) a rapid increase in the rate of creation of new knowledge; and (3) an increase in the over-all rate of change in the society. These factors, multiplied by the ability and disposition of large organizations to invest in their implementation, amplification, and exploitation, are alleged to be transforming many aspects of life in America and western Europe. Some see the rate of transformation as increasing so rapidly with the future moving so quickly into the present, and the present so rapidly toward the past, that they believe that utopianism, or other visions of a sharp break with the present, are no longer possible.[28] Allegations that the rate of change today is greater than ever before—and still increasing—are heard with a frequency considerably in excess of the presentation of hard supporting data. But the studies of Frank Lynn and others, cau-

27. In this connection see William K. Muir, Jr., "Defending 'the Hill' Against Metal Houses," in Edwin A. Bock, ed., *State and Local Government: A Casebook* (University, Ala., 1963), p. 14.

28. For apparent empirical confirmation, using data on difficulties of contemporary government and business executives in keeping abreast of changes (and consequently having little time for long-run planning or the visualization of radical alternatives), see F. Sherwood, *The Executive's 14-Hour Day* and *Planning the Future: What Does the Leader Do?* (Mimeographed papers, School of Public Administration, University of Southern California, 1965 and 1966).

F. Polak, *The Image of the Future* (New York, 1961), especially chaps. xviii–xix, attributes the decline in radically different visions of the future partly also to the disenchantment produced by the failure of past visions of the future. See also the different views of Frank Manuel and Judith Shklar in the *Daedalus* issue on "Utopia," Spring, 1965.

For a description of how knowledge and appreciation of the present can exert a general dampening effect on a powerful imagination when it is applied to future possibilities, see the picture of Tolstoy's thinking in Isaiah Berlin, *The Hedgehog and the Fox* (New York, 1957), pp. 111–112.

tiously assessed and analyzed in the 1966 report of the National Commission on Technology, Automation, and Economic Progress, lend support to some of the impressionistic statements about the high rate of change that have been made by commentators upon almost every aspect of current life.[29] One of the more estimable of these commentators has declared:

This world of ours is a new world in which the unity of knowledge, the nature of human communities, the order of society, the order of ideas, the very notions of society and culture have changed and will not return to what they have been in the past. What is new is new not because it has never been there before, but because it has changed in quality. One thing that is new is the prevalence of newness, the changing scale and scope of change itself.[30]

A second factor changing and intensifying the relationship of present to future is the growth, since 1945, of our capacity to affect the future, intentionally or unintentionally. The extreme example is our nuclear capacity for destroying civilization on the earth. But there are many less dramatic and less negative capabilities. Advances in medicine are seriously affecting the nature of the future population. Up to now most of these (such as the increase in the percentage of diabetics in the population as a result of medicine prolonging to and through childbearing age the lives of diabetics who in earlier times would have died in youth) have been widely ignored, even though it is apparent that they will have a profound impact upon the future.

Examples of increasing long-run impact can be found in many

29. Summarizing Lynn's research, the Commission concludes: "The typical time between a technical discovery and recognition of its commercial potential had fallen from about 30 years before the First World War to . . . 9 years after the Second World War. The additional time required to convert these basic technical discoveries to initial commercial application had decreased from about 7 years to about 5 years" (*Technology and the American Economy,* Report of the National Commission on Technology, Automation, and Economic Progress [Washington, 1966], pp. 1, 33). The sum of informed opinion appears to support this view, although, as may be imagined, the measurement of technological change is a complex matter about which experts have differing conclusions and methodologies. See Lester B. Lave, *Technological Change: Its Conception and Measurement* (Englewood Cliffs, N.J., 1966). For interesting differences in estimates on this subject, see the views of British (Lord Todd) and American (I. I. Rabi) Nobel prize winners in physics in Nigel Calder, ed., *The World in 1984,* Penguin, *New Scientist* series (New York, 1965), pp. 1, 9–15.

30. Robert Oppenheimer, "Prospects in the Arts and Sciences," in Boyko, *op. cit.,* p. 43.

other fields. Advances in genetics, meteorology, psychiatry, and economics, to cite just a few, have given us the capability in our present actions of affecting more of the future, regardless of whether we do it intentionally or unintentionally. And recently some strong claims have been made about capabilities for shaping the future arising from alleged advances in psychology and its derivative applications in education, advertising, and public relations.[31]

In addition to the advances just cited, one must take note of our growing ability to increase the magnitude of organized programs and projects (such as the Apollo program, the National Highway program, regional planning, larger particle accelerators, massive education programs, etc.), thus making for greater possibility of impact on the future, whether by exploitation of new advances or by the increasing magnitude of actions in existing areas. Our economy in peacetime gives us a surplus for capital investment. Aided by improvements arising from the social sciences, education, psychology, and advertising, our organizational capacity (governments, corporations, and other forms of large-scale purposive co-operation) to produce large and far-reaching effects, and to make use of the potentialities of greater investment and new discoveries, is evidently growing and not only in such obvious organizations as the United States Department of Defense, or the British Ministries of Technology and of Education and Science, where lead times of ten years are fairly common.[32]

31. For the assessment of the so-called revolution in cognitive psychology, see Platt, *op. cit.* See also Jerome Bruner, *The Process of Education* (Cambridge, Mass., 1960).

32. Wilbert Moore cited a lumber corporation that plans forest policy one hundred years ahead as an exceptional case in *The Conduct of the Corporation* (New York, 1962), p. 32. But a number of very large corporations have sectoral research and development plans with lead times of 10 to 15 years or longer, not to mention those that use 20-year or longer periods as a basis for capital investment strategy. The author is familiar with a study conducted for the Board of Directors of a large international corporation in the heavy electrical industry in the late 1950's. The purpose was to determine what was an appropriate long-term period to use in decision-making about capital investment and development activities in research and market exploitation. The recommendation, 60 years, was based partly on the particular situation of this heavy industry and partly on what could be justified in terms of the life duration of individual stockholders.

The long-term debt (bonds) of the American Telephone and Telegraph Company is close to $9,000,000,000. Many corporate bonds traded on the New York Stock Exchange run beyond the year 2050.

We appear to be in a period in which the flows of scientific and technological innovation, of economic surpluses for investment, and of organizational capacity are combining to produce more actions with more impact on a broader and deeper sector of the future than has been true before.

Toward the Conquest of the Future

A third factor changing the state of present-future relationships is the growing desire and determination to make use of our greater capacity to affect the future, to use it consciously and deliberately to create what appear to us to be desirable conditions for those who will be alive ten to fifty years hence. The combustible mixture of our growing capacity to affect the future with this growing determination to use this capacity has already set in motion action programs designed to shape or to create specific conditions in important sectors of the future. Among many possible examples, one may cite programs of family planning, conservation, education, urban planning, national economic planning, and resource development; others include long-range environmental health and sanitation programs, programs to create ample future supplies of scientific manpower, and large-scale development programs aimed at internal regions, such as the Upper Colorado Basin or the North East Region of England, or at the underdeveloped nations that are expected to form an increasingly important part of our world environment.

It seems likely that the action programs already under way are only the small beginnings of much more extensive efforts to shape deliberately larger sectors of future life. For what has increased more than action is the *desire* to shape, mold, or "invent" more and more aspects and sectors of future life. What has increased is the feeling that it is necessary, or right, or admirable to use in purposeful fashion our swelling capabilities to affect the future.

A moderate expression of such feeling is the carefully worded position taken by the National Commission on Technology, Automation, and Economic Progress:

We have become increasingly aware of the multiple impacts of social change . . . and, in so doing, we realize that we have to plan ahead. We have to anticipate social change. We need to assess its consequences. . . . Since social change is increasingly a matter of conscious decisions and social choices, and given the huge resources we possess, we can decide what kind of future we want and work for it.[33]

The Commission's conclusion is that our society is becoming much more "future oriented"; that we are increasingly able to "invent the future"; that we should do so; and that we should strengthen our institutional capacity for doing so.

Today the calls for making or consciously deciding about the future comes from almost all sides, from leaders of many different interests and "establishments": the United States Chamber of Commerce, Walter Reuther, James Reston, Whitney Young, John Gardner, the CIO, the CED, the Catholic bishops, and the National Academy of Science.[34] There may not have been such unanimity about starting to do something among eminent public men with undisputed claims to the thoughtful attention of conscientious citizens since Urban II launched the First Crusade.

According to Olaf Helmer, a leading expert in future studies, the past few years have seen the appearance of

a wholly new attitude towards the future . . . among policy planners and others concerned with the future of our society. . . . Customary planning horizons are being extended into a more distant future, and intuitive gambles—as a basis for planning—are being replaced by systematic analysis of the opportunities the future has to offer . . . the research community in particular is realizing the enormous power and responsibility it has in selecting among the multitude of possible futures. . . .[35]

33. *Op. cit.*, pp. 105–106.
34. The Executive Vice-President of the United States Chamber of Commerce, at the annual meeting of that body in May, 1966, urged the country as a whole, and businessmen in particular, to intensify efforts to plan the future and to set in motion the action sequences necessary to realize these plans. See also John Gardner's essay, *The Anti-Leadership Vaccine*, the 1965 Annual Report of the Carnegie Corporation of New York; Reston's column in the New York *Times*, editorial page, May 1, 1966; and Committee for Economic Development, *Budgeting for National Objectives* (New York, 1966), p. 12.
35. "Science," *Science Journal* (Oct., 1967), pp. 49–57. See also Andrew Shonfield's remarks about British and French attitudes toward national economic planning in *Modern Capitalism* (New York, 1965), pp. 221–236.

The general rise of the ethos of creating or selecting the future has been marked by shelves of commission reports and technical studies about sectorial problems, studies that point the way to sequences of action necessary to create improved future conditions.[36] Then there are the less widely circulated plans that guide the agencies and foundations that seek to foster critical improvements in various features of future life.[37]

Among intellectuals, one sees the growth of committees, programs, commissions, and institutes devoted to forecasting, analysis of choices, simulations of various kinds of futures, and recommendations about what should be done about different aspects of the future. A new expertise in studying and deciding the future, possibly the beginning of a new scientific field, is taking shape around the sophisticated work of Helmer and others at the Rand Corporation and at more publicized future-oriented institutions like the Hudson Institute. Another eminent example is the Futuribles series initiated by de Jouvenal with aid from the Ford Foundation. One may cite also the Commission for the Year 2000 of the American Academy of Arts and Sciences, Robert Jungk's Institut fur Zukunftsfragen in Vienna, and Organization of the Future at California Institute of Technology. These are only a few of the intellectual efforts that now focus purposefully on the state of things ten to fifty years hence.[38]

36. To cite only a few for purposes of illustration: the 1952 Report of the Paley (Materials Policy) Commission on Natural Resources and subsequent studies sponsored by Resources for the Future; the President's Manpower Report of 1964; the 1963 Robbins Report on Higher Education (in Britain); the 1960 OECD Report, *Forecasting Manpower Needs for the Age of Science;* the 1965 Plowden Report on the British Aircraft Industry; the 1964 Report of the National Academy of Sciences on *Federal Support of Basic Research in Institutions of Higher Learning* and the 1965 Report of the same body on *Basic Research and National Goals;* the Report of the 1965 Group connected with the French government's planning organization (1966); the report issued in Nov., 1965, by the Environmental Pollution Panel of the President's Science Advisory Committee, *Restoring the Quality of Our Environment;*. the 1966 Report on *Weather Modification* released by the United States National Science Foundation; and the 1964 Report of the Royal Institute of Chartered Surveyors (London) advocating a 40-year lead time for regional planning.

37. J. George Harrar, *Foundations for the Future* (New York, 1967).

38. For an initial survey of the expanding literature, see Annette Harrison, *Bibliography on Automation and Technological Change and Studies of the Future,* Rand Report AD 667213, March, 1968.

Some important references and recent examples are: OECD, *Technological Forecasting in Perspective* (Paris, 1967); "Toward the Year 2000: Work in

We have, then, the fact of our swelling capabilities to affect the future; the fact that we are setting in train increasing numbers of action programs to shape sectors of the future; and the fact that an ethos about the necessity and rightness of shaping the future has risen to the point of unchallengibility in the minds of many different kinds of opinion leaders and men of affairs. There is also the possibility that this ethos favoring "futurization" will spread throughout the society, losing much of its original restraint[39] as it is amplified by the middle men of the mass media; that it will become a prevailing political "fashion"; and that it will soak into the texture of our social values and mix with our underlying latent present needs to exploit the future. Thus, no political leader may have the credentials for mass appeal unless he personifies a hearty, present-satisfying disposition in favor of shaping,

Progress," *Daedalus*, XCVI (Summer, 1967); Herman Kahn and Anthony J. Wiener, *The Year 2000* (New York, 1967); de Jouvenel, *L'art de la conjecture*, *op. cit.;* the "Futuribles" series in Bulletin S.E.D.E.I.S. (Paris), including in No. 863, Daniel Bell's study, "Douze modes de prevision en science sociale" (Sept. 20, 1963); Harold Lasswell, *The Future of Political Science* (New York, 1963); Jean Meynaud, "A Propos de Spéculations sur l'avenir," *Revue Française de Science Politique*, (Sept., 1963), 666–668, and (Aug., 1965), 705–730; Calder, *op. cit.;* N. Dalkey and Olaf Helmer, "An Experimental Application of the Delphi Method to the Use of Experts," *Management Science*, IX (Apr., 1963); Herman Kahn, *On Thermonuclear War* (Princeton, 1960); Dennis Gabor, *Inventing the Future* (London, 1962); Gordon E. Wolstenholme, ed., *Man and His Future* (London, 1963).

"Futurism" is much on the minds of West European intellectuals and journal editors. The origin, and still most prolific source of publications on this theme, is France. In addition to the "Futuribles" and the Meynaud works cited above, see Edgar Morin, "L'avenir dans la société française," in Jean-Daniel Reynaud, ed., *Tendances et Volontés de la Société Française*, "Futuribles," S.E.D.E.I.S. (Paris, 1966), and the articles on the theme "Prospective et Utopie" in *Esprit* (Feb., 1966).

Another group of French intellectuals sponsored by the journal *Prospective* also has been active in analyzing present-future relationships. The magazine *Realitiés* sponsored a meeting of "specialists du futur" in Paris in 1966. Meynaud reports in his 1965 article, cited above, similar studies in Switzerland and a symposium of twenty Soviet scientists on the future: Serge Gouchtchev and Michel Vassiliev, *La vie au XXIe siècle* (Paris, 1964). See also the report of Lord Brain's 1966 Presidential Address to the British Association for the Advancement of Science, *Times* (London), Aug. 27, 1966, p. 11. And the series of studies on national economic planning directed by Bertram M. Gross, published by the Syracuse University Press, 1966.

39. Such as the limiting factors analyzed by Devons, Shonfield, *op. cit.;* and Samuel Brittan, *The Treasury Under the Tories* (London, 1964), pp. 298 f. See also those analyzed in Bertram M. Gross, "National Planning: Findings and Fallacies," *Pub. Admin. Rev.*, XXV (Dec., 1965), 263–273. And, in the same issue, by Charles E. Lindblom, "Economics and the Administration of National Planning," pp. 274–283.

making, or manipulating large sectors of the future. Leadership may come to be equated with aggressive aspirations to affect the future more boldly, more thoroughly, and more completely than the next man. Such attitudes may come to permeate far beyond the precincts of the originating elite or opinion-influencing groups, marking a considerable contrast to the "futurelessness" that was so conspicuous in Robert Lane's analysis of the personal outlooks of fifteen American "common men" (i.e., $2,400–$6,300 annual income range) in 1958.[40]

However, it is not necessary to conjure up these latter possibilities to make the point that efforts at molding, constructing, or creating conditions of future life, seen as desirable improvements from the perspective of the present, have increased and are likely to continue to increase in magnitude and number. The existing ethos in favor of "futurization" and our growing capability to affect the future combine to produce this result. These two forces, along with the increase in the rate of change and the development of new knowledge, are three factors that have changed the relationship between present and future. Their combined effect is to increase substantially the likelihood of control of the situations of those who will live in the future by those who live in the present. The increase in the extent of this control raises substantial difficulties for the functioning of the governmental system. It also raises the disturbing prospect of a new colonialism: the under-represented inhabitants of USA-2000 consciously being brought under the well-intentioned, but fundamentally self-serving and necessarily remote, imperium of USA-1969.

The Changing Serviceability of the Future for the Functioning of Government

In the first section of this essay I tried to describe how certain aspects of the future have had the effect of facilitating consensus and relieving pressure on the governmental process. The reader may recall the shorthand terms for some of these aspects: "cornu-

40. *Political Ideology* (New York, 1962), pp. 283 f.

copia," "ventilation and spaciousness," "hold basket," and "winch." How is the serviceability of these aspects of the future to the functioning of government likely to be affected by the changes in present-future relationships caused by the increase in the rate of change and introduction of new knowledge, by our growing capacity to affect the future, and by our apparently growing determination to make use of this capacity? I offer the following observations as an overture to a full discussion of this complex question.

The cornucopia and ventilation-spaciousness aspects of the future have, from an analytical standpoint, been considerably affected by our growing "futurization." The unmade and uncertain aspect of the future that enabled men to use it, like a projective test situation, as an almost boundless source of hope, pleasure, succor, and escape is diminishing to the extent that present long-range predictions and programs are converting parcels of amorphous future into "built up" tracts that contain specific realities or quasi-realities, tracts that are under the specific claim of someone's specific present interest in the future. Being more or less filled in by specifics, these tracts of the future are no longer infinitely malleable to fit the separate, private projective needs and desires of many different individuals. These appropriated, built up tracts can no longer be all things to all men. They are unavailable for satisfying myriad private present needs—directly and not through the action of the political system—by the projective satisfactions they offer individuals; satisfactions that have at times kept individuals from overburdening the political and economic system with demands and have at other times provided balm against deprivations felt as arising from the operation of the governmental or economic systems.[41] Whether the filling-in of tracts of the future with specific claims and predicted consequences of long-term plans has gone so far that there is now not

41. The situation might become similar to what Jacques Ellul says life is like today in industrialized countries: ". . . dreams and hope have been the traditional means of escape in times of famine and prosecution. But today there is no hope, and the dream is no longer the personal act of an individual who freely chooses to flee some 'reality' or other. It is a mass phenomenon of millions of men who desire to help themselves to a slice of life, freedom, and immortality" (*The Technological Society* [New York, 1964], p. 377).

enough amorphous future left to satisfy multivariate private projected needs is doubtful. But if "futurization" continues to grow,
the individual may have to look further and further ahead to
reach a piece of unclaimed, "unbuilt-upon" future suitable for his
projective needs. And here we face the fact that the life span may
set a limit to the individual's ability to reach this frontier.[42]

Perhaps we may assume, however, that we make up on the
"swings" what we have lost on the "roundabouts." The great
increase in our capacity to shape the future should also increase
the present sense of future possibilities available for the imaginations of citizens. This could result in a greater feeling of potency
and freedom of choice. Whether large, long-term programs for
shaping the future will open up more of the future for the projective needs of individuals than they fence in (will the moon be
more or less serviceable to projective imaginings after men land
on it?), whether they will increase or decrease the sense of
openness, liberty, and potency felt by individuals in the present
about the future, is impossible to answer. Some, like Polak—if I
interpret his two volumes correctly—are inclined to believe that
the appropriation of the future by increasing numbers of long-
term projects that make specific more and more of what was
formerly amorphous is actually destroying more of the projective
potentiality of the future than it is creating; for it is destroying
the possibility of men imagining any radical viable alternatives to
the large-scale projects already under way, and any radical viable
alternatives to the fundamental social, economic, and political
arrangements under which these long-term projects are being
carried out.[43]

Unfortunately, there is less ground for uncertainty about the
continued serviceability of that aspect of the future earlier designated by the term "hold basket": an attitude toward the future
that permits the governmental system to delay decision on some
matters, the interested parties feeling that postponement will not
irrevocably damage their prospects for ultimately achieving their

42. See Dr. A. E. Parr's hypothesis that delinquent behavior in cities is partly a
response to "the increasing predictability of the perceptual environment," in
"Environmental Design and Psychology," *Landscape*, XIV (Winter, 1964–65),
15–18.
43. Polak, *op. cit.*, "The Futureless Future," Vol. II, chap. xiv, pp. 114 ff.

political aims. This use of the future takes some of the pressure off the settlement of disputes through the political system and facilitates a broader and more tolerant consideration of public questions. With the increasing rate of change, the use of the future as a "hold basket" is less feasible, because delay brings the possibility of a totally new situation next year, and the possibility of new proposals usurping temporal and funding priority. Moreover, insofar as governmental decisions involve the appropriation of resources for large, long-term programs that become, in effect, irreversible after the first large expenditure, the hazard in having one's own proposal delayed raises the possibility that the first successful claimants in the queue will have made off with the critical resources. Hence, the pressure-relieving, "hold basket" serviceability of the future is likely to decline.[44]

One of the likely consequences of this decline is that the securing of temporal priorities for major forms of government attention and action (legislative or executive) will be the subject of more urgent and intense conflict than it is today. Struggles to dominate the temporal control points (deadlines, etc.) may increase in frequency and intensity, and greater prominence will be given to what Richard Neustadt has identified as the "action forcing" mechanisms in the governmental system. Another possibility is that there will be much greater recognition of the initiative of the President and of key congressional leaders to determine the temporal foci (i.e., how much of the future is relevant as compared to the present for bargaining, debate, and decision on any particular issue).

Access to Points of Prevision

One of the middle-range problems arising for government from the new relationship to the future is how to secure equality of access to the equipment and vantage points that accurate prevision of the future is likely to require. If the society becomes increasingly future-oriented, if shaping the future is increasingly

44. This assumes, of course, that resources will never expand to the point where they exceed claimants. When one considers that skilled manpower to manage long-term, large-scale projects is likely to remain in short supply, this seems a fair assumption. See also Kenneth Boulding, "Is Scarcity Dead?" *Public Interest*, No. 5 (Fall, 1966), pp. 36–44.

fashionable and admired as a governmental activity, and if political leaders gain standing in rough proportion to their advocacy of ambitious long-term plans deemed desirable and feasible by the public, one may witness competing political leaders attempting to outflank one another toward the distant future—in a competition reminiscent of the way the German and the French armies reached toward the sea in 1914. Higher esteem may be given to the candidates whose plans appear to be based on the longest, most accurate pictures of the future; even more than now it may be necessary for leaders to demonstrate that their programs "fit" into some alleged long-term pattern of future developments. To achieve standing and support, leaders will need to possess, or appear to possess, a substantial amount of "hard" prevision.[45] Assuming that the system rejects pure demagogic bluffing, and that alternative large-scale plans for future shaping (i.e., other than those integrally connected with the ones currently being carried out by the government) are to be tolerated, opposition leaders need equality of access to the equipment, the data, and the scarce expertise[46] upon which the ability to fashion realistic pictures of the future will depend. Since the collection of the large amounts of data needed for over-all, long-range previsions may increasingly require the resources of government or similar large organizations,[47] there is likely to be an exacerbation of the

45. See Keynes reference in 1930 to "the wealthy classes" as "our advance guard —those who are spying out the promised land for the rest of us" (*op. cit.*, p. 368). Thirty years later, the merely rich would be the last to be regarded as the group with the most valuable access to the future. For a temporally comparative view of the status of prophets in the early Middle Ages, deriving partly from the presumed monopoly of prevision, see Jeffrey B. Russell, *Dissent and Reform in the Early Middle Ages* (Berkeley, 1965), pp. 101 ff. Consider the public alarm if it were believed that a contemporary American President really felt as John Adams wrote in 1779: "There is no such Thing as human Wisdom. . . . Perhaps few Men have guessed more exactly than I have been allowed to do, upon several Occasions, but at this Time, which is the first I declare of my whole Life, I am wholly at a Loss to foresee Consequences" (*Diary and Autobiography of John Adams* [Cambridge, Mass., 1961], II, 354).

46. S. Lilley, "Can Prediction Become a Science?" in Bernard Barber and Walter Hirsch, *Sociology of Science* (Glencoe, Ill., 1962).

47. It does now. See the articles by Jantsch and Helmer in "Forecasting the Future," *Science Journal,* London (Oct., 1967). Joseph Kraft notes in *Profiles In Power* (New York, 1966): "Almost all the important problems of government go beyond the range of individual knowledge. Even to know what to think, much more to convince others what to think, about the problems of government requires mountains of detailed information that can only be produced by large staffs" (p. 67).

already existing problem caused by government agencies acting in dual, contradictory capacities: (1) as neutral sources of data and (2) as contenders, or parties at interest, in the struggle to decide how such data should be interpreted in making policy choices.[48] The ability of the government to control access to data and predictive studies prepared for it by its own agencies or by captive institutes or contractors would give it an unchallengeable advantage in prevision. If the trend toward "futurization" intensifies, continuation of open political competition may require, at the very least, that data banks used by government be available to non-governmental computer centers for use by non-governmental experts: "Forecasting the future is not a task for government alone. In fact, the concentration of forecasting mechanisms entirely in the hands of government, particularly at times when such forecasting becomes a necessary condition of public policy, risks one-sided judgments—and even suppression of forecasts for political ends."[49]

Problems Arising from the Colonial Status of the Future

To recapitulate: we are today, in a time of rapid change and the development of new knowledge, possessed of immense capabilities for affecting the future. We are also increasingly possessed by a determination to use this capacity in order to shape beneficially the conditions that will form the environment of those who live ten to fifty years hence. Increasing numbers of well-designed, well-led, well-organized expeditions are being outfitted and are setting forth to civilize, exploit, and build up sectors of unoccupied future. More and more, the lives of the inhabitants of these far-off temporal lands are going to be affected, if not largely

48. This conflict will be illuminated in several studies—including one of SST decision-making and one on Weather Modification plans—now being prepared by the Inter-University Case Program. For a case from the field of agricultural statistics, see H. Rosenbaum, *The Burning of the Farm Population Estimates,* Inter-University Case Program Series No. 83 (Indianapolis, 1964).

49. *Technology and the American Economy,* p. 106.

determined, by conscious decisions made in the mother country of the present.

Such decisions, whatever their manifest beneficial aims, satisfy underlying needs of the present. I have described in the first section some of the powerful needs and interests that cause persons and organizations in the present to want to manipulate or use the future, and that have often caused them to delude themselves about the future. These present interests, sometimes unarticulated and unrecognized, permeate our future-oriented plans and programs, whether they are altruistic or selfish, technological or educational. This is not to say that men and institutions are not capable of working altruistically to improve future conditions. It is to say that their desires, conceptions, decisions, and actions affecting the future are likely to be profoundly, and often predominantly, affected by those various kinds of present needs and interests essential for maintaining the capacity to function and for maintaining subsistence levels of well-being, orientation, and organic cohesiveness. The rate of change, the development of new knowledge, and the capability for affecting the future all may increase rapidly, but the inner core of present needs (of persons *and* organizations) to use the future to serve present purposes changes slowly, if at all.[50] I have not found any strong evidence for believing that men or organizations in countries with high-powered economies are more capable of managing their present interests in exploiting the future than those in other countries. We can, it is true, apprehend and appreciate longer chains of cause-and-effect relationships than Doob's Africans who took the ten shilling note instead of waiting for a larger, delayed reward.[51] And it is true that we seem to be more successful at saving and building up piles of capital to invest. But the continued rise in cigarette sales suggests that our capacity to overcome present needs on behalf of future health is quite limited. Some of our vaunted capacity for saving and investment is ex-

50. René Dubos, "Science and Man's Nature," *Daedalus,* XCV (Winter, 1965), 223–244.

51. Leonard W. Doob, *Becoming More Civilized: A Psychological Exploration* (New Haven, 1960). See also the studies of middle and working class children and of French villagers in Fraisse, *op. cit.,* pp. 174–177.

plained by the present gratifications arising from "bone-burying" reassurances of future security and power. Some is explained by the involuntary contributions made by individuals who have no choice but to pay the set prices (that include the profit margin) and the taxes. And many of the longer-run actions of corporations (re-investing profits rather than paying dividends) and of our democratic governments (see the record of fluoridation decisions in America)[52] are possible only because of devices that permit the circumvention of direct popular control or referendum.[53]

The permeation, not to say domination, of our future-oriented efforts by underlying present needs would not of itself establish, between those living in the present and those living in the future, a self-serving, exploitive colonial relationship of doubtful rightness, if it could be shown that the essential interests of the present coincide with the essential interests of the future. We yearn to believe that such a coincidence of interests exists. It would be an ideal world if we could shape the future to fit our present needs and at the same time enjoy the supreme additional pleasure (for The Man Who Has Everything) of feeling morally virtuous about serving the best interests of those who will inhabit our nation twenty years hence. But there are reasons against believing in a coincidence of interests of those living in the present and those living twenty or more years hence.

Our present needs to delude ourselves into believing, of our

52. Donald B. Rosenthal and Robert L. Crain, "Executive Leadership and Community Innovation: The Fluoridation Experience," *Urb. Aff. Quart.,* I (Mar., 1966), 15–38. And, by the same authors, "Structure and Values in Local Political Systems," *Jour. of Pol.,* XXVIII (Feb., 1966), 169–195. But see also the broader study by Harlan Hahn, "Public Decision-Making: A Study of Municipal Referenda" (preliminary draft, mimeo, Ann Arbor, Nov., 1966).

53. The willingness of American youth to spend longer years at educational preparation than Borneo bushmen is sometimes adduced as evidence of greater capacity to endure present deprivations on behalf of a distant reward. Apart from substantial differences in felt-deprivations, and a rather mean view of learning, this contention overlooks the tendency of young Americans to take present pleasure (1) in the status of university students, (2) in the anticipatory but presently-experienced reassurance derived from following a pattern of activity believed certain to produce long-run benefits (the bone-burying syndrome), and (3) in being able, at the same time, to complain about fancied deprivations.

The whole matter is difficult to assess, because of the need for fine subjective distinctions. Was Archbishop Cranmer actually responding altruistically to presumed needs of the future or to present needs when he held his hand in the fire a few minutes before being burned at the stake?

future-shaping activities, that we are serving the future, and not a combination of manifest and latent *present* needs to use the future, can blind us to possibilities that such activities may have negative effects upon the future that counterbalance or outweigh their benefits.[54] For example, it seems likely that much of the present belief in the "futurization" ethos is really a defensive reaction that seeks, by attempts to establish greater control over the future, a strengthened sense of orientation and security in our present lives, bewildered and unsettled as they are by the present impact of change. This is an example of self-delusion concealing a characteristic effort to use the future for important present needs. It is also likely to be self-defeating as far as its latent purposes go. For the mission of molding and inventing the future will require new technological, organizational, and governmental practices, the discovery and institution of which may further increase the rate of change.

We are only just beginning to see that the problems of raising the level of living, the quality of education, housing, and medical care of the poorest third of the nation call for immense amounts of social inventiveness, for new institutional devices, new forms of cooperation, social control, ownership, and administration. . . .[55]

There are more concrete examples of delusion about present vs. future interests resulting in the overlooking of important negative consequences. Witness the unfortunate American upper atmosphere nuclear explosions, the often unhappy consequences of excessive (and underlyingly self-serving) parental affection, and the uncomfortably wide number of possible applications of Wilde's line that "each man kills the things he loves." And one does not need to be a reactionary to appreciate the point (made by Tom Wicker, among others) that President Johnson's Great Society welfare, health, and education programs, spawned partly by his desires to remove for today's youth the obstacles he faced as a young man, may actually prevent contemporary young Americans from becoming as energetic, as wide ranging, and as

54. See the intricate examples in Carl W. Borgman, *Man's Use of Science: Some Deferred Costs* (New York, 1965).
55. Richard Titmuss, "The Irresponsible Society," *Listener,* Aug. 11, 1960, p. 208.

appreciative of opportunities as Johnson had to become when there were no such programs fifty years ago.

One reason for believing that the interests of the present and the future are different rather than the same is analytical in character. One of the powerful present needs about the future is the need to see it as sufficiently open and sufficiently pliable to make one think that it can be shaped by one's plans and actions. What this condition serves is our present need to feel a sense of potency, a sense of freedom, and a sense of potential personal consequence. This is one of the needs met by present efforts to shape the future with long-range programs of great magnitude. One may argue that an increase in the number of such programs need not create a sense of "unfreedom" and confinement of choice on the part of those who live, twenty years later, in an environment shaped by their successful outcomes. For, it could be argued, the population of 1985 will be able to achieve its sense of potency, freedom, and consequence by using the conditions we are creating for it in even more ambitious efforts to shape the life situations of those who will live in 2005.

There are three problems with this argument. One is that the method of finding freedom, creativity, and a sense of consequence by progressively ambitious shapings of the future may ultimately, if such efforts are successful, create a situation in which a man aged twenty may face an impossibly dense and unpliable life situation, created by the accretion of past future-shaping efforts, stretching further ahead than his remaining life expectancy. A second is that massive efforts at future shaping create limitations as well as potentialities, as our greater sophistication with technological and economic planning is showing us.[56]

56. See, for example, the account of the delay caused in the development and testing of the Sabin polio vaccine by the introduction of the Salk vaccine in J. A. Shannon, "NIH—Present and Potential Contribution to Application of Biomedical Knowledge," paper presented at Conference on Research in the Service of Man, Oklahoma City, Oct. 25, 1966, pp. 7–10. See also René Dubos, *Mirage of Health* (New York, 1959), and Bertram M. Gross, "Activating National Plans," in Gross, ed., *Action Under Planning* (New York, 1967), chap. vii.

John and Sylvia Jewkes have written: "It may be that the National Health Service, because of its form, has positively discouraged the allocation of resources to the purposes of medicine" (*The Genesis of the British Health Service* [Oxford, 1961], pp. 36–37). See also Alvin M. Weinberg, "Criteria for Scientific Choice," *Minerva*, I (Winter, 1963), 159–171.

Continuity vs. Growing Separation of
Generations: The Problem of Representation

The third, and possibly the most important, reason stems from the fact that ambitious, long-term efforts to shape the future require continuity of co-operative behavior for the five to twenty years needed to achieve their purposes. This means that some people will have to be "unfree" enough to fit into the designs of the originators of the future-shaping enterprises.[57] And as these programs increase in number, magnitude, and temporal scope, the number of people in the future who will have to fit the roles necessary to achieve the purposes of today's planners will have to increase. Bliss it is to be alive in the dawn of planning long-term programs for the benefit of others in the future. But to have to spend one's life filling roles created by master architects years earlier is unlikely to be experienced as "very heaven." That would seem to be the conclusion arising from the reactions of the un-crippled organization workers in the Argyris studies or from the demands at the end of World Wars I and II (and now again in 1966–68) that "old men," with limited senses of the future, should hand over the reshaping of the future world to the men of twenty and thirty who would have to do most of the living in it.[58] On the other hand, given the massive investment that some of these forward-reaching projects require (e.g., the construction of new universities, the development of new industries, the training of new kinds of technicians, etc.), it is unlikely that a nation could afford the colossal waste of canceling one before it is completed in order to switch to another.

Another difficulty about the coincidence of interests between

57. "This frank emphasis not on what people want now but on what they will want (or ought to be wanting) in the future is characteristically French in style. But leaving aside the transcendental overtones, it is in practice closely in line with the thinking of a growing body of planners elsewhere in the western world" (Shonfield, *op. cit.*, p. 227).

58. Lord Wavell made this suggestion in 1944. So did T. E. Lawrence in 1919. See also H. G. Wells, "The Optimism of the Uninjured," in *'42 to '44* (London, 1944).

present and future is the now trampled matter of the separation
of generations. Even before the Kennedys exploited it for political purposes, even before the cliché term "generation gap" replaced phonetic reading and the hula hoop as prime subjects of
Sunday-supplement concern, there was worthwhile evidence
from a wide range of unhysterical observers testifying to the
growing gap between generations as a result of increased
change.

David Apter has stated that in societies undergoing rapid political and economic change, a new generation appears every four
years. An astonishingly similar estimate has come from Ned
Rorem, an American composer and diarist. Reviewing Arthur
Honegger's autobiography in the *New York Times Book Review,*
September 11, 1966, he wrote: "Nowadays the life span of new
generations has shrunk to about five years, and musicians go ever
more quickly in and out of vogue." Bertram Gross has seen "in
many contexts, the intermingling of five or more active
generations."[59] And Françoise Gilot has described Matisse explaining to Renoir his inability to appreciate or understand the
paintings of Jackson Pollock:

. . . it becomes all the more difficult for one to understand a kind of
painting whose point of departure lies beyond one's point of arrival.
It's something that's based on completely different foundations. When
we arrive on the scene, the movement of painting for a moment
contains us, swallows us up, and we add perhaps a little link to the
chain. Then the movement continues on past us and we are outside it
and we don't understand it any longer.[60]

There is also the observation of Alan Valentine: "The man born
in 1900 could converse on more common ground with John Bun-
yan or Benjamin Franklin than with his own teen-age son."

Lionel Trilling has commented ". . . the generations don't
carry on from one another. As a teacher, I find that every job *has*
to be done over again from scratch. You can be confronted with a
generation of students, and inoculate them with certain ideas,

59. "The Coming General Systems Models of Social Systems," "Futuribles"
series, 1967.
60. Françoise Gilot and Carlton Lake, *Life With Picasso* (New York, 1964), p.
269.

and then ten years later the equivalent job has to be done all over again."[61] Both Erikson and Lane have noted a tendency in American society to confine one's range of personal interest to one's own generation and to assume that the next generation will have its own problems and peculiarities.[62]

Capping the sheafs of testimony about the difficulty of one generation sharing the same essential interests with another in current times of rapid change is the statement of a middle-aged man, interviewed by Barbara Fried for a book, *The Middle-Aged Crisis*, published in 1967: "Twenty-five years ago, a dopey 18-year-old college kid made up his mind that I was going to be a dentist. So now here I am, a dentist. I'm stuck. What I want to know is: who told that kid he could decide what I was going to do with the rest of my life?"[63]

The gap between generations, or between the interests of the same generation across a twenty-year span of its own lifetime, not only makes it unlikely that there will be a coincidence of essential interests between present and future, but it also calls into question the only other feasible means of preventing a colonial domination of the future by the present, namely, some form of representation of the interests of the future population in future-shaping decision-making. If any such method of representation of the future is to be effective, it will require an ability to empathize with those who will live in the future. But the burden of testimony about the gap between generations in the rapid rate of change we are now experiencing makes such a likelihood seem remote.

There are, however, a number of means of increasing the possibility that our present governmental decision-making will not

61. Possibly germane here is Hugh Auden's identification of surrealism as a natural response to the world of "discontinuous experiences" brought about by modern technology, cited in Paul West, *The Wine of Absurdity* (University Park, Pa., 1966), p. 230.

62. See Lane, *op. cit.*, and especially Erikson, *op. cit.*, p. 277.

63. Quoted in *Time*, July 29, 1966, p. 53. See the remarks of Lawrence S. Kubie about "Some Unsolved Problems of the Scientific Career" in Barber and Hirsch, *op. cit.*, pp. 204–205, especially about the tendency of fantasies about the future making it difficult to communicate between generations. See also D. N. Michael, *The Next Generation* (New York, 1965).

exploit the future excessively. They include constitutional changes and administrative innovations that would give greater weight to, and greater recognition of, the interests of our newest and possibly our last colonial dependency. Exploration of such arrangements is the subject for another essay.

Chapter 10

Conclusion: Some Notes on Time, Administration, and Development

Dwight Waldo

> Work is the scythe of time.
>
> Napoleon

In concluding this volume, I wish to make some further observations on the essays and to say something about directions that further thinking and research might take.

Patently what the eight authors have said does not sum, does not "reach a conclusion." The concepts and categories set forth in the first essay by Savage undoubtedly serve an orienting and framing function for what follows, but they are not adopted in any strict sense by the other essayists as the basis for their own work; nor does the work of any essayist critically rest upon or substantially develop the work of any other. To have presented a product in which this would have been the case would—among other things—have required a different type of "timing" in the enterprise itself. Not only is there great diversity in the themes treated and in the mode of treatment, but the careful reader will have noted some seeming inconsistencies or contradictions. For example, Gunnell's position is that all time is subjective, or more accurately, symbolic and social. However, at least two authors explicitly distinguish between subjective and objective time, and this commonsensical "working" distinction is implicit generally in the remaining essays: What social scientist could deny that time perception is a function of cultural-psychological factors? But how is it possible for one reared in the modern West to deny that time is *there*—frame, measure, and even "agent"?

Of course, some discussion between Gunnell and his colleagues would be necessary to determine whether there is a serious divergence; Gunnell probably would agree to a working distinction between subjective and objective time for many purposes, and his colleagues might agree that "on another level" Gunnell is correct. Still, it is not clear how much agreement could be reached. Gunnell's argument subtly interrelates not just time and development but moves to profound conclusions regarding the nature of the enterprise called social science. His argument has implications not simply with respect to the validity of much that is presented in the other essays, but with respect to the validity of much of contemporary social science.

The divergence manifested by the essays (and now twice emphasized by the editor) must not, however, be allowed to obscure the fact that there is much in common among the authors, that some themes recur several times and are developed in differing fashion. Nor is it impossible to draw conclusions from the presentations—though this statement is admittedly open to the objection that the "conclusions" are really premises or hypotheses that have been discussed at length but not verified by tests that will stand scrutiny.

What the authors share is a conviction that the temporal factor is *important* in the understanding and study of administration and development; that it is often overlooked, slighted, or fudged; and that it will pay dividends both to the student seeking understanding and to the administrator seeking control to direct increased, sustained attention to the temporal dimension. Beyond this, I think generalizations such as the following emerge from the presentations:

(1) that differing, culturally given perceptions of time are extremely important in administration and development, and that while these differing perceptions have a special relevance for development in the newer countries they also are highly significant in the older, industrialized countries.

(2) that the emergence of the Western idea of progressive time

was a matter of profound import for the direction "development" has taken in the West, and that it is not possible to understand events in the non-Western and (or) "developing world" without perceiving that the diffusion of the idea of progressive time is profoundly involved.

(3) that one of the essential functions of the leader or administrator is the "mediation" of differing time perceptions, and that this is hardly less true in a society emerging from industrialism than in a society seeking to become industrialized.

(4) that recent administrative science and even recent social science generally has paid inadequate attention to the temporal dimension in its theories and models.

(5) that sustained, arduous effort is warranted in examining the connections between the temporal dimension and such central or global concepts as "change" and "development."

(6) that on the evidence it will be useful to have both speculative thought and systematic research which seeks to establish relationships between the temporal dimension and such important factors or variables in administration-development as leadership, elites, party systems, political ideologies, administrative structures and styles, and strategies of economic development.

(7) that the temporal dimension is extremely important (and has been generally overlooked or slighted) in large-scale efforts in the transfer of administrative technologies and/or in large-scale administrative reforms.

(8) that the more thoroughly accepted is the "metaphor" of progressive time, the more relevant becomes the triad of rate, sequence, and synchronization to administrative science and technology.

(9) that profound questions are posed in a future in which—for example—the progressive time metaphor may be transformed or dissolved, ideas of change and development may themselves be changed and developed, the potential for rapid change and a desire to control the future rise simultaneously, and there is a transformation of industrial society into "post-industrial society."

The essays in this collection provide a rough geography for a

whole continent of intellectual exploration, ranging from speculation and hypothesis formulation to research of the "hardest" variety. With respect to the former, Bock's essay of course opens up a
vast terrain. But I cite also, for example, the point of view twice
expressed in the essays that a society oriented toward space is a
static society (with at most a time-sense that is cyclical), whereas
a society oriented toward progressive time is a dynamic society
and, with luck, a developing society in addition. Apart from the
interesting questions concerning the past and the present that this
poses, it presents questions of extreme relevance for the future.
To the extent that it points to important truths, what are the
implications with respect to new and increasing national boundaries? Is one world-wide trend in conflict with another world-wide
trend? What is the import for this question of the scientific-tech-
nological surge that is transforming industrial society into post-
industrial society? If the ethologists who assert that man has an
ineradicable "territorial instinct" are correct, what does this mean
for a future in which mobility is possible far beyond all human
experience?

With respect to "hard" research, the research reported by Sherwood demonstrates how currently respectable methodologies of
hypothesis formulation and data collection can be directed toward problems that "put together" time and administration. (It
may be appropriate to raise the question whether it would be
profitable to return to the tradition and technology of time-and-
motion studies in which the study of administration is so deeply
rooted, asking whether some of the tools and techniques can be
adapted to probing quite different questions than those toward
which they were first directed.) The essays by Ilchman (productivity problems), Lee (elite effectiveness), and Jowitt (Commu-
nist-world experience) point to research that cannot, perhaps,
make use of research techniques that are so well accepted, so
"hard," but which nevertheless are within the perimeter of what
is currently regarded as social science as against social theory. To
suggest another line, Diamant directs attention briefly to "circadian time," i.e., to the now well-established fact that organisms,
man included, have biologically given responses and rhythms

based upon evolutionary development on a planet with certain "natural" time cycles. There has been much research in this area, in fact, spurred by the prospect of extra-terrestial travel; and there is even a fair amount of inquiry resulting from the fact that man now travels extensively at near sonic speed levels. But I am not aware of systematic work—which obviously needs doing—seeking to relate what is known of man's circadian characteristics to questions of administration in a world in which movement in time-space is constantly increasing.

The areas of speculation and research opened up in these essays, vast as they are, by no means exhaust the possibilities for significant "time" inquiry. In illustration, I cite an essay which it proved impossible to include; this is an essay on "Reasonable Time and Real Time," by Hans H. Jecht, who was a visiting participant in the Berkeley seminar. Jecht's concern is the temporal aspect of the "Kafka problem," i.e., the problem of man vis-à-vis vast impersonal officialdom, the former with his very urgent personal problems and limited time horizons and the latter with its organizational objectives (one could be less charitable) and time expectations running into months, years, even decades or centuries. Jecht explores first the "reasonable time" concept (of individual waiting for official action) as manifested in legal systems and administrative operations. And he then explores the relevant question: To what extent can the "real time" concept and technology of contemporary electronics be used to solve this enduring and critical problem?

Other possibilities suggest themselves. For example, it might well be profitable to work with and from the concepts of "multistability" or "ultra-stability" as set forth in Ross Ashby's *Design for a Brain*; that is, the idea that "systems" to survive and function must have appropriate time cycles or constants built into them, by parts and by the whole. In quite a different vein, I feel that some exploration of the literature of linguistics, some communication with the linguists, and perhaps some mutual exploration with the linguists, would be in order. Whatever it may "be," perception of time *is* culturally shaped, and language is the key to culture. We need to understand time in other cultures; we need to understand it better in our own.

Index